Pomeranians

FOR

DUMMIES

by D. Caroline Coile, Ph.D.

D0057874

BICENTENNIAL
1807
WILEY
2007
BICENTENNIAL

Wiley Publishing, Inc.

Pomeranians For Dummies®

Published by
Wiley Publishing, Inc.
111 River St.
Hoboken, NJ 07030-5774
www.wiley.com

Pomeranians For Dummies®

Cheat Sheet

What to Check if Your Pom Seems Sick

If you suspect your dog is ill, check out these normal values. If you have any abnormal values, call your veterinarian immediately.

- ✔ **Respiration:** 10–30 breaths per minute at rest
- ✔ **Pulse:** 80–150 beats per minute at rest
- ✔ **Temperature:** 100–102.5 degrees F at rest
- ✔ **Capillary refill time:** Color returns to toenail less than 2 seconds after being pressed until it turns white
- ✔ **Gum color:** Pink
- ✔ **Hydration:** Skin snaps back into position within 3 seconds of being lifted

The Grooming Schedule

Do This	This Often
Wipe eyes	Daily
Brush coat	Daily or every other day
Brush teeth	Optimally daily; at least weekly
Check ears	Weekly
Clip nails	Every other week
Bathe	Monthly
Trim	Optional; monthly
Use a professional groomer	Optional; every six weeks

Signs of Health Problems

Any of the following symptoms signal that you need to promptly seek care for your Pom — see Chapter 11 for more info. In addition to these signs, also watch for coughing, gagging, vomiting, or difficulty breathing.

- ✔ **Anal region:** Redness, swelling; also scooting or licking the area
- ✔ **Behavior:** Weakness, lethargy, inco-ordination, stiffness, aggression
- ✔ **Ears:** Head shaking, head tilt, bad odor, debris, crusted tips
- ✔ **Eyes:** Unequal or unresponsive pupils, tearing, squinting, gooey discharge
- ✔ **Feet:** Swollen or misaligned toes, abrasions, split nails
- ✔ **Gait:** Limping, especially holding up a rear leg for a hop or two
- ✔ **Gums:** Whitish, bluish, speckled, or any color but pink
- ✔ **Mouth:** Bleeding, ulcers, bad breath, loose teeth
- ✔ **Nose:** Thick or colored discharge; crusted top
- ✔ **Skin:** Parasites, hair loss, itching, crusts, sores, lumps
- ✔ **Stool:** Black, tarry, or bloody diarrhea
- ✔ **Torso:** Swollen abdomen, weight loss

For Dummies: Bestselling Book Series for Beginners

Pomeranians For Dummies®

Cheat Sheet

Emergency Numbers

Veterinarian's phone number: _____

Emergency-clinic phone number: _____

Animal Poison Control: 888-426-4235 ($50 consultation fee)

Frequently Used Web Sites

- Need information on registration, competition, or other official matters? Go to the American Kennel Club's Web site at www.akc.org
- Want to find breeders, rescue Poms, or to just become more involved with all things Pom-related? Contact the American Pomeranian Club at www.americanpomeranianclub.org
- Looking for motels and other places you can take your dog while traveling? Check out www.dogfriendly.com
- Need information about training, competition, and behavior? Start with Dog Patch: www.dogpatch.com
- Lost a pet or want to find one for adoption? She may be waiting at Petfinder: www.petfinder.com
- Looking for veterinary information? Go to Veterinary Partner at www.veterinarypartner.com

Most Dangerous Household Hazards

- Animal baits, herbicides, fertilizers
- Antifreeze
- Chocolate
- Detergents, bleach, drain cleaners
- Doors (including garage doors) that can slam
- Electric wires
- Gasoline and oil
- Medications
- Objects that can fall
- Open-sided balconies
- Pins and needles
- Rat traps
- Small toys that can be swallowed or partially inhaled
- Socks, yarn, and long things that can be swallowed
- Unfenced pool or yard

For Dummies: Bestselling Book Series for Beginners

About the Author

Award-winning author D. Caroline Coile, Ph.D., has written 29 books and more than 300 magazine and scientific articles about dogs. She writes the monthly award-winning "Breeder's Notebook" column for *Dog World* magazine. Among her books are *Barron's Encyclopedia of Dog Breeds, Show Me!, Beyond Fetch, How Smart is Your Dog?,* and *Congratulations! It's a Dog!*

Caroline holds a Ph.D. in psychology with research interests in canine behavior, senses, and genetics. On a practical level, Caroline has lived with dogs all of her life. She shares her home with six dogs including dogs nationally ranked #1 show, #1 obedience, top field and agility salukis, and two roadside-rescue mutts — all of which provide a never-ending source of challenges, adventure, frustration, and inspiration.

Author's Acknowledgments

My unending gratitude goes to Pomeranian breeders Geneva Coats and Julie Clemen as well as the members of the *Pom Forum* discussion group. Their suggestions were invaluable, as was their critique of the manuscript.

I'm also indebted to editors Kristin DeMint, Pam Ruble, and Stacy Kennedy for keeping me in line (sort of).

And to fellow dog writer Eve Adamson — she knows why.

Publisher's Acknowledgments

We're proud of this book; please send us your comments through our Dummies online registration form located at www.dummies.com/register/.

Some of the people who helped bring this book to market include the following:

Acquisitions, Editorial, and Media Development

Project Editor: Kristin DeMint

Acquisitions Editor: Stacy Kennedy

Copy Editor: Pam Ruble

Technical Editor: Dr. Carey Wasem (www.zvah.com)

Senior Editorial Manager: Jennifer Ehrlich

Editorial Assistants: Erin Calligan Mooney, Joe Niesen, Leeann Harney

Cover Photos: © Robert Pearcy/ Animals Animals

Cartoons: Rich Tennant (www.the5thwave.com)

Composition Services

Project Coordinator: Heather Kolter

Layout and Graphics: Joyce Haughey, Barbara Moore, Laura Pence, Heather Ryan, Alicia B. South

Anniversary Logo Design: Richard J. Pacifico

Proofreaders: Aptara, John Greenough, Susan Moritz

Indexer: Sherry Massey

Special Help: Stephen R. Clark, Carmen Krikorian

Publishing and Editorial for Consumer Dummies

    Diane Graves Steele, Vice President and Publisher, Consumer Dummies

    Joyce Pepple, Acquisitions Director, Consumer Dummies

    Kristin A. Cocks, Product Development Director, Consumer Dummies

    Michael Spring, Vice President and Publisher, Travel

    Kelly Regan, Editorial Director, Travel

Publishing for Technology Dummies

    Andy Cummings, Vice President and Publisher, Dummies Technology/General User

Composition Services

    Gerry Fahey, Vice President of Production Services

    Debbie Stailey, Director of Composition Services

Contents at a Glance

Table of Contents

Introduction

● ●

So you're thinking about getting a Pom? Maybe you know you
want one but you're wondering how to find a good one. Or just
maybe you're already a proud Pom parent and want to find out
more about sharing your life with your puffy pal. Whatever your
reasons, you're off to a great start by discovering more about one
of dogdom's cutest breeds.

Have you heard the saying that small dogs are just big dogs in little
bodies? That's certainly true with Poms — the heart of a lion and
the looks of a miniature lion. That fun little package has a lot of
good stuff packed into it, and I wrote this book the same way —
lots of stuff in a fun little package. I hope you'll have fun (and learn
a lot) exploring both.

About This Book

This book is for prospective and current Pomeranian owners. It has
all the information you need to get you from your first notion of
wanting a Pom all the way through the next decade and more.
In these pages you find answers to questions like the following:

- ✔ Am I insane for even thinking about getting a dog?
- ✔ Is a tiny dog right for me?
- ✔ What's special about Poms compared to other toy dogs?
- ✔ How do I find a good, healthy Pomeranian and avoid getting
  ripped off?
- ✔ How do I get ready for my new puffball of a dog?
- ✔ How do I introduce my new Pom to the world around him so
  he's a well-adjusted dog?
- ✔ Why are frequent feedings sometimes a matter of life and
  death for tiny dogs, especially puppies?
- ✔ Is it hard to keep her coat looking good?
- ✔ How can I stop these puddles on the floor?
- ✔ Is there a secret to training this dog?
- ✔ How do I cope with bad behaviors?

    ✔ How do I know whether my dog is sick, and what do I do?

    ✔ How do I get started with the fun stuff?

You may be more interested in some of these questions than others. That's fine. Feel free to skip around. You won't hurt my feelings. Go ahead and mark up pages and highlight points, too. This is a reference book, meant to be dog-eared and dog-chewed. That just shows you've put it to good use.

Conventions Used in This Book

To help you find what you want quickly, I use a few conventions when it comes to typeface.

    ✔ *Italic* is used to highlight new terms that are defined in the text.

    ✔ **Boldface** is used to indicate the action part of numbered steps.

    ✔ `Monofont` is used for Web and e-mail addresses.

In the interest of gender quality, I vary the wording so that some sections refer to a male Pomeranian and some to a female. Unless I'm discussing the features of one sex exclusively, the text with male or female pronouns applies to both sexes.

What You're Not to Read

Of course, I hope you read every one of the golden and invaluable words in this book. But even *I* have to admit you don't have to read it all in order to be a good and informed Pomeranian owner. You can skip the nonessential stuff, and I've even made it easy for you to identify what's skippable:

    ✔ Text in sidebars: Those shaded boxes you see here and there contain interesting but not really essential information. You can save those for leisure reading.

    ✔ Text highlighted with a *Technical Stuff* icon: As much as it pains me to say this, you don't really have to read these sections — even though I think they're the most interesting parts. (Besides, they give you some great stuff to bore your friends with!) I always summarize the info elsewhere so you don't have to dig through the *why* of everything.

Foolish Assumptions

When I was writing this book, I made some assumptions — I hope
not too foolish — concerning you and what sort of information you
want to find:

✔ You're considering a Pomeranian but you know that dogs
   differ as much in personality as they do in looks; you want to
   find out whether a Pomeranian is really the dog for you.

✔ You've decided on a Pomeranian but want to make sure you
   get a good one.

✔ You're preparing for your new dog and want to make sure he
   gets off on the right paw.

✔ You're on your hands and knees, soaking up that spot on the
   carpet again, wondering what it takes to housetrain one of
   these critters.

✔ You're trying to train your Pom with commands just like you
   did your last dog, but it's not working. Is there some secret
   to this?

✔ You want to provide the best health care possible for your
   Pomeranian.

✔ You just love the breed and want to lap up as many interesting
   tidbits as you can.

How This Book Is Organized

This book is a paragon of organization. Sort of. Each of the five
parts centers on a general topic and contains chapters with specific information about that topic.

Part I: Pomeranians:
What's Not to Love?

It's easy to fall in love with a dog and particularly with a Pomeranian,
but do your circumstances allow you to bring a Pom into your life?
The chapters in Part I help you with all those initial questions
like what does the Pomeranian breed offer; what are the choices
(age, gender, color, and pet or show quality); are you and a Pom a
good match; and how do you find the right Pom for you?

Part II: When Your House Becomes Your Pom's Home

The best time to get ready for your new Pom is before you have your dog underfoot. This part shows you how to prepare your home, from Pom proofing to Pom spoiling. It gives you ideas on what to buy and where to put it. And when you're ready to bring your new dog home, this part supplies handy tips to make the trip and subsequent homecoming as nontraumatic as possible. Still, those first few days — and especially the nights! — can be challenging unless you know the best ways to deal with them.

Part III: Caring for Your Pom from Head to Paw

One of the best parts of having a Pom is the excuse to pamper and primp him to your heart's content, so this part offers information about basic dog care including helpful tips about tiny dogs. But the chapters also have information on nutrition, feeding schedules, health care, and the hereditary health conditions that Pomeranians are susceptible to. Finally, because you and your Pom eventually want to spread your wings, this chapter prepares both of you for those trips beyond your back door.

Part IV: Training Your Pom with TLC

They may be tiny, but they can still be mighty determined. And when Poms are bad, it's almost always the fault of poor training. Small dogs can be annoying — to the point that your friends may run when they see the two of you coming. And even a nip can do some damage, especially to a child. This part contains vital information on housetraining and basic commands, emphasizing the latest techniques based on positive rewards. Despite the best training, dogs sometimes come up with behavior problems that need special attention, and this part also covers those situations.

Part V: The Part of Tens

This part, a standard fare in all *For Dummies* books, offers quick lists of fun information. Want to discover some great activities for you and your Pom? Look here. Look here, too, to find out some fun Pom facts.

Icons Used in This Book

The icons used in this book help you locate certain kinds of information at a glance:

This icon highlights handy advice that can save you time, money, or effort.

This icon points to text that's worth repeating — and remembering.

This icon means *pay close attention!* It appears beside information that can save you from doggy dangers, unscrupulous breeders, and unsafe practices.

This icon appears next to explanatory information that goes a little deeper into specific topics. Although I think it is fascinating stuff, you don't really need to read it to get the point.

Where to Go from Here

Ready to get started? Check out the Table of Contents to find where you want to jump in. Or read Chapter 1, which is really the best place to start because it offers more detailed information on the rest of the book. (Chapter 1 also discusses some points you need to consider before getting a dog in general or a Pom in particular.)

If you're still not sure a Pom is for you, read on to Chapter 2 for more characteristics of the Pomeranian and more facts about owning a tiny dog.

Beyond that, feel free to skip around!

Part I

Pomeranians: What's Not to Love?

The 5th Wave   By Rich Tennant

KENNEL DOWNSTA

"You'll find that Pomeranians have a friendly, although somewhat mischievous, personality."

In this part . . .

*P*uffballs, powder puffs, tribbles, or ewoks — a Pom
by any other name is just as cute. But before falling
under the Pomeranian spell, make sure you fall in love
with the inner Pom as much as the outer Pom. And make
sure you know what you're committing to for the next
decade and more.

In this part I ask you to do some honest soul-searching
about whether you're ready for a Pom — or for any dog.
As much as you may love them, a true test of love is sometimes agreeing to wait. In this case, I'm asking you first to
consider the pros and cons of living with a tiny dog and
with a Pom in particular.

If you decide to take the Pom plunge, this part guides you
also in finding a good Pomeranian breeder. This Pom is
going to be a member of your family — make sure you
put more effort into this choice than you would for a
new toaster! After you find a breeder, I give you tips on
evaluating the litter and picking your own Pom pal.

Chapter 1

Catching Pomer-mania

Maybe it's been a long-time dream. Or maybe just a sudden impulse. Perhaps you saw one in a fashion magazine, or carried by a celebrity, or on television, or strutting at a dog show. Maybe your neighbor has one. Whatever the reason, the notion has burrowed into your brain and it just won't leave. You can't think of anything else. You have to have your very own Pom.

But before you pencil a Pom onto your shopping list, stop and think. A dog is a living, breathing being that will depend on you for the rest of his life. You'll be responsible for feeding, walking, grooming, and cleaning up after your littlest family member for the next decade or more. Think hard before entering into that kind of commitment.

The best time to make sure the Pomeranian is really the dog for you is before you bring one home. If you're thinking of meeting a puppy to help you decide, stop right now! Don't take a single step toward that puppy or you *will* be coming home with him. There is absolutely no way you can make an objective decision in sight of a pouncing Pom puppy. So read first, look later — and enjoy for a lifetime!

The Toy-Dog Extravaganza: Pom Popularity

Tiny toy dogs are all the rage these days. Keep in mind, though, that small dogs aren't for everybody.

Toy-dog breeds

The American Kennel Club places the Pomeranian in its Toy group, along with many of the other cutest dogs on earth:

Affenpinscher	Italian Greyhound	Pomeranian
Brussels Griffon	Japanese Chin	Poodle (Toy)
Cavalier King Charles Spaniel	Maltese	Pug
Chihuahua	Manchester Terrier (Toy)	Shih Tzu
Chinese Crested	Miniature Pinscher	Silky Terrier
English Toy Spaniel	Papillon	Toy Fox Terrier
Havanese	Pekingese	

Tiny dogs do have a lot of advantages when it comes to convenience, but they also take some extra care and worry. I explain the pros and cons of tiny dogs in Chapter 2, so please read it and think seriously about the good, the bad, and the ugly — as well as the snugly — before pouncing on the notion of a little dog.

Dogs aren't fashion accessories like purses, shoes, or even giant stick pins, no matter how tiny and cute they are. And just because a dog happens to be *in* at the moment isn't reason enough to get her as a pet. Dogs come in and out of style, and fads change even before a puppy can grow up. But the worst fashion statement ever is when a person buys a dog as an adornment and then discards her when she's out of style.

Now, off my soapbox and back to Poms. Of all the tiny dogs to choose from (which I cover in the "Toy-dog breeds" sidebar), Poms are different because they're the only ones that come from a Spitz heritage. I discuss this and other aspects of Pomeranian history in Chapter 2. For now, suffice it to say that Spitz dogs are the same family that pulls sleds in the Iditarod, hunts moose, and guards homes. To do these jobs, Spitz dogs need to be independent and strong willed. Poms may be little, but they have big spirits *and* big ideas.

Like all dogs, Poms have some frustrating behaviors. They bark (actually, a lot). They chase little animals. They'd rather go hunting than sleep in your lap. They roll in disgusting places, they eat disgusting stuff, and then they jump in your lap and kiss you in the face. They dig (but at least the holes are small!). They may have accidents in the house. They may have irrational fears or bizarre ideas. After all, they're dogs!

Fortunately, the good far outweighs any bad. Poms love to go places with you, whether it's a trip across the country, across town, or across the room. They're as ready to play as they are to snuggle. They're cute — boy, are they cute! Most of all, Pomeranians prove that you really can buy love.

Sizing Up Your Situation: Know What a Pom Requires

Before you contemplate getting a Pom, take a step back and think about whether you're in a position to get a dog at all. Consider these three issues:

- ✓ **Having a dog is a full-time, long-term commitment.** If you're not into commitment, be sure you think through this decision. A dog will certainly commit to you, but if you change your mind, a shelter may be his only recourse — and that's likely to be a one-way trip.

- ✓ **Dogs require your time on a daily basis.** Sharing your life with a dog means you have to be part-time groundskeeper, home-repair expert, animal trainer, nutritionist, nurse, thera-pist, recreation coach, and of course, full-time best friend.

- ✓ **Dogs usually aren't free.** The cost of buying the dog is nomi-nal compared to the cost of his upkeep through the years. But this initial cost is a consideration. Pomeranians are neither the most- nor the least-expensive breed around. You generally want to avoid bargain basement Poms and the most expensive retail Poms because neither is a good deal in the long run. Find out why in Chapter 3.

Can you commit to the friendship?

Dogs have the label of being man's best friend for a reason. They bask in your attention and soak up your love, returning your affec-tion tenfold. Poms are no exception. Yes, they can survive without human interaction, but that means you'd miss out on the real meaning of having a dog.

If you work all day and then come home too tired to do anything but zone out in front of the television and flop into bed, you probably don't have time for a dog of any breed. Leaving a dog alone all day with no companionship or entertainment is possible, but it isn't fair. Some large cities have doggy day care, or you may be able to hire somebody to come and entertain your dog every day. Even another dog to play with can make a big difference. But all this effort just to replace you? Think twice before getting a dog if you can't be her best friend.

Do you have a home fit for a Pom?

Do you own or rent your home? If you rent, your ability to live exactly where you want is a lot more difficult with a dog. You may be turned away from at least half the rental properties, and you'll pay a nonrefundable pet fee (with possibly an added charge per month) when you do find a landlord that allows dogs. And what if you move and can't find a place that allows dogs? If your future is unsettled, this may not be the right time for a dog.

A house with a yard is ideal, but Poms are equally happy in an apartment. Despite their sled-dog heritage, Poms aren't outdoor dogs because they lose heat more rapidly than they create it. In other words, little dogs get cold fairly easily. And in warm weather, the survival-of-the-fittest law dictates that little animals are easy prey for big animals. So your Pom may enjoy spending time outdoors, but he's not the kind of dog you can just lock in the backyard for the day — and certainly not for the night.

You also need to Pom proof your home, both indoors and out, by hiding any poisons, securing anything that may fall on your dog, preventing your dog from falling from high places, and protecting him from predatory people and animals. Chapter 5 alerts you to these doggy dangers.

Can you afford to feed and care for a dog?

Although the food bill for a Pom isn't as big a deal as it is for some breeds of dogs (thanks to the Pom's size), feeding a tiny dog isn't a slam dunk. They eat so little that you have to be careful not to throw off their balanced diet with too many treats. And *hypoglycemia* (low blood sugar) can be a real threat, especially with puppies. I explain all this, along with some tips on special diets, in Chapter 8.

A dog needs a bed and a bevy of other supplies (some are necessities and some are just to pamper your Pom) including food dishes, brushes, a crate, a carrying bag, toys, and all sorts of items you can't believe they make for dogs. Chapter 5 gives you some ideas for your shopping list.

In addition to the obvious financial responsibilities of feeding a dog and buying the initial supplies, you need a plan to safeguard your Pom's health on an ongoing basis. This plan includes the following:

- ✔ Finding a good veterinarian before your dog gets sick

- ✔ Taking preventive measures such as vaccinations, deworming, and heartworm treatments

- ✔ Arranging for checkups

  Keep in mind that the tests aren't just money-grabs from your veterinarian but important indicators of your dog's health.

- ✔ Deciding on spaying and neutering

  They can have some real health benefits for a Pom. As the owner, you need to understand their pros and cons.

- ✔ Knowing and watching for signs of doggy discomfort or disease

  Study Chapter 10 so you can nip a problem in the bud.

- ✔ Knowing what problems to look for in an older dog

Exact yearly veterinarian costs are difficult to project, but some averages may be helpful to you as a new dog owner:

- ✔ Yearly checkup: $80 to $130

- ✔ Yearly teeth cleaning: $200

- ✔ Spaying or neutering: $200

- ✔ Unplanned trips to the veterinary clinic several times a year: $40 (false alarm) to $80 (with antibiotics) to enough that *you* need to be hospitalized when you see the bill.

 To get a better idea on average costs for your area, call some local veterinary offices to ask about their prices for routine office visits and spaying or neutering a toy dog. You can also ask about emergency fees, but expect a charge of at least a few hundred dollars to see a veterinarian in the middle of the night.

Dogs of any breed can get sick. Dogs of tiny breeds can get very sick very fast. And Pomeranians, like all breeds, have breed-specific predispositions to hereditary disorders. You'll be ahead of the game to know which problems demand a visit to the veterinarian eventually, today, or right this very second. And you'll want to know which first-aid options, home remedies, and long-term nursing plans can help your Pom get better. Chapter 11 guides you through some of the more common health problems your Pom may encounter.

Do you have the time or cash to groom a dog?

Part of the enjoyment of cuddling with a Pom is snuggling your face in her fur and running your fingers through her coat. But that's not going to be much fun if she smells like a dead rat and feels like a solid felt pad. And that doggy breath — whew!

Grooming a Pom isn't really that hard, but it includes more than just washing and combing her coat. It involves keeping the teeth clean, the nails short, and the fleas off. Chapter 9 shows you all the moves.

If you keep to schedule, grooming takes about 15 minutes twice a week. But if you let mats form, expect to spend an hour or more dematting.

Your Pomeranian doesn't need professional grooming, but some people simply hate to groom or they want their Pom clipped. Depending on the salon and the services, expect to pay $20 to $50. If you want a groomer or your veterinarian staff to cut your dog's nails (at least monthly), it usually runs $5 to $10.

Do you have the time and energy to play with a dog?

Like all dogs, Poms need mental and physical exercise every day. In fact, they're bundles of energy (compliments of their Spitz heritage). Without enough stimulation, they can become frustrated and destructive, barking, chewing, and running in circles. Fortunately, exercising them doesn't take much space or energy on your part.

Throwing a ball in an apartment several times a day is an easy start. But you can do a lot more. For example:

✔ Challenge him with hiding games, teach him tricks, and make him work for his supper.

✔ Take him outdoors and just let him soak in the smells. A walk around the block can do both of you good.

✔ Keep him busy and thinking with interactive toys while you're gone.

✔ Take a trip together. With a little planning, your Pom can be your ideal travel companion.

Check out Chapter 16 for more ideas on entertaining, exercising, socializing, and even competing with your Pomeranian.

Do you have the patience to train a dog?

Dogs that run free, totally unschooled in manners and basic knowledge, are unpopular with people and a danger to themselves and others. Your dog deserves to be trained so she's the best that she can be. You don't need to be a drill sergeant — just smarter than the average Pom.

Training can save your dog's life. For example, she needs to come when called, especially if she's off leash and headed toward traffic. She needs to stop acting like a jerk when she's challenging the giant dog who isn't amused. And she needs to know not to bite people.

Training cements the bond between you and your Pom. In the old days, punishment-based training made training sessions no fun for man or beast. But now, reward-based training has your dog begging for the next session. You see how to do this in Chapter 14.

Do you travel much?

Does your job or hobby take you away from home a lot? If so, where will your dog stay? Boarding costs can range from $8 to $30 a day, depending on whether you want him to have a cage at the kennel or a deluxe suite complete with television privileges.

And don't forget doggy day care! Larger cities often have facilities where you drop your dog off for the day. Better day-care centers offer supervised play and training. Costs may be as high as overnight boarding, but many dogs end up pulling you to the door in their excitement to go see their friends there!

Maybe you plan to take your dog with you on the road. If you go by air, you'll pay an extra fee for him, about $50 per flight. And many motels charge a dog fee as well, usually an extra $10 per night.

Chapter 12 outlines the best ways of traveling with your furry companion.

Double-Checking Your Motives: Why Do You Want a Pom?

Chances are you've thought long and hard about getting a furry, fun-loving friend. But even with the best intentions, you may need to step back and cool off enough to objectively re-evaluate your choices and timing. After all, adding a family member is a big decision!

Recognizing your reasons for wanting a Pom

Some people jump into this commitment for the wrong reasons. Check out the following not-so-great reasons (and some follow-up responses) to see whether they come close to any of yours:

- ✔ **All the cool celebrities have tiny dogs.** Yes, but do they spend much time with their pet when the cameras aren't clicking? Besides, do they care about expenses?

- ✔ **Toy dogs are the ultimate fashion accessory.** What happens when the toy-dog fad is over? And it will be over — count on it.

- ✔ **A tiny dog is perfect for luring members of the opposite sex.** How long will that person stay before saying, "It's me or the dog!"? Better question: Which one will you choose?

- ✔ **A friend has a wonderful Pom.** Great! That means you can play with hers without spending money on your own. Besides, what are the chances yours will be just like hers?

- ✔ **Dogs are good jogging partners.** Hello! Poms? Well, that's one way to make sure you don't jog far . . . although you can carry her in a back sack and burn a few extra calories that way.

- ✔ **A dog can snap to it and do the owner's bidding.** Two words: Spitz heritage (read Chapter 2).

- ✔ **Previous pets had behavior problems.** Chances are the lapses in behavior weren't their fault. Dogs aren't perfect, and getting rid of them isn't a humane plan. Chapters 13, 14, and 15 can put an owner on the right training path.

Hesitating after a loss

You may have found yourself in the sad position of having recently lost a beloved dog. Half your friends advise you not to get another dog (at least not soon), and half advise you to get another one as quickly as possible. This situation is different for everybody.

You know you can never replace your past dog. Even if that dog was a Pom of the same sex, color, and lineage, each dog is an individual. Consider these two lines of thinking:

- ✔ If you feel you'll be constantly comparing your new dog to your old one, that's not fair. The new one can never be the same.

- ✔ If you accept that this new dog isn't a replacement but an individual that can charm you in his own way, then your new Pom isn't displacing your old dog from your heart — he's merely snuggling alongside your memories.

When you have the right frame of mind, a new Pomeranian can provide a much-needed diversion that helps move your mind in better directions. And what better way to honor your earlier dog than to want another?

Knowing when you're ready to bite the bullet

You've checked your situation, your finances, and the Pomeranian personality. You want a dog for a companion — a true friend who shares your lap by night and a jaunt around the block by day. You can't wait to help her grow into the best Pom she can be, and you're eager to try a few doggy activities with her.

You admire her combination of spunk and cuteness and don't expect her to fawn all over you. You plan on training her but aren't expecting her to be a little soldier and obey all the commands. You plan to care for and love her like any other true family member, and you hope to have her for as long as possible.

You know that to be the best Pomeranian caretaker you can be, you may need to do a little reading. Great! That's where the rest of this book comes in.

Thinking about Breeding?

As you envision yourself writing out that big check and clutching that American Kennel Club registration, you may say to yourself, "Hey, I could breed Poms." You may even start calculating how you'd recoup your purchase price with the first litter or the second stud fee. And you may think ahead a few years to the time your home is covered with hoards of puffy moneymakers, each churning out litters while you just lean back and count the cash. Dream on.

Raising puppies is hard work. If you're considering raising Poms as a business, be aware that caring for a multitude of dogs is a full-time job. You have to feed, poop scoop, groom, socialize, train, exercise, medicate, and love every dog every day. You have to be present for the whelping, and you may need to devote yourself to hand raising orphaned or sick puppies for several weeks.

Raising puppies is also expensive. To breed the right way, the potential parents need to be cleared for hereditary health problems such as luxating patellas, bad hearts, or eye problems, all of which can cost several hundred dollars.

Raising puppies is a huge responsibility in the following ways:

- ✔ You owe it to your buyers to provide only healthy, well-socialized companions, just like you looked for in your search for a puppy.

- ✔ You owe it to your dam (the puppies' mom) to make sure she survives the endeavor. Dams, especially those of toy breeds, can die in whelping. They often need Caesarean sections to save their lives. After whelping, they are subject to *eclampsia,* a potentially fatal condition that causes convulsions. It's your responsibility to make sure she emerges as healthy as when she went into childbirth.

- ✔ You owe it to your puppies to make sure they go only to the best homes. Will their family have only passing interest in them? Be impatient or cruel? You have to be ready to say *No* to families that won't be good owners.

- ✔ You owe it to the breed to maintain the high standards that breeders have maintained for more than a century. Pomeranians who are bad pets, who bite, or who are unhealthy, chip away at the breed's reputation and well-being.

If you can be the sort of breeder that you'd like to buy a puppy from, you may be breeder material. Chapter 3 highlights the makeup of a good breeder.

Chapter 2

What's in a Pom?

*F*alling in love with Pomeranians and deciding this is the breed for you is easy. But picking a dog based just on looks is as naïve as picking a mate based on looks. Sure, Poms and handsome spouses are fun to be seen with in public, but you may find you have irreconcilable differences at home. And although you can divorce your spouse and go your merry ways, divorcing your Pom can mean sealing his fate — sending him to a shelter, where he won't necessarily find a new home. So find out what's in a Pom before you decide to put a Pom in your life.

Eyeing the Standard: The Pomeranian Blueprint

What makes a Pomeranian a Pomeranian? The short answer is, DNA. But because you can't whip out your handy DNA test kit, you need to rely on what you see.

That's where the standard comes in. Every American Kennel Club (AKC) breed has its own standard of perfection that describes not only the essence of the breed but also the little details that make up the perfect specimen. The standard is the result of vigorous efforts on the part of breeders to describe the ideal Pom (both in physique and personality) when each breed was accepted for AKC recognition.

Periodically, the standard may change slightly to clarify certain points or even to make certain traits — like new colors that may have cropped up or extremes in sizes — more or less desirable. However, such changes are never made lightly. The American Pomeranian Club (APC) is responsible for safeguarding the Pom standard. The first APC standard was adopted in 1916; subsequent standards were adopted in 1935, 1960, 1980, 1991, and 1997 (the current version).

I describe the basic points of the standard in the following two sections. For the exact wording or to compare the present standard with earlier versions, go to the APC site at www.american pomeranianclub.org/standard.htm.

The gist of the Pom: General appearance

How do you describe a Pomeranian? For starters, you don't talk about the shape of his feet or any other of the important, but tiny, details. Instead you begin with his essence — the parts of the standard regarding general appearance. For the Pom, the description is

- ✔ A compact, short-backed toy dog
- ✔ A profuse outer coat and a plumed tail that lies flat on his back
- ✔ An active, alert, cocky, commanding, and inquisitive nature

Of course, there's more to a Pom than that, so the rest of the standard fills in the details. I cover these in the next section.

From head to toes: Pom specifics

The standard may seem like a lot of detail, but then they say the Pom is in the details . . . or something like that. (See Figure 2-1 for an illustration of this royal dog.) The following are only the main points:

- ✔ **Size, proportion, and substance:** He's a sturdy, medium-boned dog weighing 3 to 7 pounds (ideally, 4 to 6 pounds), slightly taller than long.
- ✔ **Head:** His expression is foxlike, with small, high-set, erect ears; he has dark, almond-shaped eyes of medium size and a rather short, fine, but not snippy, muzzle; the top of his skull is slightly rounded but not domed, and it doesn't have a soft spot; his teeth meet in a scissors bite with the top incisors just barely in front of the bottom ones.

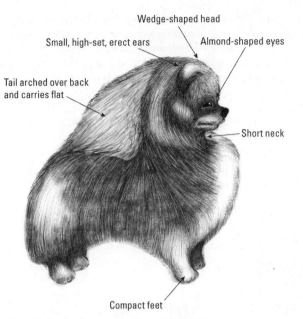

Wedge-shaped head

Small, high-set, erect ears

Almond-shaped eyes

Tail arched over back and carries flat

Short neck

Compact feet

Figure 2-1: The Pomeranian breed standard.

✔ **Neck and Body:** He carries his head proud and high; a short neck leads to a short, level back, which in turn leads to a tail that lies flat and straight on the back; the body is compact, with the ribcage meeting the elbows.

✔ **Forequarters:** His forelegs are straight and parallel to each other with strong, straight pasterns leading to well-arched, compact feet that point straight ahead; the length of his legs is such that his elbows are halfway between the ground and the highest point of his shoulder.

✔ **Hindquarters:** Viewed from behind, his legs are straight and parallel to each other; from the side, his buttocks are well behind the set of the tail; the knees are moderately bent, and the hocks are perpendicular to the ground; the well-arched, compact feet point straight ahead; as in the front, he stands mostly on his toes, not his heels.

✔ **Gait:** When he trots, his front legs reach well out in front and his rear legs push off with a strong drive, the whole impression being smooth, balanced, and vigorous. The faster he goes, the more his legs converge in a straight line toward a center line beneath his body.

✔ **Coat:** His coat is made up of two parts: a thick, soft, dense undercoat and a long, straight, glistening, harsh outer coat. The thick undercoat makes the outer hairs stand off from his body, giving him a puffball appearance. The coat is heaviest around the neck and the forepart of the chest and shoulders; it is shortest on the head and legs. The coat on the rear of his legs down to the pastern and hock is feathered; his tail is profusely covered with long, harsh, straight hair.

✔ **Color:** All colors and patterns are equal in desirability:

• **Black and tan:** The tan is rich and clearly defined over the eyes, on the muzzle, throat, and forechest, on all legs and feet, and below the tail.

• **Brindle:** The base color of gold, red, or orange has strong, black, vertical stripes.

• **Parti-color:** Colored areas appear on white; a white blaze is preferred.

✔ **Temperament:** He is extroverted, intelligent, and vivacious; a great companion and a competitive show dog.

Beneath the Fur: Pom Anatomy 101

A Pom may look like a puffball of fur, but beneath it lies a real dog that has all the same parts as other dogs — and wolves! No one expects you to become a canine anatomist and know the names of every part of your Pom's body. But knowing the basic parts helps you understand the breed standard, and it comes in handy when you're trying to describe your dog's boo-boo to the veterinarian.

Basically, your Pom's body is like yours. Sort of. But if you could get down on all fours, stand on your fingers and toes, and grow a tail, you'd have a better idea of how your parts matched up. (Just don't do this when you're expecting company!)

The following is a list of the more common parts:

✔ Your dog's toes are his *fingers*.

✔ His hand, or *pastern,* is actually off the ground.

✔ His *elbow* is way up there almost to his chest.

His *upper arm* is next to his body.

✔ His shoulder blades reach up to form a high point above his spine; this point is called the *withers*.

✔ His heels (or *hocks*) are in his hind legs and are well off the ground.

✔ His knee is called a *stifle*.

✔ His lower back is called his *croup*.

Figure 2-2 illustrates parts of Pomeranian anatomy. It's helpful to locate them on your own dog for practice and then compare them to your own anatomy for fun!

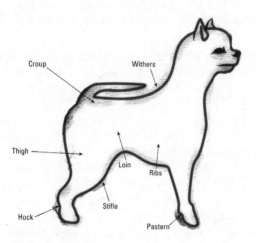

Figure 2-2: The Pom anatomy.

Small Package, Big Personality

Poms sure look cute — but you know how looks can be deceiving! Luckily, there's no deception in the Pom's case. These little spit-fires act as cute as they look. This section contains my top eight traits that make Poms so unique.

Great balls of fire!

Poms are full of energy, their little pistonlike legs moving in a blur as they rush from one place to the next. If Poms were big dogs, they'd travel miles every day and drive their people quite insane. Fortunately, they're small, and even though they travel great distances, they can do it all inside your home by scurrying from room to room.

The Pomeranian genealogy

Pomeranians descend from one of the most ancient lines of domesticated dogs, the Spitz family. Spitz-type dogs were associated with hunter-gatherers at least 6,000 years ago.

The Spitz have retained many of the traits that helped their ancestors (European wolves) survive in cold climates. They have thick, weather-resistant coats for warmth; small, furry ears that are less susceptible to heat loss and frostbite; a bushy tail to cover the nose when sleeping; and a muzzle of moderate length to warm incoming air.

Over time, various subtypes of Spitz breeds developed according to the needs of the geographical regions. For example, some Spitz were used as sledge dogs, some as herders, and, last but not least, some smaller ones as house dogs whose main function was to sound the alarm at danger. Sound familiar?

Little is known about the Pomeranian dog of long ago except that it was a Spitz dog weighing about 30 pounds, not the tiny darling we know today. The breed's home country is Pomerania, in what is now part of northern Poland and Germany. Poms were prized pets not only in Pomerania but also throughout Europe, attracting notables such as Michelangelo, Mozart, and Isaac Newton.

The Pomeranian came to Britain in 1767. In 1888, Queen Victoria spotted an especially small Pomeranian while she was on a trip to Florence, Italy. (*Marco* weighed only 12 pounds when most Pomeranians were weighing closer to 20 pounds.) She brought him home and exhibited him at an English dog show, thus setting the trend for smaller Poms. When specimens started to mature below 8 pounds, they were dubbed *Toy Pomeranians*. Marco was also a red sable at a time when most Poms were white, black, or white and black. But by the end of the 19th century, most Poms were small and red. Ah, the pull of royalty!

By the beginning of the 20th century, Pomeranians were one of the most popular breeds registered or shown in England. The smaller size and greater variety of vivid colors did much to make the breed a dog of fashion that no well-dressed lady could be without.

Poms were also catching on in America, although, without the royal example, the trend was a little bit slower. In 1888 the first Pom was entered into the American Kennel Club's (AKC) stud book, and in 1892 the first one was exhibited at an American dog show. The AKC officially recognized the Pomeranian in 1900, the same year the Pomeranian Club of America was founded. The breed grew in popularity, becoming one of the ten most popular AKC breeds in the 1930s. It again entered the top ten in 1994, where it remained for many years.

Nonetheless, don't let their small size fool you into thinking you can ignore them. In a pinch they can exercise on their own, but they need the mental exercise that only you can provide. Without that stimulation, a Pom finds his own entertainment and challenges — and then exercises his mind by getting into trouble!

He needs the chance to stretch his legs and expand his mind every day. This means you need to play with him, make sure he gets a workout, and train him every day. Just like the big dogs, he looks forward to outdoor adventures like a romp in the yard or a walk around the block. Make your outings adventurous by exploring new routes and places every day. Nobody likes to get in a rut — a bored Pom is a bad Pom, but a tired Pom is a good Pom.

Cuddle-up pup

What about being a lap dog? Poms enjoy cuddling in your lap and being spoiled, but only after they've had a chance to run around and be dogs.

Poms are affectionate but not fawning. They tend to be very attached to their family, often choosing one member as their special person.

Perky and playful

Poms just want to have fun! This fun-loving fuzz ball is always eager to play a game. For instance, he loves to play big-game hunter with tiny, stuffed, squeaky toys and may find a thrown ball irresistible.

He won't back down from a game of tug of war, but be careful not to pull too hard or he may go flying — *and* he can do all this inside your apartment! (But be sure you get outside too. See the previous section "Great balls of fire!")

Fit and fancy-free

Pomeranians descend from one of the most ancient lines of domesticated dogs, the Spitz family, which has been associated with hunter-gatherers for at least 6,000 years. (See the sidebar "The Pomeranian genealogy" for more on their background.) But a Pom doesn't just look like a miniature Spitz. She also acts like the tough northern dog whose ancestors pulled sleds and sounded the alarm if intruders came calling. That's no work for sissy dogs.

It's the Spitz

Pomeranians are the smallest of the dogs considered to be in the Spitz family. Spitz breeds tend to have wolflike or foxlike wedge-shaped heads, small ears, thick double coats, bushy tails curled over the back, and a stocky build. They are independent by nature. Other Spitz breeds include the Akita, Siberian Husky, American Eskimo Dog, and a host of others.

Spitz dogs have always relied on their own thinking to get the job done. In the same tradition, Pomeranians don't just sit around scratching their ears, waiting for your next command — they're already acting out their own plan. As a result, Poms are constantly checking out new sights and don't mind telling your company they're not welcome. (Yes, they can be a little suspicious of strangers — it's the Spitz way.) That's why early socialization and training are vital for Pomeranians.

The little brainiac

Pomeranians are incredibly bright (although their independent nature means they often use their intelligence to get into mischief). And they won't be bullied into compliance — their Spitz ancestry makes them too good at digging in their heels. That's why positive, reward-based training methods work so well with them. When you convince your Pom that your way pays off for him, he becomes your apt and willing pupil. In fact, many Pomeranians have attained high honors in obedience trials, and they're adept at picking up new tricks.

Bold and brash

One of the less-bright traits of Poms is forgetting their size. They tend to approach much larger dogs with brash cockiness, almost daring them to cross the line. The bluff often works — the big dogs back away from this mighty mouse — but not always. As a Pom owner, you want to make sure your dog doesn't overestimate herself.

Watchdog extraordinaire

Smaller Spitz dogs were used as watchdogs, and the Pomeranian certainly doesn't disappoint in that regard. This perky patroller is always on the alert, sounding the alarm if anything is even slightly amiss.

Sometimes they can get carried away in the barking department, so it's important to train your dog when to bark and when to obey your command to be quiet. Holding his tongue is a challenge for most Poms, though! After all, he does have very strong opinions, and he expects you to listen to them.

Protection dog — not so much!

Of course, if a burglar decides to ignore the barking, your Pom probably isn't too much help in ripping him to shreds. Nevertheless, at least one Pom has been proclaimed a hero for attacking an armed intruder and saving his mistress. I was so impressed that I include him as one of the most famous Poms in Chapter 17.

All Things Considered: The Pros and Cons of Poms

As cute as Poms are, you'd expect them to be the most popular dog in America. In fact, they're not far from it. Toy dogs have been steadily gaining in popularity since the turn of the millennium, with an almost alarming increase in their numbers. Pomeranians were among the top-10 most popular AKC breeds in the mid-1990s; since then, they've been passed by other toy breeds but they still remain in the top 15.

Even with all their advantages, though, Poms aren't for everyone. This section can help you see how Pom perks and pitfalls balance out for you.

The not-so-great points

On the down side, no dog, not even a Pom, is perfect for every person and situation. While small size has big advantages, it also has disadvantages worth considering, as do some other Pom characteristics. For example:

- Toy dogs can be seriously injured by jumping off of furniture, being dropped, or being stepped on.
- They can trip you easily.

✔ They're too fragile for very young children to play with safely.

✔ They can't go jogging with you, can't get far hiking, can't do a good job of protecting you, and can't do some dog sports aimed at larger dogs.

✔ Housetraining can be more of a challenge in toy dogs compared to large dogs.

✔ They can be killed by larger dogs, wild predators, or even birds of prey.

✔ Poms in particular need attention to their coat.

✔ Poms can also bark a lot.

The great points

One reason for the upsurge in toy dog popularity is that it makes sense to go small! Consider these other reasons:

✔ Small dogs cost less to board, medicate, and generally care for.

✔ They can chew on one kibble like it's a feast.

✔ Because less goes in, less comes out, and you aren't faced with elephantine poop piles or puddles.

✔ You can carry a toy dog in a purse-sized bag and take her with you to places big dogs aren't allowed.

✔ Busy schedules, small yards, and maybe a bit of laziness all make small dogs more appealing when you consider the exercising element.

✔ Small dogs don't need to go outside in bad weather to get some exercise. On snowy days, you can play fetch, tag, or your own crazy games indoors!

✔ They don't push you out of your bed or eat you out of house and home.

✔ They don't drag you down the sidewalk, kill the neighbor's cat, or jump through your windows to attack the mail carrier.

When you've decided a toy dog is just the ticket, you have so many breeds — Affenpinschers to Yorkshire Terriers — to choose from. So why a Pomeranian?

Uniqueness

Poms have their own way of standing out among the toy dogs:

- ✔ Poms are among the smallest of all the toy breeds.

- ✔ They're among the more energetic and adventurous of toys.

- ✔ They enjoy meeting challenges and can succeed at many dog sports.

- ✔ Poms love to play, but they also enjoy cuddling.

Color varieties

Poms come in one of the widest varieties of colors of any breed: white, black, brown, red, orange, cream, blue, sable, black and tan, brown and tan, spotted, brindle, and combinations of these colors and patterns.

The earliest Poms were white or sometimes black and white or solid black. When the red-sable Marco came on the scene (see the sidebar "The Pomeranian genealogy" for more on this guy), he aroused interest in other colors.

In the early 1900s, an orange English Champion named Mars came to America and created not only a sensation but also a demand for more orange! By the 1930s, Poms were being shown in a wide variety of colors, with blacks enjoying popularity. In the 1960s, black and tans, formerly unacceptable, were deemed acceptable by the Pomeranian standard. Since then, black and tans have become some of the top-winning Poms in the country. In 1996, brindle was finally recognized as an acceptable color.

Chapter 3

In Search of Your Soul Mate

So, you've decided a Pomeranian is for you. Just as important, you think this is the right time and you have the right place for a Pom. You're ready to zip out and pick up the first cute one you see. Whoa — hold on there! Even though you're tempted to grab the classifieds, run down to the pet shop, or log onto an online pet site, you have other questions to consider.

In particular, you need to decide exactly what you want in a Pom. So in this chapter I lay out the preliminary options you need to consider, such as gender, age, quality, and quantity. I also offer pros and cons, recommendations, and even guidance on the cost of your new Pom friend.

I promise it's almost time for you to go out and get the Pom of your dreams. But sit tight — you get to that part in Chapter 4.

Before you begin your hunt, you also need to know what source will be best. Not all Pom sources are equal, so I provide a little caution to help you find that perfect Pom. In this chapter I give you a close-up look at the best places for Pom shopping as well as the places to avoid. I also show you how to carefully size up breeders and other sources, and I give tips on adopting abandoned Poms.

Boy or Girl? Choosing the Right Gender for You

How do you know whether to buy all your new puppy items in pink or blue until you decide boy or girl? How do you know whether to call your new puppy toys *baby dolls* or *action figures?* Of course, the Pom or Poms you choose don't really care about such human distinctions — they just want you to love and take care of them. However, to ensure that you'll provide the right care, you do want to understand the different gender needs and challenges.

Whether you choose male or female is primarily a matter of preference. Gender doesn't indicate personality even though some people consider males to be more loving and females to be a little smarter. But these are broad generalizations; you can easily end up with a cuddle-loving female or a smart-as-a-whip male. And although females tend to be a little smaller, the difference is somewhere between tiny and teensy. Unless competing for the world's smallest dog is your goal, size isn't a big consideration when choosing your Pom's gender. A bigger concern is a Pom *in heat.*

The main points to consider? Females come into season for about three weeks twice a year; males tend to lift their legs and mark in the house. But if you plan to have your dog neutered, you won't have to worry about these problems. *Spaying* involves removal of the uterus and ovaries. Although humans who undergo such surgeries take a long time to recuperate, dogs, especially young ones, recover within a couple of days. *Castration,* on the other hand, involves removal of the testicles.

In addition to the bloody discharge and wanderlust that are commonly associated with a female dog in heat, a female dog that hasn't been spayed will shed her coat a month or two after her season. Your once-beautiful puffball becomes a scrawny little rat for a bit because, like all unspayed females, she has hormones raging through her body. *Note:* A female Pom will lose her coat whether she *whelps* (gives birth) or is just in heat.

There's nothing you can do but pull out the vacuum (for the rug, not the dog!) and know that her hair will look as pretty as ever in a couple of months. But if you are trying to keep her looking pretty for a special event in just a week or two and she hasn't started shedding too much, the best advice is to not wash her. Washing, especially in warm water, loosens the hair follicles. By the time you dry and brush her, you may find half her hair in your brush!

Age Matters: Choosing Your Match

As long as your Pom is past the age of consent (at least 8 weeks of age), does it really matter how old he is when you bring him home to meet the family? Maybe not as much as you think. I touch on some pros and cons of older versus younger Poms in this section, but don't let age alone deter you.

The benefits and drawbacks of maturity

Most people think *puppy* when they think about getting a new dog, but adult Poms offer many advantages over puppies. If you work outside the home, have children, or live in an otherwise hectic household, consider an adult dog. For additional info and even more reasons to adopt a senior, check *Senior Dogs For Dummies* by Susan McCullough (Wiley).

Many breeders have adult dogs available that may be retired breeding dogs or show dogs that never quite turned into championship material. Be forewarned: They're still oh-so-capable of winning your heart!

Rescue groups also have adults available. In fact, always consider a rescue when considering a new adult dog. (See the end of this chapter and Chapter 4 for more information on rescued Poms.)

If you're choosing an adult Pom, what you see is what you get — no need trying to predict what his adult personality's going to be. Of course he may be a little shy at first (more so than a puppy), but as long as he's not hiding and growling, that reaction is normal.

He also has more sense than puppies and knows enough to wonder why this stranger (you!) is so interested in him. Will he take a treat from you? That's a sign that he's not really upset. If he's still uneasy, ask the breeder whether you all can go to some neutral territory. Some dogs are more apprehensive when a stranger invades their home.

Consider these other benefits and concerns of caring for an adult Pom:

> ✓ **Affection:** Some people are concerned that an adult dog won't form the attachment to you that a puppy would. Fear not — Pomeranians form bonds very quickly. Within a short period, your adult Pomeranian will feel like she's owned you all her life.

If the dog's really shy or aggressive, though, she needs a more experienced owner. You don't do yourself or the dog any favors by taking on a challenge that you don't know how to manage.

✔ **Behavior:** Mature Poms are often already housetrained, but whether they catch on depends on how they've been living. If they've been in a kennel, they're usually easier to housetrain than if they've been running loose in the house untrained. Regardless, they're generally past their destructive chewing stage, although a few errant chews may still happen. Senior Poms don't need to be fed every few hours or walked every few minutes, and they even know a cool trick or two.

✔ **Habits:** Of course, older dogs may still have bad habits like using the bathroom where they want, barking at shadows, or ignoring your calls. They may have come from bad situations such as puppy mills or abusive homes, where they received bad training (or none at all). For these reasons, find out as much as you can about an older dog's background before you bring her home. Taking on more than you can handle isn't fair to either of you.

✔ **Health:** How is his health? The older the dog, the more likely health problems are to show up. As your last step, have a veterinarian examine him. If the dog has health problems, the veterinarian may be able to advise you as to whether the problems will worsen.

And remember, nobody's perfect! He's probably wondering about your temperament, too.

The joys and trials of youth

Ah, glorious youth! The age where the eyes sparkle, the teeth gnaw, and the rear end leaks like a sieve. Wait a minute — tell me again why everyone wants a puppy? One reason is obvious — Pom puppies are just so darn cute. Period.

Puppies have a couple of benefits, though, that pack a serious punch:

✔ **They learn to do things your way.** Simply put, it's a lot easier convincing your new dog that your way is the right way without her pointing out, "That's not how they did it where I used to live!"

✔ **You can train your dog to do special tasks or live in special circumstances.** You may have a special job planned for your Pom (like being a therapy dog) or simply special requirements (like living with cats or other pets). Exposing her to any special circumstances early in life helps her take them in stride later on.

Deciding Whether Two Poms Are Better Than One

Poms are social animals, which makes them such great companions. Without another dog in the house, your Pom looks to you to be her buddy. But when you're not home, who does she have for company?

Give some strong thought to two Poms if you live alone and work out of the house (or travel a lot) and you have no other pets.

You don't need to worry about competing with your Poms for their affection because they have plenty of love to go around. They can thoroughly enjoy each other when you're gone and be happy to fully enjoy you when you're home. You have twice the fun, twice the cuddling, and twice the floorshow. Watching two Poms at play is better than any television show ever made. Best of all, two puppies can comfort or entertain each other when you're trying to get some sleep at night!

Although two dogs may become especially attached to one another (making you feel a tad neglected), you can easily remedy the situation by separating them and focusing your attention on each, one at a time. Make this time special by training, or playing a game, or taking them for a car ride, one playmate at a time.

 If you decide to get two pups, you'll find that opposite sexes tend to get along the best. *Note:* That suggestion is assuming you plan to have them spayed and neutered. Otherwise, opposites become too attractive and it's a mistake. Besides, most good breeders don't sell what may appear to be a breeding pair of *pet-quality* puppies (see the following section for more about this term) unless you agree to early spaying and neutering. Responsible breeders don't want you rushing off to breed puppies, whether irresponsibly or naively.

What about more than two dogs? My answer to that question is to consider how many hands you have and succumb to my advice that two is pushing it at the start. One day, you may be able to handle three Poms. But take it from somebody (me) who has had every number of dogs, from 1 to 13, at a time: After three, it only gets harder!

Considering Your Goals: What Pom Type Would You Like?

The term *quality* isn't necessarily about how *good* a dog is; it's more about his *type*. Poms have three qualities: *pet* (also called *companion*), *show,* and *breeding*. Although *pet* is the lowest quality and *breeding* is the highest, the Pom that's best for you will always be top quality in your eyes!

Dogs from hobby breeders are generally graded as either *show* or *pet* quality. The third type, *breeding* quality, can't be determined until the dog is an adult.

The higher quality you demand, the longer your search will take. A couple of months is a reasonable time in which to find a pet-quality Pom, but plan to wait a year or so for show quality. Finding a true breeding-quality Pom may take a few years.

Pet (or companion) quality

A pet-quality dog has a trait that prevents him from winning in the conformation show ring. The trait can be major (like being way too big or having very little coat), or it can be minor (like having toes that point out or the wrong-shaped ears). A common problem in male Poms is the failure of one or both testicles to completely descend into the scrotum.

A pet-quality dog is still in good health and has a good temperament. Being a pet or companion is the most important role any Pom can assume, so it's the very best quality for most people.

Good breeders usually sell pet-quality puppies with the requirement that that they be spayed or neutered or that they be registered with AKC limited registration (see Chapter 4). If your dog does turn out to be higher quality than initially guessed, only the breeder can change the limited registration to full registration. Of course, no one can un-spay or un-neuter the dog! Regardless, spayed, neutered, or limited-registered dogs can compete in every other venue of competition except conformation showing.

Show quality

Show-quality dogs, like pet-quality dogs, must be in good health and have good temperaments. In addition, to have a reasonable expectation of becoming champions, they must portray the qualities of the breed standard.

Expect to pay considerably more for a show-quality dog than a pet-quality dog. *Note:* A breeder who doesn't show his own dogs is unlikely to produce show-quality Pomeranians. At least one parent should bear an American Kennel Club (AKC) Champion (CH) title in front of its name, and the remainder of the pedigree should be peppered with champions.

If you want a show-quality dog, your wait will be significantly longer than if you want a companion-quality dog. And the more you demand in terms of quality and specifics, the longer you can expect to wait for that perfect puppy. At the very least, expect to wait a couple of months. The reason for this wait is twofold:

- ✔ So many factors can change with age. If you really have your heart set on a show-quality puppy, you may need to buy an older puppy (at a higher price) that has greater assurance of turning out as planned.

- ✔ Poms have small litters (two to four puppies) and only a small percentage of those litters may be show quality.

If you decide to get a show-quality dog, keep these points in mind:

- ✔ **Flaws may emerge at a later age.** Maybe a puppy keeps on growing and growing or the coat falls out. Hey, nobody's perfect. Dog shows are fun, but they make up only a miniscule part of the time you share with a dog. Don't let it bother you, and try competing in one of the many other areas open to you and your Pom.

- ✔ **Be fair to the breeder.** If you buy a show-quality dog, plan to show it. Hobby breeders work hard to produce these show-quality puppies. Their payback isn't the purchase price but the thrill of seeing their protégés win in the show ring, especially for a novice owner. Promising to show their future star and then hiding him from the world is not good form.

- ✔ **You need to earn the breeder's trust.** If you've never shown a dog before, most breeders will be hesitant about entrusting you with a top show-quality puppy. A good way to earn their trust and respect is to earn an obedience title with another dog, perhaps by first buying a companion-quality puppy.

Breeding quality

Breeding-quality dogs come from impeccable backgrounds and are usually exemplary show dogs. A few may have a fault that prevents them from shining in the ring (such as a crooked ear or a size that's out of the standard), but they possess other merits that more than make up for it. Above all, these dogs are free of serious genetic disease. Don't expect a good breeder to sell you a breeding-quality dog as your first Pom. You'll need to prove yourself by competing with your current Pom and by not rushing out to breed any dog you happen to own.

If a breeder tries to tell you a tiny puppy is breeding quality, the breeder probably has little idea of what breeding quality really means (except the ability to produce puppies). A show-quality dog is difficult to identify as a puppy; a breeding-quality dog is impossible.

Perusing Pedigrees

A registered dog comes with a *pedigree,* a story of who begat who that can be traced back to the first Poms in this country. Most pedigrees only show you who's who for the last three to four generations. On the registration paper, your puppy's litter is on the left-hand side. From there the pedigree works back, generation by generation, moving left to right, with the *sire* (the male) always above the name of his progeny, and the *dam* (the female) always below.

Early spay-neuter

Many adoption groups and some breeders sterilize puppies before they're adopted, even if that means as early as 8 weeks of age. They take special precautions (minimizing surgical time, keeping the puppy warm, withholding food for as short a time as possible, and being extremely careful with their comparatively delicate tissues) to avoid hypothermia, hypoglycemia, and excessive bleeding in the pup.

Given these precautions, puppies sterilized at early ages have shorter recovery times and fewer complications than pups sterilized later. Some limited information suggests that females spayed at a young age have a higher incidence of urinary incontinence, but that tends to be more of a problem in large breeds.

If you want a top-quality dog, look for titles in the pedigree. For example, the letters *CH* stand for *champion* and designate a dog that has won based on the breed standard. The letters *CD, CDX,* and *UD (Companion Dog, Companion Dog Excellent,* and *Utility Dog)* or *RN, RA,* and *RX (Rally Novice, Advanced,* and *Excellent)* after a dog's name are various obedience titles. They signify dogs that have demonstrated minding skills in obedience trials.

If you don't plan to compete with your dog (and most people don't), these titles still demonstrate a breeder's sincerity in using the best dogs and her intent to do more with her dogs than just breed them. Of greater importance are health clearances. ***Note:*** Titles and clearances on dogs farther back than the grandparents aren't significant.

Look especially for whether the litter is *inbred* (the litter has the same dog appearing behind both the sire and the dam). Fewer generations between that dog and the litter generally mean a more-inbred litter. See Figure 3-1 for a sample pedigree of an inbred dog — this is what you *don't* want to see.

Although inbreeding is a tool used by many breeders, the average pet owner gains nothing by having an inbred dog. Inbreeding increases the chance of two recessive genes appearing in a puppy, increasing the chance of certain recessively inherited health problems such as progressive retinal atrophy or a generally weaker immune system.

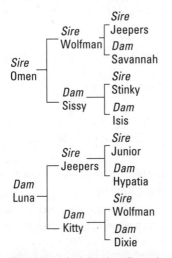

Figure 3-1: An inbred pedigree has the same dog behind both father and mother.

Evaluating Pom Sources

Finding a Pomeranian isn't hard. Your challenge is to find one that will live a long and healthy life. So you want to find a breeder who's careful about the dogs she breeds, the way she raises them, and the homes she sends them to. The problem is that such breeders don't always make themselves easy to find because they have a long waiting list of good homes.

How do you know when someone's a good breeder? Two steps: First, understand the various sources for dogs, and second, know how to evaluate the quality of each source. The primary sources for Poms are

- ✔ Pet stores (supplied by commercial breeders)
- ✔ Backyard breeders (found usually through newspaper ads)
- ✔ Serious breeders (also known as hobby breeders)
- ✔ Rescue groups and shelters

Pet stores and commercial breeders

Pomeranians, with their stuffed-teddy-bear looks, are popular pet-store puppies. They appeal to impulse buyers who take one look and whip out their credit card. In contrast to pet stores that tend to rely on impulse buyers, good breeders most likely turn away impulse shoppers because they want to ensure a good fit between owner and dog.

Some pet stores rely on uninformed buyers who don't know:

- ✔ Puppies are hauled across country to the stores by the truckload.
- ✔ These pups come from large, commercial-breeding operations that often keep hundreds of dogs in cramped cages, sometimes in squalid conditions.
- ✔ This breeding stock is bought and sold at auctions, with low price usually being the deciding factor.
- ✔ Poor temperaments, poor resemblance to the breed, poor structure, and poor health don't matter; it's all about profit.

Pet-store puppies are often raised in a wire-floored cage, sometimes stacked on top of one another. In the worst situations, urine and feces from pups on top fall down on puppies below, who then grow up without the normal canine disgust for stepping in their own waste. This scenario can make housetraining a potential nightmare because the pups never experience doing their business outside on the grass. Also, socialization, which is so vital for puppies, is absent or minimal. Sadly, a pet-store Pom, though surely cute, is probably no bargain, especially with the large retail-price markups (more on pricing in Chapter 4).

Not every commercial breeder has such bad conditions. Some of these breeders realize that the best way to raise salable puppies is to produce puppies under healthy circumstances. The problem is that you can't tell which puppies come from which type of commercial breeder after the pups are in the pet store.

Newspaper ads and backyard breeders

Another place to find a Pomeranian puppy is in the newspaper's classified section. These ads are often placed by people referred to as *backyard breeders*.

A backyard breeder may be operating a small-scale puppy mill. In other words:

- ✔ He may keep dogs of different breeds, selling the puppies to make extra money.

- ✔ He puts up roadside signs advertising puppies and even sells puppies at flea markets.

- ✔ He keeps the dogs in poor conditions, seldom has their health tested, and provides minimal socialization for the dogs.

Ferreting out a bad-news backyard breeder is easy: Ask whether he'll have other litters coming any time soon. If he replies, "Sure, what breed would you like?" tell him "None."

Sometimes a backyard breeder is a family that decides to breed a litter from their pet Pomeranian. And they may have a variety of reasons: They want their children to experience the miracle of birth; they want to add a new Pom that looks like the one they have; or they want to see whether they can make a few dollars. Although they're possibly a bit naïve about the whole breeding process, their intentions are good. As Pom owners, they care about the pups and will care about you. The puppies may be well socialized, but their parents may not have been health tested.

Beware the claims of rare

If a breeder claims a dog is rare because of color, size, or an unusual trait, this statement should raise a caution flag. Some colors are more common than others, but no Pom color is rare, and certain colors don't make a dog more valuable.

The same is true of size. The Pomeranian standard specifies the average weight to be 3 to 7 pounds (4 to 6 pounds for show dogs). Within this range, one size is as good as another. Smaller sizes can be more difficult to keep healthy, so aim for the top of the standard.

A family backyard breeder may not be the ideal place to buy a puppy, but they are better than pet stores or small-scale puppy mills. This is definitely a situation where you as the buyer must beware and ask lots of questions.

Hobby breeders who are really serious

For some Pom lovers, breeding healthy, high-quality Pomeranians is an obsession. They compete in conformation shows or performance events and virtually center their lives on their dogs. These serious breeders are usually referred to as *hobby breeders* — although their dedication surpasses that of most hobbies. Many people are under the false impression that breeders breed to make money. But hobby and serious breeders don't. It's not a business; it's a love affair. And almost invariably, they spend much more money on their dogs than they can ever hope to recoup

If you want a high-quality Pomeranian, serious hobby breeders are your best source. However, they're also more difficult to find, so a little sleuthing may be needed. Here are good sources for information:

✔ **National Clubs:** The best place to start is the American Pomeranian Club national breeder referral list (go to www.americanpomeranianclub.org and click on <u>APC Info</u> and then <u>Member Roster</u>). You can find contact information for local members who may be breeders or who can direct you to breeders.

You can also contact the club's national breeder referral person by clicking on <u>APC Info</u> and then <u>Breeder Referral Info</u>. The breeder referral person often knows who has litters in your area or who has litters of various colors if you have a preference. Most, but not all, hobby breeders are members of the national breed club.

Joining the club means agreeing to a code of ethics that covers integrity in breeding. Of course, signing the code doesn't guarantee people will follow it any more than joining the club makes them magically good breeders. But it's a start.

✔ **Regional Clubs:** In addition to the national club, many regional Pomeranian clubs exist. (The national site can refer you to a regional club in your area; click on <u>APC Info</u> and then <u>Regional Clubs</u>.) Getting to know local Pomeranian breeders is one of the best ways to meet their dogs in person and to let the breeders know what a good home you have for one of their puppies.

✔ **Dog Shows:** Another way to meet breeders is by attending a local dog show. You can find upcoming shows at the American Kennel Club's Web page for upcoming events at `www.akc.org/events/search/` or check out `www.infodog.com`. The latter site also includes the specific times Pomeranians are shown at particular shows.

Although Pomeranian exhibitors are usually happy to talk to you, the one time they'd rather not chat is right before they go in the ring. Make arrangements to talk to them after judging is over.

✔ **Dog-Specific Magazines:** Several sources are available.

   • A Pomeranian magazine like *The Pom Reader* or a magazine aimed at toy breeds like *Top Notch Toys* are excellent places to find top breeders. Go to `www.dmcg.com` for more information.

   • All-breed dog magazines like *Dog World* (`www.animalchannel.com`) also contain advertisements from hobby breeders.

✔ **Veterinarians:** Local veterinarians can often be a good source. After all, they know breeders, so they know which breeders take good care of their dogs!

✔ **Internet:** You can join one of the many Pomeranian discussion lists on the Internet. Start your search at `www.yahoogrops.com` and look for breeders there, but you must evaluate these breeders carefully.

The next section equips you to separate the wheat from the chaff when it comes to serious Pom breeders.

Finding Good Breeders

Okay, so it's time to grill the breeder! Not really, of course. You want to listen carefully as he shares his enthusiasm for his dogs. In fact, you're establishing a relationship, not just buying a dog. Besides being your best source for a puppy with good health, good temperament, and good looks, a good breeder also becomes your mentor and friend. For example:

- ✔ You can always ask questions, share anecdotes, and find help at a moment's notice.

- ✔ You find that you're part of an extended family of puppy owners, and you can keep up with littermates throughout their lives.

- ✔ If circumstances arise that force you to surrender your dog, a good breeder is there to make sure your dog's taken care of.

The following series of questions (and the right answers) can help you determine the good breeders from the bad ones:

- ✔ **Can I visit in person?** Good breeders may actually require that you visit in person so they can meet you and see how you interact with the dogs. The breeder has no valid reason for not allowing you to visit except if you have a sick dog at home. If they say "No" to a visit, say "Good-bye," hang up, and dial the next number on your list.

- ✔ **Do you specialize in Pomeranians?** Dealing with one breed is so challenging that serious breeders stick with the breed they're passionate about. Unless she's building an ark, a breeder who has two of everything (multiple breeds) is more likely a small-scale puppy mill. (Check back to "Newspaper ads and backyard breeders" for more on this breed of breeder.)

- ✔ **Do you always have puppies available?** Breeders who *always* have puppies may not be able to give each litter the attention it needs. You want your puppy to experience the breeder's home, not just his kennel or garage. However, if the breeder has years of experience, a great deal of success, the proper facilities, and good help to make sure the dogs are properly cared for and socialized, then the constant breeding may not be an issue.

- ✔ **Are the dogs registered with the AKC or United Kennel Club (UKC)?** A good breeder registers her dogs. Although other registries exist, only the AKC and the UKC are considered reputable.

✔ **What sort of health concerns do you screen for?** If they claim Pomeranians have no such concerns, you know you're dealing with the wrong people. If they say Poms need no health screening, walk away. If they say they've had a couple of problems, keep listening. No line is completely free of health problems, and you may have just met an honest breeder.

But at the same time, be careful. You may have just met a really stupid breeder who doesn't know any better. See Chapter 4 for a list of tests to look for.

✔ **Do you participate with your dogs in conformation shows, agility trials, obedience trials, or therapy work? Have the dogs earned any titles?** Participation indicates an above-average commitment to the breed. Titles indicate an above-average dedication to the breed plus better-than-average quality of the dogs (Refer back to "Considering Your Goals: What Pom Type Would You Like?" for definitions of *quality*.)

✔ **Can I see the pedigree?** The pedigree should always be available for inspection. If it's not, this is not a reputable breeder.

✔ **What sort of paperwork comes with the puppy?** Several kinds of paper should be available:

- You can expect a medical history, a pedigree, and a registration slip.

- A good breeder also includes written care instructions, a contract, and a warranty.

  No breeder can guarantee everything, but he should warrantee the puppy's health for the first week and perhaps offer a partial refund in the event of certain hereditary diseases.

  A contract should cover a plan for the puppy if you can't keep her. For example, a good breeder stipulates that you must return the puppy to the breeder to prevent the puppy ending up in a shelter or being passed from person to person. *Note:* In most cases the breeder does not give a refund for a returned puppy that's grown up because placing an adult dog is usually difficult.

✔ **Do you have any breeding requirements?** Some breeders require you to breed your dog and then share the litter with them or to provide free stud service. This is never a good idea. You may wish to spay or neuter your dog, and you don't want to be obligated to breed.

✔ **Do you require that the puppy be spayed or neutered?** This is not an issue about competition. Good breeders often require you to spay or neuter your dog because they're concerned about the future of the puppy and the breed. The dog they sold you is probably companion quality, which means she's a wonderful dog but not show or breeding quality; as such, she shouldn't be bred.

Good breeders are also concerned about your taking the plunge into breeding. Breeding responsibly and knowledgably isn't something you can just jump right into, and you may end up being sorry you ever had such a foolish idea.

An alternative to required spay-neuter is AKC limited registration, which means that if you breed your dog, her offspring can't be AKC Registered.

✔ **When can I take a new Pom puppy home?** The answer to this question is an opportunity to evaluate the breeder. Breeders out for a buck are eager to get a puppy off their feed bill as soon as possible. Backyard breeders who don't know any better may also let you take home your puppy whenever you want. No puppy of any breed should leave its breeder before 8 weeks of age. For more info on when the pup can leave the breeder, see Chapter 4.

✔ **How much do puppies cost?** Good breeders charge neither bargain-basement prices nor exorbitantly high prices in comparison to other breeders. Although prices vary by region of the country, a good companion-quality Pomeranian from a reputable breeder should cost $300 to $900. See Chapter 4 for more details on price.

✔ **Do you have any previous puppy buyers I can talk to?** Good breeders keep in touch with their puppy buyers. If they claim not to have any contact information, that's a bad sign. Good breeders are also proud of their puppies and know their puppies' owners are proud, too. For privacy reasons, they may ask that the former buyers contact you rather than vice versa. But if they flat out say "No," walk away.

As you check out serious breeders, you may quickly discover that they're also evaluating you! In fact, if you *don't* feel they're curious about you as a potential pet owner, it can be a red flag. For example, when a breeder only seems concerned about your check clearing, you may want to move on to another breeder.

Good breeders make sure their puppies go where they'll be loved for a lifetime. For that reason, the breeder usually checks out the following:

✔ They ask about your experience with dogs and pets in general and toy dogs in particular.

✔ They ask about your home and family and where you plan to keep the dog.

✔ They're very upfront with you about expenses, exercise, training, grooming, health care, and safety issues.

✔ They often require that you neuter or spay your dog, and may ask you to wait for several months for a litter. During this cooling off period, they're making sure you're not just impulse buying.

Rescuing Abandoned Poms

It's hard to believe, but many Poms are out there needing a secure home and a family to love them. Reasons for abandonment abound, but most often it's just the wrong home for the right dog. Maybe an owner simply got tired of the Pom, couldn't deal with the barking, or had life changes that left him unable to care for a dog. Poms get abandoned just like other dogs.

Whether they had a loving owner or not, rescued Poms are often apprehensive, confused, and even frightened. They may cling to their foster owners or new families, afraid that they'll lose these recent saviors. But with time, love, training, and stability, these Poms gradually adapt to their new circumstances and become exceptional family companions.

You may fear that adopting a rescued Pom means taking on somebody else's problems or that rescued dogs come with emotional baggage. These occurrences are rare. In fact, the top obedience Pomeranian of all time was rescued at 8 years of age from an animal shelter.

A rescued Pomeranian is the deal of a lifetime but certainly not free. Because rescue groups realize that people tend to value pets that they've invested in and because these groups need to recoup their expenses to continue the services, they charge a reasonable fee. Expect to pay about $200 or so for a Pom from a rescue group.

To the rescue!

Even if you can't take on the long-term responsibility of a dog, you can do your part for rescue. Rescue groups always need supplies, money, and volunteers.

Volunteers can help rescue, bathe, groom, socialize, train, and transport Pomeranians. Most of all, volunteers can help foster by providing a temporary home while a Pom awaits a forever home.

Here are ways you can find Poms in need of homes through rescue groups or shelters:

- ✔ **The American Pomeranian Club:** The club maintains a national rescue network that you can access through their Web site at www.americanpomeranianclub.org. Click on APC Info and then Rescue. The Rescue link also lists local rescue contacts around the country.

- ✔ **Petfinder:** This group maintains a national database of dogs of all breeds in shelters. Go to www.petfinder.com and search by Pomeranian.

  You can also narrow your search to just local shelters. Dogs from shelters tend to cost a little less than dogs from breed rescue groups, but they often don't go through as much screening or preparation.

- ✔ **Pomeranian Club of Canada Rescue (Canada):** Access this group through their Web site at www.toyrificpoms.com/pomrescue/index.htm. This group focuses on Poms in Canada.

- ✔ **Pomeranian and Small Breed Rescue (Canada):** You can reach this group at www.psbrescue.com.

Chapter 4

The Final Selection: Picking Your Perfect Partner

So far, so good. You've found a good breeder (or two or three), seen a bevy of Poms of all ages up close and personal, and you're still certain you want a Pomeranian. Terrific! (If you haven't read Chapter 3, it's loaded with ideas for getting to this point.) But as visions of all those bouncing Pomeranian puffballs dance in your head, how do you narrow the choice to the one (or two) that will be coming home with you?

Funny you should ask. This chapter eases you through all those steps — from setting eyes on your dream Pom to signing on the dotted line. I give you background info on fair prices, interactions with the breeder and her pups, and the all-important health questions. The last few sections cover the red tape: payments, paperwork, and registration. I also include the info you need to feel comfortable dealing with an alternative source — rescue programs and shelters. (Please read Chapter 3 for an introduction to these two resources.) At last, the best part is about to begin!

Knowing the Right Price: A Quick Guide

Talking money and filling out papers isn't nearly as much fun as playing with your new Pom, but it's a necessary part of buying a purebred Pomeranian. A good breeder knows all the procedures, but you're wise to have some knowledge of the basics as well.

When's the right time to ask about price? That's difficult to say. If you make price the first question on your list, the breeder may get the impression you're just out for a bargain puppy — a big turnoff for good breeders looking for good homes. On the other hand, talking for hours or making multiple visits only to discover the puppy is out of your price range sounds pretty silly.

The best time to bring the subject up is before you visit but after the breeder tells you briefly about the puppies — and perhaps after you tell the breeder about yourself. Be upfront; you know good-quality Poms can be costly, so you want to make sure you can afford one from this breeder before taking up any more of his time — or yours.

Although I can't tell you specifically how much you'll pay for a Pom, I can give you an idea of what factors affect the price:

- ✔ **Region of the country where you live (or buy your Pom from):** More urban and affluent areas charge more. (No shocker there!)

- ✔ **Age of puppy:** Younger puppies tend to bring more than older puppies or adults that may not be considered as cute unless, of course, the older puppy is show quality (See Chapter 3). Then it goes for quite a bit more than the others because its show prospects are more certain; see the next bullet.

- ✔ **Pedigree and show quality:** Puppies from parents with titles or *health testing* (veterinary tests to show they are clear of various hereditary health problems — see Chapter 11) generally cost more.

  A show-prospect puppy may range from $900 to $1,500. An older puppy that is definitely show quality ranges from $1,500 on up.

- ✔ **Who you buy your puppy from:** Usually puppies from pet stores cost the most, followed by hobby breeders, then backyard breeders. (Refer to Chapter 3 for info on all these Pom terms.) Newspaper ads by backyard breeders in your area can give you a good idea of low-end prices, and local pet-store prices represent the high end.

- Pet-store prices range from $1000 to $1,500.

- Breeder prices for a healthy puppy range from $300 to $900.

- Rescue prices range from $100 to $300, with less expensive dogs coming from shelters and slightly more expensive ones coming from rescue groups.

In general, the lower prices are for older dogs or dogs that require neutering or spaying.

In the long run, the dog from the hobby breeder is the best bargain because it's been screened for hereditary health problems and brought up under healthier conditions. But the rescue dog gives you the most love for your buck!

If the breeder has a waiting list, she may require you to place a deposit to save your spot. This step is customary, but be sure to get a receipt that spells out any agreements (like the sex and health of the puppy) and guarantees your money back if no puppies become available within a specified time period.

A deposit is also necessary if you've selected a puppy before he's old enough to go home. Be sure you have some way of identifying that pup when you go back to pick him up! Take a photo — you'll want one anyway. If the puppies all look alike, ask the breeder to paint some of your puppy's toenails with some nail polish you've brought along.

Visiting the Breeder

After you've narrowed down your choices, you can make a visit to the breeders on your list.

Most breeders are not large-scale kennels and aren't set up for visitors to just drop in. Breeders may have a small kennel or raise puppies in their home, and they may work out of the home during the day. So trying to visit as many breeders as you can just for the fun of it isn't a good idea. As much as they love talking Poms, breeders do need to attend to their dogs and other responsibilities. Narrow your choice breeders down to just a couple of contenders; then expand your list only if those don't seem right.

In order to prevent your being the Typhoid Mary of the Pom world, breeders prefer you don't visit one kennel right after another, and you certainly shouldn't stop by the dog shelter on the way. Wash your hands before you visit the kennel and be prepared to leave your shoes outside.

Taking a look around

The visit to a kennel allows you to see how the breeder is raising the puppies, how the other dogs in the household look, and last but not least, how you get along with the breeder. Be sure to pay attention to the following:

- ✔ **Are the facilities clean, with sufficient room for the dogs?** A good breeder doesn't keep his dogs in cramped, dirty cages. This applies to every dog on the property, not just the puppies.

- ✔ **Do the puppies have time outside and access to grass?** Puppies raised entirely inside may *imprint* (learn to prefer) the surface they're forced to relieve themselves on, making housetraining difficult.

- ✔ **Do the puppies have access to people?** Puppies need some time in the house so they get plenty of socialization. If they're in a separate kennel, ask whether they get to come in the house or how the breeder socializes them.

- ✔ **Are all the dogs friendly and healthy looking?** They don't have to love you, but you don't want them snarling at you either. Are their coats well groomed?

When it comes to appearance and demeanor, make allowances for any old dogs and for the dam, whose coat has probably fallen out after *whelping* (giving birth). Ask to see pictures of her before she had puppies. She may not be thrilled with you around her puppies, but she should be comfortable with the breeder. ***Note:*** Don't expect to see the sire, which may live elsewhere.

Getting personal: Specific questions to ask

When you're on the premises and looking at the pups, here are a few more questions to bring up:

- ✔ **What was the purpose for breeding this litter?** Good breeders mate specific dogs to bring out the best qualities of both, and they're delighted to explain their reasoning. They can point to the good health of the parents, their exemplary temperaments, or their conformity to the breed standard. If the breeder is evasive or the answer sounds off, then beware.

✔ **Can I see photos of both parents and other relatives?** Good breeders may have you regretting you asked this question as they proudly pull out photo album after album of Trixie's ancestors. Bad breeders — Camera? Photos? Huh?

✔ **How do the parents compare to the Pomeranian breed standard?** That is, can the breeder point to a dog and say this one has the correct foxlike expression, but her ears are a little too large and her skull is a little too domed? A breeder who says her dogs are perfect or advises you to ignore the standard is no longer a good candidate.

✔ **How soon can I take my puppy home?** No puppy of any breed should leave its breeder before 8 weeks of age. Pomeranians, like many toy puppies, are generally held longer; the breeder often insists on keeping them until they're 10 to 12 weeks old.

The Poms' small size, along with their susceptibility to hypoglycemia (see Chapter 8), makes early placement somewhat risky. In addition, puppies pick up valuable lessons about being dogs by staying with their littermates and mom. Puppies separated too early can have problems relating to other dogs for the rest of their lives.

The Big Test: Interacting with Potential Pups

After you've selected and visited your breeder (see the previous section), he may want to choose a puppy just for you based on your previous discussions. (The breeder knows the puppies better than you possibly can during your short visit, and a good breeder tries to match puppy to person based on personality.) But if you have a choice (and even if the breeder has chosen one for you), you still need to make sure this is the right puppy for you.

This section gives you helpful hints on setting the stage for this all-important interaction and carefully selecting the new love of your life.

Getting the ground rules right

When you're at the breeders and ready to interact, keep these suggestions in mind as the breeder brings the puppies to you:

✔ **Sit on the floor with the puppies.** This arrangement encourages them to come and see you and allows you to interact more freely with them. It also eliminates the chance of tripping over, stepping on, or dropping one of them!

✔ **Wait for them to come to you.** Make note of which puppies come up to interact with you by climbing in your lap or playing with your fingers. Put those pups on your *yes* list. Don't chase or grab at the puppies. Nobody likes that.

✔ **Give every available puppy a fair shake.** Just because one isn't the sex or color you initially had in mind, don't write it off. You may lose out on the best dog for you.

If all the puppies look alike, you may get one confused with another. If you know you're definitely not interested in some of them, ask the breeder to take them out of the mix. Or have the breeder put different-colored ribbons on them or on their collars.

Try to visit the breeder more than once before the puppies are ready to go. Puppies often act and look very different from one visit to the next. The breeder may want you to bring your children just to see how they interact with the dogs. If you bring young children, bring another adult to supervise them. *Note:* If you can't keep your children under control for a couple of hours, the breeder may decide yours is not a safe home for a small puppy.

What if you change your mind? It's possible you could lose your deposit unless you have a valid reason. Of course, if the breeder changes his mind, he is obliged to return any deposit.

Finding love at first sight

Of course, just as with people, a puppy temperament that suits one person may not be the best for another. If you have a quiet household and a patient personality, yours may be just the home for that hesitant puppy; if you're an adventurer, you may find your match in the wildest puppy. But for most people, the middle puppy, neither quietest nor wildest, is the best choice.

As you observe these little Pom prancers at the breeder's, note these personality traits:

✔ **Confident:** Pom puppies are generally confident. They should carry their tails high and be eager to interact. Beware any puppy that hides in a corner, keeps his tail tucked, cringes at sudden noises, or growls when you approach. This puppy will need special training and is not for the novice owner.

✔ **Independent:** Take each puppy that's on your *yes* list into another room, away from its littermates. The puppy should take the separation in stride, and you should be able to get her interest.

While still separated, see whether the puppy tends to follow you. That bonding is always nice, but don't discount the puppy who gets distracted exploring all the new stuff. Regardless, you don't want the puppy that huddles on the ground, too scared to move. He may grow out of it — but not without a lot of work.

✔ **Playful:** Is the puppy interested in toys? Will he fetch? This quality is important if you like to play or if you have children. (It can also help you figure out which kinds of toys to buy!)

✔ **Affectionate:** Will the puppy allow you to hold her for a few seconds? Give her a couple of chances. You're asking a lot of a pup to pluck her from the middle of playing with her brothers and sisters and then expect her to snuggle calmly in your lap.

Still can't decide? Having a hard time saying *No* to the little puppy who seeks you out, tumbles into your lap while playing, and promptly falls asleep? Maybe letting your dog choose you really is the best approach. The only problem is that you may find yourself with an entire lap full of Pom pups! If you can't take two, maybe it's time to ask the breeder to make the final choice for you.

Screening for Good Health

Like all popular breeds, Pomeranians have their own set of heredi-tary health concerns. Small breeds, for example, tend to have *patellar luxation* (knee problems), and Poms develop this problem more than any other breed. They also tend to have *alopecia X,* a coat problem where their hair falls out. No one can guarantee these conditions will or won't appear, but puppies from parents without these problems are less likely to develop them. That's why testing the parents for various disorders is important.

Relying on the breeder's expertise and integrity

Good breeders are aware of these hereditary problems and do their best to avoid producing them in new litters. Ask the breeder whether any of the following health concerns are in a particular Pom's ancestry:

✔ **Alopecia X:** This condition is one of the Pom's most common breed predispositions. No screening test is available, but ask the breeder whether it's common in the line. Because the condition is more common in males than females, some researchers believe it's sex-linked (passed from mothers to sons).

✔ **Eye conditions:** Poms can suffer from *entropion* (the eyelid turns in on the eye) and *progressive retinal atrophy* (the light receptive cells die, and the dog becomes blind). Neither problem is especially common in the breed. Screening tests are available, and you have some assurance if the parents have been examined by a veterinary ophthalmologist and registered in the Canine Eye Registration Foundation database.

✔ **Patellar luxation:** Also known as *slipping kneecaps,* this condition affects a large percentage of Pomeranians — in fact, a higher percentage than any other breed. Although the mode of inheritance is unknown, all breeding stock should be examined.

The Orthopedic Foundation for Animals (OFA) maintains a registry (available online) of Poms that have been checked and recorded with them. Go to their Web site at www.offa. org, click on Search OFA Records, and then choose Pomeranian and Patella. Breeders are not required to register their dogs with the OFA, but they should have a veterinary report attesting to the condition of their dogs' knees.

✔ **Patent ductus arteriosus:** This is the most common heart problem seen in puppies and is particularly common in Pomeranians. Researchers believe it is caused by the interplay of several genes. Ideally, the parents, the parents' siblings, and other relatives should be screened by a veterinary cardiologist.

Other conditions like *tracheal collapse* (the windpipe can't stay open when breathing) and epilepsy have no screening tests or clearance registry, but you're wise to ask whether the litter's line has a history of them.

No hereditary line is totally disease free. A breeder may not know or may not want to tell, but that's one good reason you take the time to select a reputable, experienced breeder in the first place.

Checking up on a puppy's health

Healthy puppies are chipper little nippers. They play hard and they sleep hard. If they're awake, they should be bouncy, even if they're still pretty clumsy.

None of the puppies in a litter should have signs of potentially contagious diseases. (If one puppy's sick, you can be sure the rest are on their way.) Signs of common illnesses that you can check for yourself include

- Diarrhea or signs of recent diarrhea, such as a reddened or irritated anus

- Vomiting (excuse the occasional regurgitating that can happen when playing too hard right after eating or drinking)

- Dehydration, which can indicate a recent bout of diarrhea or vomiting

  Test for hydration by gently picking up a fold of skin and letting it go. It should snap back into place instead of forming a tent.

- Repeated sneezing, sniffling, gagging, or coughing

- Extremely runny or gooey eyes

- Snotty nose

- Dirty, smelly ears, or head shaking, which can indicate ear mites

- Pale gums, which can indicate anemia from heavy parasite infestation

  Healthy gums are bright pink.

- Thin with a potbelly, which often indicates intestinal parasites

- Dirty, crusted, or reddened skin

Now check out the individual puppy you're interested in:

- **Teeth:** Are his teeth straight? Do they meet with the front top teeth just in front of the bottom teeth?

  This detail isn't that important if you don't want show quality. However, some puppies' *occlusions* (the way the teeth meet) are so off that the pup may have difficulty eating. Other puppies' bottom fangs are too narrow and stick into the upper gums or the roof of the mouth when the puppies close their mouths. Both of these problems often require expensive dental work for the puppy to be comfortable.

- **Eyes:** Check again for irritation. Do the lids fold in on the eye? That condition may be entropion (see the first bullet list in this section). Although many puppies grow out of it, the problem may require surgery if it persists into adulthood.

✔ **Limbs:** Check for signs of limping. Puppies are always throwing themselves around and falling, so some limping may be excusable. But limping at an early age may also indicate severe patellar luxation (see the first bullet list in this section), which will probably require surgery. If the puppy of your choice is limping, ask to come back another day and check on him or request that a veterinarian check him out.

✔ **In males:** Check to see whether both testicles are descended into the scrotum. Okay, this isn't easy. You probably can't feel anything there until at least 8 weeks of age or so. But by that age, the tiny testes (which may only be the size of a BB) should be in or almost to the scrotum.

Gently run your hand backward from around the penis and you should feel the slight lump that is the testicle. Most testicles are completely descended by 10 to 12 weeks of age, although some late bloomers may take as long as 5 or 6 months. Neutering a dog with undescended testicles is a more involved surgery than neutering one with normally descended testicles.

Any purchase should be contingent on getting a clean bill of health from a veterinarian within 48 hours of taking possession of the puppy. (Chapter 5 tells you how to find a good vet and schedule the first appointment, and Chapter 7 gives you a rundown of what to expect at that appointment.)

Paying for Your Pom and Handling the Paperwork

When you've made your choice, you probably can't wait to crack out the cash and start signing the papers to make him all yours! But this process takes some time, so sit down and try to concentrate on paperwork, not puppy play.

Money matters

By this time you and the breeder have reached an understanding about price. Few breeders accept credit cards, and most prefer cash or a money order instead of a personal check. Some breeders accept installment payments, usually keeping their name on the registration papers until you've paid in full.

Paperwork you receive

When you pay for your Pom, the breeder should give you the following:

- ✔ AKC registration slip
- ✔ Bill of sale
- ✔ Copy of the pedigree
- ✔ Record of the puppy's medical information
- ✔ Any contract or health guarantee
- ✔ Contact information in case of future questions
- ✔ Care instructions

Other paperwork you can buy

When you buy a registered puppy, the registration is part of the price. However, the pedigree isn't necessarily included. Most breeders include one (and I hope you got to see one before you made your purchase), but it's usually typed or handwritten and not certified. This copy of the pedigree is just fine for almost every need you will ever have.

However, you can still buy an official certified pedigree from the AKC. You would need it only on rare occasions, like trying to register your dog in a foreign country.

You can also purchase a DNA profile for your dog. Upon request, the AKC will send you a swab to collect cells from the inner lip of your dog. Send the swab back in the provided envelope (along with a small fee). A few months later you'll receive a certificate suitable for framing that shows the pattern of several marker genes used in verifying parentage. The genes don't tell you whether your dog has a particular gene-causing disease, but they can identify your dog as well as any fingerprint . . . or paw print . . . or nose print.

Registering Your New Friend

Most AKC puppies are sold as part of a registered litter, and because you've gone through the trouble to buy a purebred dog, the next step is to register each pup from that litter. (The breeder seldom registers the individual dog unless you've chosen an older dog.) Registration costs $20 but goes up by $35 if you take longer than a year after the litter is registered.

Include the following information on the registration form, which the breeder provides (see the bullet list in the previous section):

1. **Your name**
2. **Your address**
3. **Your dog's name**

   Usually you get to select a name for your puppy. But often the breeder requires that the kennel name (only its first name usually) be part of the registered name.

   Some breeders also use *litter identifiers;* they request that you name your puppy starting with a certain letter or theme. That way other breeders — for example, if you were to compete with your dog — know that all the puppies whose names start with a *D* or with a name of some songbird, for example, are littermates.

Registration is a bargain. It comes with a free 60-day trial health-care policy, a free first visit with a participating veterinarian, a puppy-care brochure, e-mail certificates for deals at dog.com, and of course, a registration certificate. Registration also enables your dog to participate in AKC events.

Transactions of a Different Bird: Adopting from Rescues or Shelters

Rescued Poms have had their hearts broken, and they need secure, permanent homes where it won't happen again. That's one reason rescue groups are picky about where these dogs go. They don't want you adopting a dog only to have it or its offspring turn up in the shelter again.

In contrast with shelters that may not have the staff to get to know every dog individually, rescue groups often send their Poms to live in foster homes while they're awaiting forever homes. This extra attention gives the rescue group an advantage over shelters when matching you with the right Pom. Rescue groups tend to incur more expenses per dog on average because these groups are more likely to save dogs that need medical attention. Expect to pay a slightly higher adoption fee compared to a shelter.

Rescue groups do most of their initial screening and matching through the internet or by phone, whereas shelters tend to rely more on personal visits. If you visit a Pom at a shelter, remember these tips:

✔ Ask whether you can take her outside or to a quiet room, away from barking dogs.

✔ Plan to spend a long time getting to know her.

✔ Remember, she's probably a little shellshocked from being in the shelter situation. Her full personality will take a while to blossom after she comes home with you.

Most rescue groups begin the adoption process by having prospective owners complete an application. Applicants may be asked to provide veterinary references, and the rescue group or shelter may schedule a phone interview or in-home visit. Although this process may seem invasive, it is intended to ensure the best match of Pom, owner, and circumstance. Here's what you can expect:

✔ Expect to provide proof of home ownership or permission from your landlord to have a dog.

✔ Expect to wait for the dog to be neutered or spayed; this is often done only after the dog has found a home.

✔ Expect to pay a reasonable fee that covers the dog's surgery, vaccinations, and board. Your adoption fee helps the shelter or rescue group recoup their expenses and be ready to help the next dog in need.

✔ Expect to be asked the following questions:

- What happened to your last dog?

- Do you have experience with small dogs?

- Who will take care of the dog?

- How often are you home?

You should ask questions, too, which will help you get to know a dog:

✔ Does this dog have any medical or behavioral problems?

✔ Why was she given up for adoption?

Rescued Poms' vaccinations are brought up to date by the adoption group, and the Poms have a complete medical examination. They may be microchipped, meaning they have a tiny chip with identification permanently embedded under their skin.

Many rescue groups and shelters provide temperament testing, basic training, and behavior consultation. Also, adopting from a rescue group provides you with a safety net if problems arise.

Many groups provide you an opportunity to become a club member, to participate in rescue reunions, and even to become part of a rescue team.

When you rescue a dog, you also clear a place for another dog that otherwise may not have a chance. And you bring home a very lucky dog to an even luckier home.

Part II

When Your House Becomes Your Pom's Home

"Honey! The Pomeranians have gotten into the neighbor's yard. I'm going to go round them up."

In this part . . .

Take a last breath BP (Before Pom) because — for better or worse — your life will never be the same. And make no doubt about it, your life will be both better and worse. With preparation, though, the better can far outweigh the worse. That's where these chapters come in.

You want to relax and enjoy your new dog as much as possible these first few days, but that can only happen if you've prepared well before you bring her home. By stocking up on supplies now, you won't find yourself running to the store every few minutes for one more essential. And by Pom-proofing your home now, you won't find your Pom undoing everything just as fast as you can do it.

First day, first night, first week — you know what they say about first impressions. Make these first weeks a great beginning for this lifetime friendship.

Chapter 5

Prepare to Be Pomerized!

In This Chapter

▶ Purchasing the gear and setting up house

▶ Preparing your home and yard to be accident free

▶ Introducing . . . your new veterinarian

*Y*ou probably plan on celebrating your Pom's birthday in years to come, but did you know that dog owners celebrate another day? It's called *Gotcha Day* — the day your new dog comes home, steals your heart, takes over, and says the doggy equivalent of "Gotcha!"

Just like any party, you have a lot to do to get ready for your Pom's first Gotcha Day! In this chapter, I tell you everything you need to start out right.

Collecting Pom Paraphernalia

Sure, you can get by with some food, a leash and collar, and maybe some wire for an enclosure. But where's the fun in that? You want to shop! And a new dog gives you the perfect excuse to blister that charge card. Chapter 8 tells you about all the gear you need to feed your Pom, but here I discuss all the other odds and ends that you need to give her the comforts of home.

Housing and transporting

You can't always hold your Pom in your arms — tempting though that may be. And you can't let her run amok when you're not watching her. You need a place to confine her, for her safety as well as your home's. Crates and exercise pens can save you hours of frustration, lots of money, and sometimes, your sanity.

Crate

Not only does a crate prevent little Poopsie from depositing little poopies all over your house, but it also prevents her from gnawing through your chair legs while you think she's sleeping soundly at your feet. And a crate gives her a bed of her own, a safe haven where she can go when she wants to put out the *Do Not Disturb* sign.

Crates come in three materials (you can see examples of them in Figure 5-1):

- ✔ **Wire:** Wire crates are easy for you to collapse (especially the ones designated *suitcase design*). Be careful not to throw your sweater or other valuables on top of the wire crate when it's occupied. An industrious dog can pull most materials through the grating — not a fashionable look when she's finished with it.

- ✔ **Plastic:** Plastic crates were developed for airline travel. They're very cozy but they don't allow the visibility and ventilation of wire crates.

Figure 5-1: Crates come in plastic, wire mesh, and cloth.

✔ **Cloth:** Cloth crates are only for dogs that have been crate-trained; unsupervised puppies have a habit of chewing and digging their way out — not good for them or you.

For housetraining purposes, your goal is to buy a crate that's just large enough for your puppy to turn around, stand up, and lie down in. It's not a playpen, and if it's too big, she'll be tempted to use the far end as a bathroom. (See Chapter 13 for more information on using the crate for housetraining.)

The crate is the puppy version of a toddler's crib. Use it at his naptime and when you can't watch him, but never as a punishment or a place to store him when you're not interested in him. If you plan to use the crate as your babysitter when you're at work all day, every day, you need to rethink getting a dog.

Exercise pen

If you can't leave your puppy in a crate while you're at work, what can you do? Let him run loose? Only if you happen to live in a kennel. Lock him in a bathroom, laundry room, or kitchen? Not a good idea. He has plenty of ways to get into trouble in those areas.

The solution is an indoor yard or exercise pen (also called an *X-pen;* see Figure 5-2). This is a 4-x-4-foot pen that's typically wire. They come in different heights, but a 2-foot-high pen is fine for your little goofball. In fact, a baby's playpen works well as an indoor X-pen for small dogs. (If you have a baby that still uses it, this idea won't work; you'll be vacuuming it constantly!)

You can take the X-pen outside if you want your puppy confined in the yard. In this case, a wire top for the pen (sold separately) is particularly handy. Pom puppies are so tiny that large mammals and birds consider them prey. A secure top may not dissuade a coyote, but it can stop an eagle from swooping down and carrying off your dog. Also be sure she has shade and remember to check on her often. Better yet, sit outside with her.

Carrier

One of the perks of having a Pom is that you can carry her with you around town in a bag that looks almost like a purse. These soft pet-carriers are available at prices that range from affordable to extravagant (think designer variety carriers). Regardless of the budget, look for one that's well ventilated, sturdy, and easy to carry. Flip ahead to the color section of this book to see what a carrier looks like.

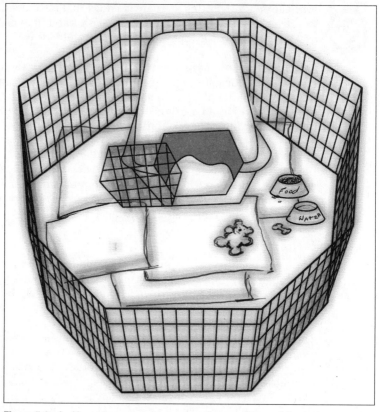

Figure 5-2: An X-pen is a good place to confine your Pom while you're away.

Carriers come in handy other times as well:

- ✔ On trips to the veterinarian

  The carrier helps her feel more secure and makes your job far easier because you're not trying to hold her on your lap or keep her from running up to the other patients.

- ✔ For your regular walks in case you ever need to swoop her up to safety

- ✔ Of course, for that stroll down Rodeo Drive

Car-safe restraints

Just as you don't want any member of your family riding in the car without a seatbelt, you need to make sure your Pom doesn't become an unguided missile in case of an accident. The safest place for your dog to ride is in a sturdy fiberglass or wire travel kennel that's secured to the car (you may be able to use a seatbelt to secure the kennel). The next best option is a travel bag, also secured. For an adult Pom, you can use a seat harness.

Dining ware

Your Pom needs two bowls: one for food and one for water. Although he can use your bowls for his food and water, most people prefer to have special bowls for their dogs. Some tips to remember:

- ✔ The best bowls are of stainless steel because they're easy to clean and impossible to break.

- ✔ Ceramic has the advantage of being microwavable in case of leftovers, but it can crack.

- ✔ Plastic bowls are generally the worst choice. They scratch, and the tiny scratches are hard to clean. In addition, a few dogs have allergic reactions to them and develop a pinkish nose when they eat from plastic.

Walking supplies

One of your Pom's daily highlights is going walking with you. You'll probably walk in different types of places, and you may find that different circumstances call for different walking outfits — for your dog, not you!

Collar

You need a small buckle collar for your Pom puppy. But don't even think about getting a choke or chain collar for your Pom pup! A small-size collar may be a challenge to find, so look in the cat section. The collar should be loose enough for you to get a couple of fingers between it and your Pom's neck.

Never leave the collar on her unattended because she can easily get her lower jaw stuck in it. Don't ask how — they just manage to do it!

The collar is just for training purposes right now. In fact, you may also want to train her to a small harness, which has several advantages. For example, your Pom can pull on a harness without damaging her throat (a problem in some toy breeds), and in case of emergency, you can safely lift your dog up by the harness. (A collar, on the other hand, would simply slip off.)

Leash

Poms also need lightweight leashes, but you may have trouble trying to find the ideal one because most of them are for larger dogs. If you can't find a small dog leash, try the cat department. A *show lead* (a leash normally used for exhibiting dogs in conformation shows) also works well because it doesn't have a heavy clasp and is very lightweight. These are available from most online pet supply catalogs. I show some harness and leash choices in Figure 5-3.

a   b   c

Figure 5-3: Be sure your leash is strong but lightweight. A well-fitting harness may be more comfortable for your Pom.

Avoid chain leashes because they feel like an anchor on your Pom puppy's neck. They're also good at whacking the dog in the face.

Retractable leashes have their place and are very popular, but they also have shortcomings. First, the good news: A retractable leash allows you to stand under cover while your dog goes potty in the rain. (Yeah, that would be the day!) It also gives your dog a little more range to sniff out his surroundings.

Now the bad news:

- ✔ People are careless with these leads. When they let the dog wander to the end of the extended leash and she makes a sudden turn, she ends up in the road, splattered by a car. Or she runs up to a big dog — and gets chewed up.

- ✔ People use these leashes everywhere they take their dogs, but they're not practical for populated sidewalks and public areas.

- ✔ Because dogs have to pull against the leash to extend the leash, they learn to always pull when on leash — even when you don't want them to.

- ✔ If you accidentally drop your end of the leash, the plastic handle scuttles toward the dog, making a racket and often scaring her. If she takes off running, the handle clacks along behind so she keeps running in a panic — a bad situation.

Identification

Talk to the breeder or your veterinarian about having your Pom microchipped (see Chapter 10). You can also have her tattooed. (No, this isn't the butterfly-in-a-seductive-place kind of tattoo — it's an identification number or her American Kennel Club number on her inner thigh. Well, I guess that *is* kind of seductive.)

Plan to get some lightweight identification tags. Although the best ones attach as a flat plate to her collar, they can be a hassle because you have to keep changing her collar as her neck grows. The other choice is a hanging tag, which is problematic because it's so large on a tiny dog. If you go the hanging route, be sure to get the smallest one available. Again, consider products designed for cats.

Chewies and anti-chewies

Puppies explore with their mouths. They also feel the need to chew, chew, chew. By giving your Pom something safe to chew, you can help save him from unsafe chewies. Even so, he's apt to go hunting for more chewing adventure. What's a choosy mother to do?

- **Chewies:** Puppies like to chew. They like to chew your hands, your furniture, your clothes, and your wallet. Fortunately they also like to chew rawhide. For many breeds, rawhide can be a bad idea because the dog rips off hunks, swallows it, and then chokes. As long as you get a rawhide chewy — too big for him to swallow hunks off of — and supervise your Pom as he chews, he should be fine.

- **Anti-chewies:** You can buy sprays that make an article taste so bitter that your dog practically foams at the mouth when he licks or chews it. Bitter Apple is the best known of these products.

Tools for setting boundaries

A puppy needs boundaries — to keep her safe and to keep your home from becoming a shambles. Boundaries also help you train your Pom by preventing her from getting into trouble. Fortunately, setting Pom boundaries is fairly simple.

Baby gates

You can't always keep your puppy in a crate or X-pen (see "Housing and transporting" earlier in this section), but you can't always be chasing her from one room to the next either. The solution is to set up baby gates between rooms. Be sure you don't use the old-fashioned accordion style, which can close on a puppy's neck and strangle her. If you have too many doorways or your doorways are too wide for standard baby gates, just prop a long, sturdy piece of cardboard across the opening. (Make sure *you* can step over it so you don't have to move it all the time.)

Ramp

Will you allow your Pom on the furniture? The time to decide is now. If you don't plan to have her on furniture as an adult, simply don't lift her up there now. If you want to hold her or play with her, get on the floor with her. (That's a good idea anyway.)

If you do plan to let her up on furniture, you need a way for her to get down safely because she can injure herself if she jumps down. Pet ramps are available to help small dogs hop up and down off of beds and furniture safely. You can also make your own with some covered foam steps or plywood ramps. Just make sure the ramp can't collapse or fall over.

Fence or kennel

Many Pom owners get along without a fenced yard by walking their dogs on leashes on regular schedules. But if you have a yard and plan to let your dog loose in it, at least part of it needs a fence. Ideally, a fenced area extends from the back door so you can just open the door to let her out. (You can even add a doggy door and make your life that much simpler.)

A fence that's not escape proof is pretty much worthless. Make sure your tiny Pom can't squeeze through or under it. And even though he can't get over it, your fence must be tall and strong enough to keep out bigger dogs and dangerous animals.

What about the underground electric fences that give your dog a warning beep and then a small shock when she gets too close to the boundary? Not a good idea. Although these fences keep your dog in, they can't keep potentially dangerous dogs out.

If you plan to leave your dog unsupervised outside, a covered kennel run (see Figure 5-4) is your best choice.

Don't place a run at the back of the yard. Your dog will be miserable there and you'll tend to forget him. If you plan to leave him in the run — or anywhere outside — for any amount of time, make sure he has access to shelter.

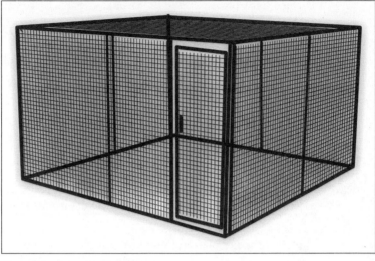

Figure 5-4: A covered kennel run.

Grooming gear

Eventually you'll want a well-outfitted grooming kit, but for a puppy you need only the essentials:

- ✔ **A soft-bristle brush** is an ideal introduction to grooming.
- ✔ **A medium-tooth comb** helps you reach down to the skin.
- ✔ **Rinseless shampoo** is the best kind for a puppy.

If you plan to *really* groom your Pom at home, a few more items are necessary (see Figure 5-5). How many supplies you need, though, depends on how good a job you want to do. At bare minimum, you need

- ✔ Medium- and wide-tooth combs
- ✔ Slicker brush (a brush with many tiny, bent tines to pull out dead hair)
- ✔ Pin brush (a brush with straight tines to fluff the hair)
- ✔ Bristle brush (a medium-texture brush is best for Pom coats)
- ✔ Scissors (blunt tips are safer for not stabbing your dog)
- ✔ Toenail clippers (for dogs — make sure you get the kind for small dogs)

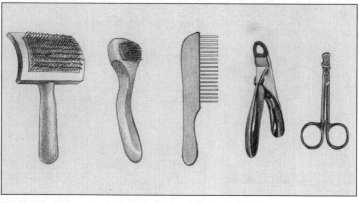

Figure 5-5: The more you groom, the more types of supplies you'll want.

✔ Mat rake or mat-breaking tool (for getting out mats)

✔ Water spritzer bottle (to moisten the coat before brushing)

Another useful item is a grooming table that lets you groom at a comfortable height. Some tables have a grooming arm that tethers your dog in place. As long as you teach your dog not to jump off, you can use any table with a nonslip surface.

Do not leave your dog (any dog!) on any kind of table unsupervised, especially if he's tethered.

Cleaning up after your pup

Being a puppy owner means becoming a cleaning expert. You can't just leave your Pom's poop all over your yard (or someone else's, for that matter), and indoor accidents are inevitable. This section walks you through the basics of doing the dirty work.

✔ **Poop scoop:** A poop scoop isn't your most exciting purchase, but it may be the most useful. And it's far better than makeshift trowels and buckets because it's designed to make the job easy.

When you're walking your dog down the street, the easiest scoop is a cheap sandwich bag (avoid the thick, zippered ones).

✔ **Carpet cleaner:** Get the kind with enzymes because they destroy the odor-causing molecules rather than simply covering them up. Find them at pet supply stores.

✔ **Air freshener:** Spray before company comes — assuming you want these guests to come back.

Toys and other fun stuff

Just like children, puppies need to learn how to have fun with toys that entertain and educate because

- ✔ Toys give puppies something to chew on and toss about in place of your valuables.

- ✔ Toys help develop puppies' brains and coordination.

- ✔ Puppies that never learn to play with toys tend not to understand toy playing (an important activity throughout their lives) as adults.

Also like children, puppies of different ages appreciate different kinds of toys. For example, very young puppies like small, soft toys, so cat toys are often ideal. But because the toys are so small, you must supervise play with them at all times. Puppies, like children, can choke on toys that are too small.

As your puppy matures, he may start liking balls, squeakies, and tug toys. By the way, tug toys have gotten a bad rap in recent years because domineering dogs can get the wrong idea of who's boss if they continually win the game. But chances are good that your Pom isn't a little Napoleon and has no delusions of being stronger than you.

Just to be on the safe side, when you initiate tug games, always end the game after *you* win. And no matter how weak you are, you surely can win a tug game against a 2-pound puppy!

Special interactive toys are good distractions for puppies and adult Poms that have to be left alone. These toys challenge your puppy to dislodge sticky food treats, thereby occupying and rewarding him over a long time period. Remove these toys when you return (you can store them in the freezer if they still have food in them) so your dog looks forward to them the next time you leave. Try rotating several interactive toys with different challenges to prevent him from getting bored.

Make sure the toys you buy don't have small pieces that your dog can pull off and swallow, and make sure he can't burrow into it and discover electronic guts. Avoid bean-filled toys, which can pose a hazard if your dog manages to open them up.

Preparing for Emergencies

The time to prepare for the unexpected is now. Prepare by getting your first-aid kit together, making an emergency plan, and knowing how to handle common crises.

Stocking the first-aid kit

Keep your first-aid kit orderly so you can find each item in a hurry. And when you've used something up, replace it! The single most important item is the emergency phone number of your veterinarian, but you also need the following:

- Activated charcoal
- Allergy medication
- Antidiarrheal medication
- Antiseptic skin ointment
- Corn syrup
- First-aid instructions
- Hydrogen peroxide
- Instant cold compress
- Latex gloves
- Liquid bandage

- Ophthalmic ointment
- Pen light
- Rectal thermometer
- Scissors
- Self-adhesive (cohesive) bandage
- Soap
- Sterile gauze dressings
- Styptic powder
- Syringe
- Tweezers

Making an emergency plan

Even when you know what to do, it's hard to think straight when an emergency jumps in your face. You need a plan:

- Carry the emergency number of your veterinarian with you in your wallet or store it in your cellphone.

- Know where the emergency veterinarian is and drive there beforehand to make sure you know the way. It's too easy to get lost when you're in a panic.

- Never leave your car in your driveway with only fumes in the gas tank. The last thing you need is a stop at the gas station so you can make it to the vet.

Designing Spaces Fit for a Small King or Queen

You don't have to add an addition to your home just because royalty is moving in — but a little redecorating is in order. Where will Her Highness be staying?

By day

You want your Pom where she can interact with you but also keep out of trouble. Use your baby gates and doors (see the earlier section "Tools for setting boundaries") to keep her in a room with you, unless she'd be underfoot. Then place her in a crate or X-pen, which you should locate where she doesn't feel isolated. (Check out the first section in this chapter for more on these setups.)

When you're away

Your Pom needs a safe place to spend the day when you can't be with her. To give her all the comforts of home, do the following:

1. **Place the X-pen on a dog-proof floor (such as linoleum).** For a carpeted floor, lay down an old shower curtain to protect it.

2. **Put the crate or bed in one corner of the pen, bowls of food and water in another, and a doggy litter box (see Chapter 13) in another.**

3. **Throw in some toys and your puppy is ready to kiss you good-bye for the day.**

You can refer back to Figure 5-2 for an example of your puppy's X-pen palace.

By night

What goes in your puppy's bedtime bed? Consider the following items to be sure he sleeps tight:

- A soft blanket
- A stuffed animal for cuddling

✔ A stuffed puppy comforter that has a place to insert a warm pad (You warm it in the microwave before insertion.)

These comforters also make a soft noise that sounds like a heartbeat (much better than trying to slip in a traditional clock!).

✔ Any creature comforts that make your puppy feel like he's with M-O-M.

Pom-Proofing Your Home and Yard

You hear all the scare stories about baby proofing. But puppy parents have those worries and more. Human babies don't have fangs that can gnaw through wood; they can't run under furniture at full speed; and they can't squeeze into tiny places you never knew you had.

One way to Pom-proof your house is with a room-by-room search. To get you started, this section has one list for general safety violations and then a list for each room. Just to be thorough, I also list some of the problems your puppy can get into when he's outside your house.

Generally speaking . . .

Many hazards aren't restricted to just one room; the following widespread dangers can be tough to anticipate:

✔ **Exterior doors:** Keep all doors securely closed. A screen door is an added safety device. Any open door should have a doorstop so the wind can't catch it and slam it shut on your puppy.

✔ **Glass doors:** Running into a glass door can cause severe injuries. Place stickers on glass doors at Pom eye level so she knows when the door is closed.

✔ **Stairways:** A fall on a stairway is like a tumble down a canyon for little Pomeranians. Open-backed steps are an invitation to disaster. Always keep a baby gate (see the earlier section "Tools for setting boundaries") between steps and your Pom.

✔ **Uncovered electrical outlets:** Whatever could be in those tiny holes? If the puppy licks hard enough, she may find out — she may even see sparks. This charge is definitely not good for her tongue or her general well-being. Buy outlet covers at hardware or baby supply stores.

✔ **Electric wires:** Do you have a jungle of vinelike wires under your desk? Perhaps you just have an occasional wire to a lamp or phone. That has to be fun to pull on . . . until the lamp or phone comes crashing down on her or your computer goes on the fritz!

✔ **Space heaters:** Your puppy can get a painful burn if he gets too close to a hot space heater. He can also knock one over, which just may start a fire. Keep these heaters out of his reach.

✔ **Ashtrays:** Put ashtrays and any nicotine products out of reach. Better yet, quit smoking — that second-hand smoke doesn't do your cute puppy any good.

✔ **Coins:** Paper currency may go through your puppy's digestive system, but coins can be an expensive meal if your puppy swallows them. They may get stuck along the path, or in the case of pennies, sit in the stomach and dissolve, releasing toxic zinc. Your puppy is not a piggy bank! Keep coins away from him!

✔ **Purses:** These are a Pandora's box of puppy perils that may include drugs, cigarettes, coins, and maybe even some pepper spray. Keep purses away from purse-snatching Poms!

✔ **Unattached bookcases, vases, and statues:** What's up there? Puppies like to jump onto just about anything. Make sure she can't send your oh-so-curious belongings — or the whole bookcase — toppling over, especially onto her.

✔ **Blinds with long cords:** Those hanging strings are fun to jump at and tug on until he catches his head in a loop and chokes. Cut the loops, shorten the cords, or buy childproof protectors for them.

Kitchen

Puppies love kitchens because they usually combine people, good smells, and dropped food. But kitchens can be dangerous for a small dog, especially when you're cooking.

✔ **Cabinets:** To puppies, cabinets are like secret caves filled with treasure. But the cave holds dangers like poisonous cleaners and degreasers. Remember to either place bad stuff elsewhere or secure all your cabinets with child safety latches.

✔ **Plastic bags, wrap, and aluminum foil:** Put these items out of reach. They may be fun to chew, but they sure are difficult to digest.

✔ **Plastic canisters:** It was funny when Winnie the Pooh got his head stuck in the honey jar, but if your puppy gets her head stuck in just-the-right-size jar, it can form an airtight seal around her head and suffocate her. It's happened.

✔ **Puppy underfoot:** Puppies fancy themselves gourmet chefs in the making. They want you to shake up all the ingredients, so they run between your feet when your hands are full. And by sticking their heads in the open refrigerator, they also ensure that you don't close the door too soon. Unfortunately a Pom puppy's skull probably isn't as strong as a refrigerator door. Keep the little chef out of the kitchen while you're cooking.

Dining room

Your Pom's second favorite room just may be the dining room — especially if you have messy eaters in the family!

✔ **Swinging door:** If you have a swinging door, stop it from swinging or take it off its hinges.

✔ **Hanging tablecloth:** Can the puppy jump up and snag the tablecloth? Yes. Can the puppy jump out of the way of the fine china plummeting toward her as she drags the cloth off the table? Maybe.

Family room

The family room is a great place to cuddle and play with the puppy, but don't just walk out and leave her alone to find trouble. She may not have to look far.

✔ **Fireplace without secure fire screen:** A fireplace fire is as big as a forest fire to a Pom puppy! He may not realize just how hot it is until his fur is ablaze. And he can catch your house on fire by removing a burning stick and then throwing it down on your papers. Even if you have a fire screen, don't leave your puppy alone around a fire.

✔ **Sewing or knitting basket and craft kits:** Needles and pins can perforate any part of the digestive tract. And thread, yarn, or any long, stringlike object can cause the intestines to accordion, which is potentially fatal. Also, castor beans (used in some beading projects) contain *ricin,* one of the most damaging chemical toxins of plant origin.

Bedrooms

I know you want to relax, but don't go sleeping on the job. There's still plenty of mischief possible in the bedroom!

- ✔ **Toys:** You were careful to buy puppy toys that she couldn't rip apart and swallow, but what about other stuffed animals she may find around your house? Swallowing parts of toys can cause blockages — not to mention hard feelings with the kids.

- ✔ **Open closets:** Missing a shoe? Whose fault is that? Close the closet door!

- ✔ **Diaper pail:** Yuck! But when you say "Yuck!" your dog says "Yum!" Dogs do eat soiled diapers. Besides the disgusting sight, diaper material can cause blockages. Solution? Keep diaper pails out of reach. Simple.

Bathroom

The bathrooms can be the most dangerous room in the house for people. What about for dogs?

- ✔ **Pills:** Childproof caps aren't puppy proof, so he can just gnaw right through. And with his tiny body weight, it takes only a fraction of a pill to wreak havoc on his body. Even small doses of pills like acetaminophen and ibuprofen that are safe for people can be deadly for dogs.

- ✔ **Toiletries:** Razors, perm solutions, hair coloring, suntan lotions, deodorants, and rubbing alcohol are just a few examples of items you need to keep out of your puppy's reach.

- ✔ **Drain cleaners:** Drain cleaners are designed to dissolve organic material. You puppy is all organic material. Don't let them mix.

- ✔ **Toilet with open lid:** Your Pom puppy is probably too short to reach, but where there's a will there's a way.

Laundry room

Most sensible Poms steer clear of any room that involves work, but sometimes an adventurous one goes exploring And some owners use the laundry room as quarters for their dog. Make sure you spot the dangers before he does.

✔ **Detergents, bleach, and lye:** If your puppy finds a box of white stuff, she can have a great time simulating a snowstorm, flinging white powder everywhere. But that powder burns eyes and throats, and bleach can be blinding or fatal.

✔ **Open dryer door:** Snatch something out of the dryer, leave the dryer door open, and walk away. Who walks in? Your puppy, looking for a soft, warm place to snuggle. Then you go back and decide you need to dry those clothes a little longer. If the tumbling doesn't get him, the heat will.

Garage

Your Pom doesn't need to have NASCAR aspirations to find all sorts of entertainment in the garage. Unfortunately, he'd be safer driving a race car than nosing around the contents of a typical garage. Best advice? Keep him out altogether!

✔ **Antifreeze:** A sweet treat on the garage floor beckons to your puppy. But just one lap of antifreeze containing *ethylene glycol* can kill him. Even if he merely licks his paws after walking through it, he can become extremely ill. Use only antifreeze with *propylene glycol,* which has reduced toxicity. And be sure to clean up any spills.

✔ **Fluids:** Gasoline, diesel, oil, kerosene, brake fluid, carburetor cleaner, windshield fluid, paints, paint thinners, acetone, mineral spirits, pool chlorine, wood stain, furniture polish, glue, and batteries are all potentially deadly. Keep them up and away.

✔ **Tools:** Tools can seriously injure you when they fall on your foot. Imagine what they can do if your puppy knocks one down on his own head. Keep him away from cords and work areas.

✔ **Car:** Always check on the dog's location and put him up before moving the car.

✔ **Garage door:** Broken necks and backs can come from garage doors being slammed carelessly, and even automatic doors may not stop in time. Never leave your Pom loose when the garage door is shutting.

✔ **Power tools:** Would you let a toddler hang around when power tools are in use? Then don't let a puppy around.

✔ **Nails, tacks, and screws:** These aren't meant to go inside a puppy's digestive tract, and they'll cost you one very large veterinary bill to extract.

✔ **Herbicides, rodent poisons, slug bait.** They're designed not only to kill but also to taste good. But they taste good and kill dogs, too. The fatal effects may show up days later, long after you've assumed he's fine.

✔ **Fertilizers:** These have one simple guideline: What's good for a plant is bad for a puppy.

Outside

Of course, doggy dangers aren't limited to the indoors. Check your yard for trouble spots, whether man-made or natural.

Man-made accessories

The outside of your home isn't usually designed with the safety of a tiny dog in mind. Check out your outdoor living space for danger.

✔ **Decks, balconies, and upper-level open windows:** Most railings weren't designed to keep tiny dogs from slipping through. Put temporary fencing or other barriers around the edges.

✔ **Unsealed deck wood:** Pressure-treated wood contains arsenic; if the wood isn't sealed regularly, the arsenic can leach out and be toxic to a puppy that licks the wood.

✔ **Weak fence:** A weak fence is a ready-made challenge course. Every time your Pom finds a way out, it reinforces his determination to keep trying. Show your pup from the start that this is one challenge he can't meet. Make sure the fence meets the ground. For Poms that love to dig, extend some wire underground toward the inside of the yard.

✔ **Unfenced pool:** Just like toddlers, dogs can fall in swimming pools and drown. They may swim for a while, but when they get too weak to hang on to the side, they eventually go under. Keep the pool securely fenced, give him swimming lessons, make sure there's a way out, and make sure he knows how to *find* the way out.

All things natural

Even a suburban backyard can seem like a jungle to your little Pom — and a dangerous one unless you know what to look for.

✔ **Predators:** Don't let your small puppy outside alone, and consider a mesh-top exercise area (refer to Figure 5-4) if large eagles and other birds of prey are around. Other predators include

• Coyotes and mountain lions that look for an opportunity to snatch a small dog if he's alone in the yard

- Alligators that consider dogs a delicacy

- Unfortunately, bad people who may want to steal a Pomeranian puppy

✔ **Wild animals:** Beware of poisonous snakes, snapping turtles, giant marine toads, and various animals that may injure a curious puppy in self-defense. Inspect your yard for insect hives, underground nests, and fire-ant mounds.

✔ **Treated lawns:** Wait at least 24 hours before letting your puppy on a treated lawn or around treated bushes.

✔ **Nut trees:** Nuts can be fun to play with and even to crunch on. But the nuts can cause blockages and have to be surgically removed.

✔ **Poisonous plants:** Many plants can be bad for your puppy. To be on the safe side, don't let her graze among yours. Check your plants against the complete listing online at www.aspca.org or consult with your veterinarian. Some common poisonous plants include

• Azalea	• Milkweed
• Castor bean	• Mistletoe
• Corn cockle	• Oleander
• English holly berry	• Philodendron
• Foxglove	• Rattlebox
• Jerusalem cherry	• Rhododendron
• Jessamine	• Water hemlock
• Lily	

✔ **Tree limbs:** Rotted limbs can fall on a small dog, killing him. Even falling fruits and pine cones can hit a dog in the head with fatal results.

✔ **Cocoa mulch:** Cocoa mulch has a sweet taste, but it contains theobromine, the same ingredient in unsweetened and semi-sweet chocolate that's fatal to some dogs.

Exercising caution during holiday decorating

Have you stopped to think about how a puppy may affect your holiday traditions? Besides making sure you no longer travel alone guilt-free, your puppy can quickly show you how not to decorate your house.

Christmas

Santa brings good puppies a stocking of gifts, but bad puppies get in a ton of mischief. Christmas tree lights, ornaments, popcorn strings, extra electrical cords, tinsel, candles, and angel hair can be enticing but dangerous to puppies. Ribbons, twine, and foil wrapping (and the gifts they wrap) can also pose dangers.

If you wouldn't leave a particular gift on the floor *unwrapped,* then don't leave it on the floor *wrapped.* (It's just a matter of time.) This rule is especially true of edible items; your Pom's nose isn't fooled by some flimsy wrapping paper!

Christmas parties mean lots of opportunities to slip out the door, get stepped on by guests, or be overwhelmed by company. Unattended alcoholic beverages, coffee, chocolates, nuts, illicit drugs, and cigarettes beckon to a curious Pom. Some owners err by tying festive ribbons around Fido's neck and then letting him play unsupervised. Place him in a secure area or crate during parties or hectic times.

Outside your home, salts used to melt ice on walkways can irritate a dog's paws. Some of these salts are poisonous if your puppy licks her paws. And be aware: She can get frostbite or become hypothermic if she's left out in the cold. Use common sense — if she acts cold, she is cold!

Christmas cactus isn't toxic, but many holiday plants are. Keep this list in mind:

- ✔ Mistletoe and Jerusalem cherries are highly toxic, particularly the berries.
- ✔ Holly berries are somewhat toxic.
- ✔ Poinsettia is not as toxic as most people think, but it still can cause gastrointestinal irritation.

Thanksgiving

Thanksgiving means turkey leftovers that a dog can be truly thankful for. But too much turkey can make a dog sick because large amounts can cause pancreatitis in susceptible dogs. Share a little turkey with your Pom, but don't overdo it (and be sure his helping doesn't have bones).

Independence Day

More dogs are lost on the Fourth of July than on any other day. They can become so frightened of loud fireworks that they escape and just run in terror. Your dog also can be burned by sparklers and injured if she chases firecrackers. Leave your Pom at home (in a soundproof room if possible) during fireworks.

Halloween

Sure, it's fun to dress up and see how the dog reacts. But one monster after another at your door can make your dog go nuts. Put her away if she overreacts to trick-or-treaters, and remember to keep Halloween candy well out of reach.

Finding a Vet and Scheduling the First Appointment

Plan to line up a veterinarian even before your puppy comes home; you want him to have an appointment during that first week for a health check and any scheduled vaccinations. Be sure to bring his vaccination and worming record with you (see Chapter 4 for more info on these records) so the veterinarian knows which treatments he's already had.

But first, you want to find a veterinarian you like. Because the two of you will form a partnership in caring for your Pomeranian's health for years to come, you should choose carefully. Although the closer the clinic, the better, sometimes it's worth driving right past the clinic down the street for a veterinarian more suited for your needs.

And there are other factors to consider: What hours is the clinic open? How does it handle emergency situations? Some veterinarians trade off with each other for off-hours duties; larger towns often have a dedicated pet emergency clinic. Clinics with more than one veterinarian have several advantages such as appointment availability and collaboration between veterinarians in difficult cases.

Before your puppy becomes a regular patient there, check out the facility. Ask for a tour. The clinic should be clean and have safe, sanitary overnight accommodations. Look for American Animal Hospital Association accreditation, which is given only to hospitals meeting certain standards. And of course, the fees shouldn't make you pass out when you get the bill — at least no more so than the other clinics in town.

Chapter 6

Coming Home

● ●

In This Chapter

▶ The first journey: Bringing your Pom home

▶ Connecting with the family

▶ Surviving the first night — you and your Pom!

● ●

*C*ongratulations! It's a Pom! The big day is finally here. You've Pom-proofed your house and filled the puppy basket with necessities — you're ready to welcome your new addition!

But wait! You have a few more preparations to make before you're ready to roll. For example, you need a way to comfortably trans-port your new addition and a game plan for introducing her to the new house, family, and other pets, if you have them.

Your happy homecoming will be exciting, but you still want to manage that excitement. Remember, your little Pom may be more than a little anxious about leaving the only home she's ever known and saying good-bye to Mom and the other kids. You want her first impression of her new home and family to be a happy occasion, not a terrifying misadventure.

With the suggestions in this chapter, you can make this event a good memory. I provide you with solid advice on the first trip home, the first hours around new faces and surroundings, and . . . the first night alone.

Making that First Trip Safe and Sound

You've picked out your Pom; now it's time to pick him up and bring him home. Whether it's a trip across town or from a neighboring state, plan to coordinate your pickup with the breeder.

Scheduling the pickup time

Schedule your arrival time early in the day; you're likely to be at the breeder's a while and you want to get home well before your pup's bedtime. The breeder will want to give you care instructions (feeding, grooming, and early training) and make sure you understand them. These guidelines may seem overwhelming, and you may end up feeling frazzled. If only there was a book about Pomeranians for new owners that could help you know what to expect. Oh, wait! You're reading it, aren't you? So don't worry — you'll do fine on the first day.

Be sure to confirm your arrival time with the breeder so he doesn't feed the puppy right beforehand. This timing should lessen the possibility of car sickness or nervous diarrhea. Yuck!

If you work during the week, arrange to get your new dog on a Friday or just before your vacation time. That way you can spend plenty of time with him and be able to nap when he naps. With any luck, you won't feel like a walking zombie from sleep deprivation on Monday morning.

Preparing to drive Miss Daisy: What to bring

Ready to hop in the car and cruise to the breeder's? Not so fast! That car may not look — or smell — so pretty when you get home unless you bring some stuff with you to make the trip go a little more smoothly. And chances are your little one doesn't have much car-riding experience.

Here are the necessities for your trip:

- **Another adult:** Even a good friend may not be so thrilled if you pack her in with the rest of the gear, so save the front seat for her. She can ride along with you and lend an extra pair of hands. You'll be grateful for the help if the puppy starts fussing.

- **Carrier:** Just as a new baby doesn't ride home from the hospital in your arms, neither should a new puppy — or even an older dog. Regardless of the length of the trip, bring a dog carrier with a towel in the bottom. Bring extra towels in case of accidents.

- **Cleanup supplies:** Some rinse-free shampoo and paper towels are also handy just in case he has an accident and gets it all over himself.

- **Drinking water:** Bring some bottled water or an empty bottle that you can fill with water from the breeder's home. Changes in water can give some dogs upset stomachs. Why risk it in the car?

- **Money:** When you head to the breeder's place, don't forget your money! Unless the breeder has indicated a personal check is acceptable, bring cash or a cashier's check.

- **Toys:** Be sure to bring something (a chew toy or even a stuffed animal for cuddling) to occupy him.

- **Food:** If the trip will last a couple of hours or longer, bring some of the same food he's been eating. *Hypoglycemia* (low blood sugar) is a concern in these little ones (see Chapter 8 for more on this), so don't put off a meal too long just because you're traveling. Ask the breeder ahead of time what your dog has been eating; either buy a small bag of it in advance or ask the breeder whether you can buy a few days' supply from him.

  Have your pup's first meal waiting at your home. Even if you don't have a long ride, chances are the breeder won't feed her right before she leaves for your house.

  Note: Even if you've selected the ultimate canine ambrosia, start by feeding the same food the breeder has been feeding her. She's facing enough changes without having to cope with a new food that may upset her tummy — and your housetraining plans. If you plan to switch her to another food eventually, be sure to do it gradually. Abrupt changes in diet can lead to puppy diarrhea.

- **Collar and leash:** Bring a secure leash and collar just in case you have to take him out. You don't want him bolting away, falling down a storm drain, hiding under a parked car, or doing any of the hundreds of dangerous tricks a loose puppy can do. But be forewarned; he probably doesn't know how to walk on a leash. Don't get your hopes up for much walking or relieving.

If you've planned an overnight trip to collect your Pom, read about traveling with a Pom in Chapter 12. Bring a playpen or exercise pen and place plastic sheeting beneath it.

Your new pup may not look like the pup you chose a few weeks ago. If you're concerned, say so. Good breeders would never switch puppies on you, so if you've chosen a trustworthy breeder (check out Chapter 3), you don't have to worry about this scenario. Chances are, your puppy has just changed with age. However, if she no longer looks healthy, ask whether you can come back at a later date to get her. A good breeder doesn't want you leaving with a sick puppy any more than you do.

When the dog flies home

To collect your dog from the airport, give yourself plenty of time to locate him.

✔ If he's flying air freight, he may go to the air freight office, which may not be part of the main terminal.

✔ If he goes to the baggage pickup, he must be hand carried from the door. (He won't be placed on the conveyor belt!) Be sure you're there to meet him, and have identification with you in case you're asked for it.

He probably messed his shipping crate, so be ready with extra towels and cleanup supplies. Also bring some scissors to cut the plastic cable ties that airlines often add for extra security. You can't open the crate unless you can cut through those ties. (And try not to look dangerous while wielding your scissors or knife in the airport!)

Technically, you're supposed to keep your dog in the shipping kennel until you're outside the terminal. Obviously, this doesn't work with big dogs, so most airports allow you to take the dog out right away as long as you don't abuse the privilege. In other words, keep him in your arms and on a leash until you get outside. If you find a grassy area, give him a chance to urinate.

Managing a Happy Homecoming

As you pull into your driveway, it hits you — your life will never be the same! You now have a new little one ruling over your every move. Your household may become a tiny Pom dynasty, but that's a small price to pay for Pomeranian pleasures.

Now, did you catch the emphasis on *little, tiny,* and *small?* As tempting as it may be, this is not the time for a welcome home party with friends and neighbors. Stop a minute and try to view this from your pup's low-down-close-to-the-ground perspective: Your little Pom (whether pup or adult) was driven in a big, unfamiliar car to a big, unfamiliar house to meet big, unfamiliar people. And there may be some big, unfamiliar pet mates to boot.

Your new Pom needs to figure out who's who and how to be brave in her big, new world. Being greeted by a wall of noisy new faces, reaching hands, and sniffing noses isn't going to help. Let her focus on just you and your family this first day and night.

Gaining a sense of place

Your first goal is to give your new Pom a sense of place, to become familiar with his surroundings. Keep distractions (like other people and pets) to an absolute minimum because your Pom has a lot of sights and smells to process. Consider these suggestions:

- ✔ **Calm the kids.** If you have children, they'll likely be excited to see the new puppy. But they have to be calm or else wait in another room.

- ✔ **Secure other animals.** Make sure all your other animals are put up.

- ✔ **Take him to the grass.** Introduce your Pom to the spot you've decided will be a good bathroom (read more about this in Chapter 13). He probably won't use it because he has no idea what you want. But at least you've given him a chance.

- ✔ **Show him the Pom-approved spaces.** After he's had a little time to check out the outside bathroom, take him inside and let him loose in the part of the house you've designated as Pom friendly (Chapter 5 has more details on this step).

  - Start by introducing him to the places most important to him: his eating area and sleeping area. Put a bit of food in his bowl so he'll get the idea.

  - He may be glad to be out of his crate, so don't expect him to go back in for a while. He's also probably curious about this strange new world, if a little scared. But don't overwhelm him with a tour of the whole house — even if you live in a one-room apartment. Leave something for later!

Always stay with him as he explores. He may never have been loose in a house before, so he's a prime candidate for trouble. If he chews on an electric cord, give a harsh warning sound like *Ahgt!* and remove him from temptation.

Don't be surprised if he has an accident inside almost right away. That's why you want to take him back to the bathroom area several times while he's looking around. Review your Pom's *gotta-go* signs in Chapter 13, and be ready.

Meeting the family

Now that your new Pom has had some time to begin settling down in her new environment, you can begin introducing her to the people in your family. If it's just you and another adult, then you may have accomplished this mission during the ride home. If you have children, especially young ones, they'll need to develop a little care and a lot of calm for your Pom.

Here are a few guidelines for your kids to follow when they meet the new dog for the first time:

- **Patiently take turns holding the new dog.** Avoid any fighting over the puppy or any rough handling. Small dogs are fragile, and even the best-intentioned children can end up causing injury.

- **Use indoor voices and avoid being too loud around the dog.** Screaming with excitement may put the dog on edge.

- **Avoid chasing the puppy.** It's hard not to get carried away with a game of chase! But a fun game to the two-legged chasers may feel like a run-for-your-life situation to the chasee.

- **Sit on the floor nearer the new dog's level.** The Pom can easily move from one seated person to the next without being dropped or tripping a child. *Note:* A puppy can trip a toddler, but the toddler's still big enough to squish the puppy if he falls on her.

This is such an exciting time, and kids tend to forget all these guidelines when the Pom starts bouncing around. If you take time to explain that these guidelines help the dog feel safer and more secure, your children will most likely show care as they meet the new member of the family.

Everyone in the house needs to know how to hold a puppy (see Figure 6-1). Always pick the dog up with one hand cradled under her chest (never by her legs, nape of neck, or anywhere else). Then rest the dog against your chest and hold her securely underneath with your other hand.

Saying "Hello" to doggy or kitty

If you have other animal family members, chances are they're very curious about the little intruder you've allowed in their home. "Surely," they think, "you don't intend to keep *that* thing in the house, do you? Woof! Hiss!"

Even if you have abnormally friendly dogs and cats, oversee these introductions carefully to ensure that the bigger or rougher animals don't injure the small Pom. You also want to be sure the established animals don't become jealous of the newcomer. If you have more than one other pet, make these introductions one at a time.

Figure 6-1: How to hold a Pom correctly.

Meeting dog to dog

The best place for new dogs to meet is in neutral territory so your resident dog doesn't start acting uppity and territorial. You can go to a neighbor's yard or for a walk side by side — assuming your puppy will walk on a leash! For meeting one or more other dogs in the house, place the puppy in his exercise pen or crate before letting the other dogs into the room, one at a time, to see him. You can also sit and hold the new Pom on your lap. ***Note:*** If your other dog is large, avoid holding your Pom up above him because dogs have a tendency to jump and grab at things held up in the air.

Either separate the dogs by a barrier or have them both on leashes. Some dogs use the barrier as an excuse to start *fence fighting,* which means acting ferocious as long as something's between them. If this fighting starts, you can separate the two dogs, place them on leashes, and try again.

Keeping an eye on the dogs' behaviors

Watch how the resident dog and your newcomer react to one another. A puppy will probably be curious but cautious. Some pups get excited, in which case you need to prevent her from jumping all over the resident dog or from starting a chase-me scene. An older new Pom may be laid back, frightened, or have a devil-may-care attitude — you never know.

Meanwhile, a resident dog may be curious, approach the puppy, and try to sniff. These are all good signs. Watch for these other signs that the introduction is going well:

- ✔ Your resident dog is sniffing, with ears relaxed or held slightly forward.
- ✔ Your resident dog is in a play bow position, with front legs on the floor and butt in the air (see Figure 6-2).
- ✔ You can distract your resident dog with a treat.

Some dogs rush up to the new dog, overwhelming her. Even if the resident dog's intentions are friendly, the newcomer can become so frightened that she tries to bolt, which can trigger a chase response in the other dog. *Note:* If the resident dog is bigger, you may have a cops-and-robbers chase scene right in your own home! Don't allow any chasing or rushing at this point.

Some dogs approach stiff-legged, like they do with a strange adult. This response can be appropriate, but after the dog figures out the newcomer is a youngster, he needs to stop the tough-guy act and sniff nicely.

Figure 6-2: The play bow position means a dog is in a good mood.

Watch for these trouble signs. You may want to stay close or at least keep the resident dog on a leash:

- ✔ Your resident dog is walking stiff-legged.
- ✔ Your resident dog is staring intently at the Pom.

✔ Your resident dog jumps at the Pom without play bowing (see Figure 6-2).

✔ Your resident dog growls or snarls at the Pom.

Fostering a friendly canine relationship

Try not to rush a new dog's relationship with your other dog — they probably won't become instant buddies. As they get to know one another during the next week, make sure you lay the groundwork for a good relationship. Here are a few guidelines:

✔ Your resident dog is the king or queen and should remain so. This fact means he gets fed before the new dog, gets loved before the new dog, goes through doors before the new dog, and basically gets treated like royalty in comparison. This show of favoritism is tough when you're so enthralled with the new dog, but the perfect recipe for jealousy is to push the resident dog into the background while you gush over the newcomer.

If an older dog has a hard time getting over this jealousy, she may lash out to put the usurper in her place. The reaction is the older dog's misguided attempt to show you exactly who's more deserving.

✔ There's no need to lock the older dog away whenever the puppy comes out to play. However, allowing the puppy on your lap while you make the older dog stay on the floor isn't a good idea.

Make the puppy's presence a sign of good times to come. For example, when the puppy eats all those extra puppy meals, give your older dog a small treat too.

✔ Puppies often come with a get-out-of-trouble-free pass with older dogs. This apparent liberty means the pup can crawl on them, bite them, and do all sorts of tricks that an adult dog doesn't allow another adult to do.

Your older dog's tolerance doesn't mean she likes that kind of play. Make sure your grown dog has an escape route (perhaps a high sofa she can get on or her own crate) so she can get away from the little pest. And be ready to put the pest up.

✔ Allow your adult dog to warn an irritating puppy. In other words, let her growl at times (like an older sibling tells a younger one to leave her alone!). If you don't allow this response, the dog may tolerate the pesky pup too long and jump the pup — without warning! If your puppy doesn't heed the warning, help him out by removing him and placing him back in his exercise pen.

✔ Keep your puppy from eating out of the other dog's bowl, especially if the other dog is larger. Although you don't want to encourage food-possessive behavior, it's a natural reaction when dogs are around other dogs. Until your puppy understands proper etiquette, he needs your help to avoid dumb stunts.

Meeting the cat of the house

Cats rule! Or at least they think so. Your Pom will probably try to make friends with your cat, but your cat may have other ideas. Most cats don't like strangers rushing up to them, especially ones that lick, nip, and yip. For this reason, have your Pom in a pen or on a leash when you introduce her to the cat. And make sure the cat has a higher place to jump to so he can look down and feel superior to this little vermin you call *family* (Hrmph!).

If the dog starts to chase the cat (or vice versa), put an end to it immediately. If the dog gets too fresh with the cat, the cat's likely to swipe her with his paw. Don't punish the cat; just hope the dog is smart enough to need only one lesson.

As with older dogs (see the previous section "Fostering a friendly canine relationship"), follow this advice:

✔ Make sure you don't give your cat reason to be jealous of the new Pom.

✔ Heap on the attention and treats to your cat when the puppy's around.

✔ Make sure the cat has abundant puppy-free zones in the house.

Settling In on the First Night

You've made it through the first day — your pup is safe in your home, introductions have been made, he has begun sizing up his new kingdom (inside and out!), and he has some idea of where his next meal is coming from. Nice job! Just a few more hours and you can say your first day is really over. This section helps you call it a success by giving you suggestions for the nighttime challenges.

Starting a routine from the get-go

Just like young children, young dogs benefit from a bedtime routine. Naturally, the first part of establishing a routine involves picking a set bedtime for every night. Here's one to consider:

1. **About 30 minutes before bedtime, feed your young puppy his last meal of the day.**

   Reduce this to a snack for older puppies.

2. **About 20 minutes after your dog eats, take him out to the bathroom.**

   He must take care of his business before hitting the sack.

3. **Take him to his sleeping quarters and settle him inside.**

4. **Go to bed.**

   At least, *try* to go to bed. If your Pom is experiencing some anxiety, read the next section for guidance on what to do next.

5. **If he awakens in the middle of the night, carry him out to the potty place again.**

   This is not a time for playing. Give him a few minutes and return him to bed. Even better, set an alarm clock for the middle of the night so you, not the puppy, decide when he goes out. No fair hitting the snooze!

This cycle may repeat throughout the night, but it really does get better!

Calming those first-night jitters

When the first night falls, you place your pup in her crate (see the previous section for the steps that precede this and Chapter 5 for more on the crate), say "G'night," turn out the lights, and all's well. Right? Maybe. Scared and lonely, a Pom pup does what most pups do in that situation: She screams and cries in an attempt to be reunited with her family.

Your Pom puppy is coping with a situation you can't even imagine for a human baby — she's suddenly removed from her family and home, the two elements that have made her feel secure her entire life. This situation is far less traumatic if the breeder separates the puppies for increasing lengths of time before they leave, but this preparation may not alleviate the sudden stress of a new home.

Even older or pre-owned Poms are nervous in a new setting. After all, how would you like to find yourself suddenly spending the night in a stranger's house? Try these suggestions:

- Give your Pom a place he can call his own — a crate, bed, or special corner of the couch — to help him feel at home.

- A treat or chewie can help keep him in place and convince him this new place is pretty neat!

You may have been told to ignore your wailing puppy so you don't spoil or reward her for crying. But what does that really teach her? Only that in the most frightening situation she's ever encountered, nobody's there to help her — no matter what she does. Her real mother would never treat her that way. Some dog behaviorists now believe this traditional advice may contribute to separation anxiety (see Chapter 15) in adulthood.

This new attitude doesn't mean you spend the rest of your life rushing in at the slightest cry, offering your dog a floorshow or a buffet. It simply means that you take her out of the crate, attend to her basic needs, comfort her, and place her back in the crate, much as you would a crying baby. (Okay, so the crate's not a good visual for a baby, but you get the idea.)

You've already decided on sleeping quarters for your puppy in a place not too far from your family activities (Chapter 5 covers this topic). But if that choice means she's all alone in a remote part of the house at night, it can get awfully lonely over there! You may have to amend your plans. The easiest solution is to bring her sleeping quarters into your bedroom, at least for a few nights (and with your spouse's approval of course!).

What about your Pom sleeping on your bed? This isn't a good idea, mostly because of safety concerns. Consider these possibilities:

- A Pomeranian puppy is so small you can roll onto him in your sleep.

- Even if you're a light sleeper, he can still fall off the bed.

- The bed may be so large that he feels comfortable making one corner his personal bathroom — bad for your bed sheets, your sleep, and his housetraining.

If you want to hold him for a while as he drifts off to sleep, fine, but then carefully place him in his own bed for the night. If you sleep alone, you can place the crate on the bed. This way you can stick your fingers in it so he can gain some comfort from you.

Chapter 7

Starting Off on the Right Paw: The First Few Days

In This Chapter

▶ Making the rounds with family, friends, and other animals

▶ Just say "Ahhhh": First visit to the vet

▶ Fitting in: Crates, cars, and schedules

▶ Training through play

▶ Curbing bad habits early

*Y*ou never get a second chance to make a first impression! And this is your big chance to make a good impression on both a future best friend and a beloved family member. Gulp!

Now that I've put the pressure on you, you can calm down. In fact, that's my number-one piece of advice for these first days: Keep it calm — your new Pom has enough excitement just meeting you and your family. But beyond that, I have a few tips that may come in handy when it's time for your pup to meet new people, go new places, and become a proper member of your family.

Getting to Know Your Pom

A Pomeranian puppy makes new attachments quickly, and even adult Poms begin to think of their new owners as family within a couple of days. For your new dog's sake, keep visitors to a minimum for the first day. After all, if a parade of people pop in, how can he figure out which ones really matter?

Keeping the newness of it all in mind

During these first days you'll help your new dog form friendships with other family members and get used to her new surroundings.

Research shows that these tasks are significant because at about 12 weeks of age, she naturally becomes more hesitant about novel situations and strangers. The more situations she's exposed to before then, the fewer challenges remain that can wig her out.

With socialization, it's the quality — not the quantity — that counts. As with all things puppy, you need to introduce new experiences gradually, never pushing your pup past the point that she's scared. Keep these points in mind:

✔ Your children are no doubt anxious to play with the new dog, so make sure they don't get too rambunctious and that the puppy has time to herself. Too much harassment and she may start hiding whenever they show up.

✔ The same is true for her new canine and feline family. Have all pets play inside at first or in a confined area outside so they can't run out of control and out of your reach.

Bonding with humans big and small

Before you start introducing your Pom to other people, at home or away, keep in mind and share these strategies, which can make introductions go much more smoothly:

✔ **Hold your dog in your arms.** This way new faces don't tower over your Pom as people greet him, and you don't have to ask them to sit on the ground!

✔ **Keep people from rushing up or creeping slowly up to him.** Rushing is startling and creeping is, well, creepy. Creeping is actually too much like stalking and can unnerve some dogs.

✔ **Remind strangers *not* to look the dog in the eye when they say hello.** To a dog, that direct stare is threatening. A perfect way to scare the bejeebers out of your Pom is to have somebody creep up to him, bend over, stare him in the eye, and then reach out to pet his head. Be prepared to clean the pee off the floor.

If the dog's uneasy, the person can face sideways, which is less threatening, or sit on the floor and wait for the dog to approach. When your dog's at ease, the person can gently rub the pup's chest or neck.

✔ **Encourage people to rub your dog under the chin or on the chest instead of petting him on the head.** Like humans, dogs don't like being pounded on the head.

At home

Help your pup with these gradual steps in socialization:

- ✔ **Plan for your puppy to meet only one or two people at a time.** These people must be gentle and nonthreatening. You can have them offer him a treat to cement the friendship — sort of the opposite of what people tell their children ("Hey, little dog, want a piece of candy?").

- ✔ **Stage a puppy party for people and your dog.** Invite people to your house and, one at a time, have them greet your puppy. They should walk up to you and your dog casually and then nonchalantly put out a hand for your dog to sniff.

Near home and beyond

For now, avoid places where other dogs congregate. But after your veterinarian assures you that your puppy's vaccinations are sufficient, try to take your pup to as many places as possible.

Make each exposure a good experience by doing the following:

- ✔ **Go for a walk around the block and see who you bump into.** You can try to direct a meeting by picking up your dog and perhaps handing the stranger a treat to give to your pup.

- ✔ **Introduce your Pom to children, especially if you have no children at home.** The best plan is to avoid random children; instead, invite only children that are calm and obedient to visit your home and meet the puppy.

- ✔ **Avoid the all-dogs-like-me person.** If you meet this person, tell him your appendix just burst and then scurry away.

- ✔ **Explore public places (like sidewalks, parks, and some outdoor cafes) that welcome dogs.** Avoid taking your puppy to a crowd with the idea of her meeting lots of people at once. She can be stepped on, and people can terrify her if they all try to reach and pet her.

Going to the Vet for Your Pom's First Checkup

Plan to take your new puppy for a health check within a couple of days of bringing her home. In fact, your contract with the breeder may specify a required time frame for this checkup to keep the health guarantee in place.

Checking out the doctor

Your Pom's life may depend on your selection of a veterinarian, so — next to you — this person may be the most important one in your pup's life. You can ask for recommendations from local breeders, kennel-club members, or trainers, but of course, you'll ultimately want to see for yourself by making an appointment.

Take note of how well the veterinarian listens to your concerns:

- ✔ Does he communicate clearly?

- ✔ Does he treat your dog gently?

- ✔ Does he regularly treat Poms or toy dogs?

  Ask how many of these patients he has and whether he feels comfortable doing surgery on them. Chances are he has quite a few such patients, but it never hurts to ask.

I like to schedule some routine appointments at first so I can check out the veterinarian. But you can simply ask to visit and tour the facilities. If you don't like one clinic, try another.

Making the first appointment a success

This first visit has more importance than the basic checkup; it should be a time for your puppy to discover that going to the veterinary clinic is fun. To make the most of this visit for you, the pup, and your veterinarian, keep the following suggestions in mind:

- ✔ Bring any health records the breeder provided and a stool sample (from the Pom, of course!) so the doctor can check for intestinal parasites.

- ✔ Use a travel bag or small crate to take your dog to the clinic.

- ✔ Keep her close to you in the waiting room and keep her from barking at other animals. They may have serious illnesses, and their owners will appreciate the courtesy.

Bring favorite treats so the veterinarian and staff can give them to your dog. It's always best if the first exam doesn't include needles or cavity searches. If an injection is necessary, ask the doctor to replace the syringe (after drawing the vaccine) with a tiny-gauge needle before sticking the dog. This way the injection hardly hurts at all!

This first appointment allows the veterinarian to diagnose any common puppyhood problems (like worms) and discuss your Pom's vaccination schedule and heartworm prevention regime.

The veterinarian also

- ✔ Listens to your pup's heart to make sure she doesn't have a potentially serious problem
- ✔ Weighs your puppy
- ✔ Checks your Pom's teeth and gums
- ✔ Probably examines ears and eyelids
- ✔ Perhaps checks the knees for early signs of patellar luxation
- ✔ May give vaccinations

Vaccinations are a medical procedure. The veterinarian must determine the schedule of shots according to your Pom's body and how it works even though it may not seem like the most convenient schedule to the owner.

Before leaving the clinic, be sure to ask about heartworm and flea prevention (if the doctor hasn't mentioned it) and schedule an appointment at the appropriate time for your Pom's next vaccinations.

Consider just visiting the clinic's waiting room sometimes so the pup has experiences there where nothing bad happens. Sure, she has to get shots sometimes, but drop in another time just to say "Hi." The staff will appreciate your efforts to make their patient comfortable, as this casual visit makes working with her easier on the staff in the long run.

If you're acquiring an adult Pom, schedule a checkup for her within a few days of welcoming her home. At this initial check, the veterinarian performs all the checks that a puppy gets at its first visit plus probably a heartworm check.

Acclimating the Pup to His New Life

Although meeting people and other animals is one of the most important missions you have for your puppy these first weeks, it's not the only one. This is also the best time to introduce your puppy to new experiences. Do you plan for him to ride in a car?

Stay in a crate? Go to the groomer or veterinarian? Learn some tricks? What else? Make a list and try to expose him to each situation now.

Making a crate feel like home sweet home

Your Pom may have already spent some time in a crate. With luck, he has had good experiences. But more often his experiences have been limited to the trip from the breeders and perhaps his first night away from home, both kind of scary.

Take time now to acclimate him to the crate. The following are a few good reasons:

- ✔ The crate provides a secure place where you don't worry about your Pom.

- ✔ Crates provide a safe means of car travel and a safe haven when staying with friends or at hotels.

- ✔ A crate-trained dog fares better if he has to be crated at the veterinary hospital or needs bed rest at home while recuperating.

- ✔ Crates help in housetraining. (I knew you'd like that one!)

Getting her to like the crate

As with all new routines, getting your Pom to look at the crate as something other than a holding bin will take some time and deliberate moves. The following steps can help you achieve success:

1. **Leave the door open and toss some treats just inside the door at first.**

   Gradually toss them farther and farther inside after she's stepping in to get them.

2. **Toss in a larger bone she may want to chew on. Tie the treat to the inside of the crate if she tries to take it outside.**

   Now she has to stay inside if she wants the goods! You also can use a toy filled with treats.

3. **Untie the treat and close the door while she feasts, only for a few seconds at first. Open it as soon as she finishes.**

4. **Keep repeating this routine.**

   Within a day or so she should be running to the crate as soon as she sees you with treats. If you want, you can now introduce a cue like *Bedtime!* for her to go in the crate.

5. **Gradually extend her time in the crate, always giving her chew toys or interactive toys to occupy her.**

6. **Try to let her out before she has a chance to get bored or vocal. If she begins to protest, wait until she's momentarily quiet before letting her out.**

7. **Continue to extend the time she must be quiet before you release her.**

How long will it take? For some dogs, about a day. For others, a millennium. Every dog is different, but the earlier you start, the better your chances of it going well.

Some words of caution

The crate is one of the safest spots your puppy can be, but you must do your part.

✔ Remove your Pom's collar while he's in his crate. Collars, especially choke collars or collars with tags, can get caught in crate wires and strangle the puppy.

✔ Discourage chewing on the wire by spraying it with anti-chew preparations and by making sure your pup has no issues with being crated (see the training steps in the previous section). If your puppy tends to chew on the wire, he can get his jaw or tooth caught.

Overuse can create serious behavioral problems. Think of the crate as your child's crib — a safe place to sleep but not a place for your pup to grow up or be punished.

Contrary to popular opinion, crates don't seem to make young pups feel more secure. In fact, crated pups (especially those not already familiar with the crate) tend to cry even more than uncrated pups when separated. If he cries, try leaving your pup in an exercise pen or small, safe room when you first start teaching him to be home alone. You can leave a crate with an open door accessible to him.

Encouraging independence and relieving anxiety

As important as socialization is for your Pom, her acceptance of being alone is equally vital for her well-being. Don't put this step off just because it's not as much fun as her other lessons.

When you understand your puppy's anxiousness *and* your role in helping her feel secure, you're more prepared for the job ahead of you. Like her other training, this process takes time, patience, and a plan.

It's in the genes . . . and the screams

Dogs are very social animals. From an evolutionary viewpoint, a puppy alone is vulnerable, not likely to survive unless he does whatever he can do to get back to his family. A puppy that finds himself all alone gives out a distress vocalization (okay, a scream) which brings his mother running.

Without his mother (or his caregiver, now that he's in your home), a puppy keeps crying until he's too exhausted to continue. But exhaustion is not the same as being okay. He begins to associate being crated or left alone with being frightened, and this distress is likely to build on itself, creating a lifelong problem.

Your puppy is seeking security. Comfort him from the beginning to prevent him from becoming so stressed in the first place. Then, when you begin encouraging his independence, you need to know *how long* to leave him as well as *how* to leave him.

Leaving, but just for a while

Your pup needs to understand that when you leave her you always return. She builds this confidence by being left alone for very short times that gradually lengthen to longer times. Try these steps:

1. **Start by occasionally leaving the room for just a minute before popping back in.**

2. **Move to a longer time period only when your pup seems content and calm at the current time period.**

   The object is to return before your pup gets restless or anxious.

3. **Gradually build up to 10, 20, and 30 minutes away from your pup.**

The biggest barrier to success is leaving the pup alone too long. Nobody ever got over being scared of being deserted by being ignored. Be patient, and go slowly. You'll make much more progress if you return while she's still calm at 10 minutes than if you wait until she's having a fit at 11 minutes.

How do I leave thee?

The fact that you leave and return isn't a newsworthy event, so do it without ceremony — no long good-byes or joyous reunions!

Distressed puppies are too upset to eat or play. However, giving your pup something to occupy and comfort him while you're gone is useful.

- Mirrors and soft cuddly toys seem most effective at calming separated puppies.

   Try soft, warm, dog-shaped toys that even have a heartbeat, simulating the pup's littermates.

- Interactive toys that challenge your puppy to dislodge sticky food treats are good distractions for bored, but not distressed, puppies.

- The buddy system (that is, having another dog or cat around) may help your Pom, but don't rely on it. Your other pet may not always be there to babysit.

Getting used to riding in the car

Your puppy may have had a couple of car-riding experiences so far — to the veterinarian for shots (oh great!) and to her new home with you (oh no!). Chances are, neither ride was much fun. Combine those thrills with the fact that lots of puppies get carsick, and your Pom may think the car is one awful contraption.

Your job is to make your pup associate the car with good times. Try these suggestions:

- **Go for very short rides to fun places *before* nausea and diarrhea can even begin to churn.** For some dogs this means opening the car door, setting the puppy inside, driving 20 feet, and getting out to play — or to let him puke. (Hint: If he pukes, you've gone too far.)

- **Check your driving habits.** The more often the speed changes, the more nauseous your puppy gets. If you live in hilly country, try to maintain a constant speed up and down hills.

✔ **Bring the puppy to the front of the vehicle.** Although a crate is usually safest, riding in a crate can increase motion sickness in some dogs. Looking out of a window can help alleviate some cases of motion sickness. Experiment with somebody holding your pup — and a lot of towels and plastic sheeting. (Sounds like a bad joke, doesn't it!)

✔ **Give your Pom gingersnap cookies; they may help alleviate carsickness.**

✔ **Ask your veterinarian about motion sickness pills for your dog as a last resort.**

Enjoying Playtime

Play is one of the reasons we have dogs. Sure, it cements the human-canine bond and all that stuff. But the real reason is that it gives us an excuse to act like idiots. You don't want to pass up that chance.

Play also provides a safe arena in which puppies can pick up new behaviors and develop self control.

Engaging the hesitant Pom

If your puppy's hesitant about playing, start with cooperative instead of competitive games. Such games include

✔ Learning fun tricks

✔ Playing fetch

✔ Searching for hidden treats

✔ Playing alongside you with toys that squeak or are easy to manipulate

These games can gradually build to more competitive games; for example, cat toys dangled on a string may become a low-key tug game.

Outsmarting the push-and-shove Pom

Some Poms are pushy when they play. They not only prefer more competitive games but also try to control them! Conventional wisdom says that such games give your dog too much control, but you can play them and still call the shots.

For example, if a game of fetch ends up a game of keep-away or tug of war, use it to encourage cooperation. Take these simple steps:

1. **Come up with a game-over word, like** *Give.*

2. **Teach your Pom (in an enclosed area) that** *Give!* **means** *Trade!* **because you trade him a treat for whatever he has.**

3. **Walk away and ignore him if he refuses to give up the prize.**

This game becomes a handy command for around the house — for those times he's playing keep-away with your $20 bill or new package of razor blades.

Drawing the line with your nipping Pom

Although many new dog owners worry that their little puppy is a budding Cujo, most puppies grow out of nipping on their own. You want to make sure, though, that play stays fun and that she stops nipping when you request. Those barracuda teeth can hurt!

Play it cool

Puppies react roughly with one another, escalating their fighting until the going gets so rough that one of them cries "Uncle!" and leaves. Most pups quickly figure out that if they bite another dog too hard, it's game-over.

You can reinforce clean fun with your pup with the same tactics.

1. **When your pup chomps down on you, yelp sharply and withdraw from him, standing still and ignoring him for 20 seconds or so.**

2. **If he stops nipping and instead behaves, quit your statue act and give him a treat.**

Because your yelp may encourage him to play even harder, you may have to experiment with several versions before your dog realizes you're serious. (The neighbors are going to love this!)

Focus on the positive

Nipping is fun! So give her something to do that's equally fun. Reward her for not nipping by giving her a toy to carry, a ball to chase, a chewie to chew, or a tuggy to tug. If she knows a trick, reward her for doing it.

You also have to do your part to minimize the nipping in the first place:

- ✔ Avoid wriggling your fingers in front of the puppy's face and then yanking them out of reach as she lunges for them.

- ✔ Keep from shuffling your slippered feet around on the rug while your puppy pounces on them. Well, okay, that is kind of fun, but it can lead to her biting your ankles.

- ✔ Convince the rest of your family and any visitors to discourage puppy nipping.

Rarely, the biting is not in play, so it's important for you, as the owner, to spot the signs of true, aggressive biting. Snarling, with ears back, is a sign of possible trouble — especially when combined with protecting food or assets, being picked up, or being told to move.

If you're still concerned, see Chapter 15, where I discuss aggression.

Growling is a natural part of a pup's playful nipping. Did you know that what seems like a growl may actually be a laugh? Dog laughter is a rough sound made only when exhaling, and it's typical of dogs playing competitively such as in tugging games. Unfortunately many people misinterpret the sound as a growl and even punish their dogs — just for laughing.

Laying Down the House Rules

One of the best parts of adding a Pom to your family is spoiling him rotten. After all, you're not going to undermine his chances at becoming a business tycoon or college graduate. And he's hardly equipped physically to be a canine serial killer. Who cares whether he's spoiled, right?

Not quite. You don't want your friends to start avoiding you because of that obnoxious brat that's always biting at their heels, and you don't want your own life and household taken over by a furry Napoleon.

Explaining the laws of the loveseat

Most Pom owners welcome their pups on the furniture, but even little Poms have muddy paws, chew holes in the cushions, and leave fur on the furniture. If you don't want her on the furniture, you can

> ✔ Get furniture that's too high for her to jump up on.
>
> ✔ Teach her early on that her place is elsewhere.

You can always let her up when she's older, but you can't easily ban her after she's enjoyed the lap of luxury.

Getting up on the furniture is no cause for getting down on your pup. Simply follow these guidelines:

> ✔ **Lift her down to a place of her own.** (It has to be a really good place to compete with that sofa and its view, though.) A deluxe dog bed in an equally entertaining spot that has a good vantage point should get her attention.
>
> ✔ **Train her to go to that place on cue by rewarding her when she goes there on her own.** As she starts to eagerly run to her bed, give her the cue *Place!* and reward her after she's there.

If your Pom sneaks onto forbidden furniture, it's not the end of the world. In other words, forget the booby traps, shock pads, or rough handling.

A far less traumatic dissuader is newspaper, aluminum foil, or another uncomfortable surface on the furniture. Most dogs quickly decide their own bed is preferable! (Then again you can just give in — after all, a Pom was meant to share your sofa!)

Keeping his chompers on chewies, not chairs (or shoes!)

Like babies, puppies chew when they're teething. But unlike babies, they keep it up when they're well past teething. And just when you think you're safe, they seem to go through a super chewing stage near the age of 1 year. They chew papers, cushions, chair legs, rugs, shoes — pretty much anything of value. What to do?

The best-laid plans . . .

You can meet with some success if you combine the following moves:

> ✔ Keep your important, valuable items out of sight as much as you can.
>
> ✔ Watch your pup as much as you can.
>
> ✔ Slather horrible-tasting products like cayenne pepper or commercially available bitter tastes on those tempting items that you can't move out of his reach.

✔ Wrap aluminum foil around your chair legs. Your puppy won't find it very enticing to bite . . . but your guests will ask who your decorator is.

✔ Try to guide him toward chewing more acceptable objects. (See the next section for ideas on this.)

Choose his chews carefully

The kinds of objects your puppy chews on at an early age tend to be his favorites the rest of his life. When you find your pup chewing on your belongings, simply take the object from him and replace it with a more acceptable object. Here are some suggestions:

✔ Make sure the new object doesn't resemble items you don't want him to chew — old shoes, socks, stuffed animals (if you have children who collect them), carpet remnants, and so on.

✔ Try rotating his toys so he only gets a few at a time. Every few days put one set away and replace them with some other toys. This way he has the excitement of new toys every few days.

✔ Engage him with interactive toys like the ones he has to work at to extract food. Fill these with bones, soft cheese, canned dog food, or peanut butter, and then freeze them to make them last even longer.

Punishing him does little good, and you can make matters worse if you punish him right when he proudly brings you the trashed treasure. Congratulations! You've just trained him to take your treasures to a secret location so you never get them back!

Part III
Caring for Your Pom from Head to Paw

The 5th Wave   By Rich Tennant

"I've got the salad spinner down here! I'm drying the dog."

In this part . . .

"All you add is love" or so the saying goes. But in Pom World, it's definitely an understatement. In addition to food and love, you add coat care, tooth care, nail care, eye care, and ear care. You add vaccinations, parasite prevention, and unwanted pregnancy prevention. You add the know-how to recognize and cope with the minor and major illnesses from puppyhood to senior citizen, and you add the ability to act on emergencies.

You also add care, whether your dog is on the road with you or staying behind. And you add preparation in case the unthinkable happens and your little dog is lost.

Love is an essential ingredient — but you need to add much more. The chapters in this part show you how.

Chapter 8

Eating Out of the Pom of Your Hand

. . . .

In This Chapter

▶ Realizing the challenges of feeding toy dogs

▶ Understanding nutrients and ingredients

▶ Deciphering dog food labels

▶ Taking the fat off or putting it on

▶ Feeding dogs with food-sensitive disorders

. . . .

*F*eeding a little Pom seems pretty simple: Buy a giant bag of dog food, open it up, and let your dog tunnel his way from one end of the bag to the other. Replace the bag once a year or when he gets to the other end, whichever comes first.

Of course you know better — and want better. One of the joys of having a tiny dog is the luxury of feeding him only the best. But tiny dogs have big challenges when you try to decide *the best* for them.

Your Pomeranian thinks you must be the greatest hunter on earth as you return from the grocery store with bag after bag loaded with food. Eating is one of a dog's great joys in life. Help him be happy and healthy by hunting down the best and tastiest foods.

Avoiding Toy Dog Food Follies

It's not unusual to see people buy giant bags of dog food filled with giant chunks of food suited for giant dogs — and then feed those chunks to their tiny dog. But that's like handing your baby a lobster and telling her to have at it. The intention may be good, but it's not right for her size. Like your baby, your Pom needs not only age-appropriate food but also size-appropriate food for reasons of safety, nutrition, and enjoyment.

Feeding bite-sized bits

Look at those tiny teeth and jaws! You can't expect your Pom to munch down those rocks of kibble that larger breeds practically inhale. He's likely to just give up chewing and swallow them whole, which makes for a bad situation.

Too many dog treats and kibbles are actually choking size for a Pom. In fact, many popular training treats (which are purposefully small — about ½ inch in diameter — for larger dogs) are the perfect choking size for a Pomeranian.

To ensure your Pom's snack-time safety, try the following tips:

- ✔ Squish some dog-training treats to make them flatter.
- ✔ Try human donut-shaped cereals.
- ✔ Tear off bits of flat string cheese.
- ✔ Give her small pieces of thin deli meats.

Many dog food companies now make dry food specifically for small dogs. Besides being easy to swallow, it's usually more nutrient-rich and higher in calories. For more on dry dog foods, see the later section "Perusing the Pet-Food Aisle."

Watching out for low blood sugar

It's no hype: Low blood sugar, technically known as *hypoglycemia*, can kill. This emergency condition is related to feeding, and you see it mostly in small, young, stressed, or active dogs.

Pomeranian puppies and some adults can't store enough readily available *glycogen* (the form of glucose that their bodies keep in the muscles and liver for energy). When the glycogen runs out, the body starts breaking down fat for energy. But because puppies have very little fat on their bodies, they quickly deplete this energy store. And when that store is empty, the brain (which depends on glucose to function) starts having problems. The puppy may start to get weak and sleepy, perhaps wobbling and stumbling if she has to move. If she doesn't get glucose soon, she can have seizures, lose consciousness, and die.

Don't worry too much about hypoglycemia. For most Poms, it's just a puppyhood concern, and they outgrow it by 7 months of age or so. But all Pom owners need to be aware and ready, especially if your dog stresses easily. Just feed regular, frequent meals that contain complex carbohydrates, and be on the lookout for lethargic or otherwise odd behavior.

Keeping blood sugar at a healthy level

Hypoglycemia sounds scary, and it is! But you can take a couple of steps to make sure your Pom never experiences it.

- ✔ **Don't let your Pom puppy go more than four hours without eating.** If that's not possible (like in the middle of the night), make sure he's warm, confined, and quiet so he doesn't use much energy.

- ✔ **Make sure his foods are fairly high in protein, fat, and complex carbohydrates.** Complex carbs slow the breakdown of carbohydrates into sugars. This steady breakdown leads to more efficient use of the carbs rather than a roller-coaster ride of highs and lows.

    Complex carbohydrates are mostly from the whole-grain groups, such as corn, rice, and wheat. Although you can't just feed your Pom a loaf of bread, you can feed him a good-quality commercial dog food that contains some grain-based ingredients.

- ✔ **Avoid simple sugars, such as sweets and semimoist foods.** However, keep those foods on hand in case your Pom starts having signs of hypoglycemia.

Reacting quickly to a blood-sugar deficiency

If you suspect your Pom is becoming hypoglycemic, you need to get some simple sugars into her. Follow these steps to perk her up quickly:

1. **Try to give her corn syrup (a good choice for quick energy), but if she won't swallow it, rub it on her gums and the roof of her mouth.**

2. **Feed her semimoist foods (the kind that look like fake meat and come in a clear pouch) if she'll take them. But don't put anything in her mouth that can choke her!**

3. **Keep her warm and call your veterinarian.**

    If you've gotten enough sugar in her, she should start showing signs of improvement while you're on the phone — within a couple of minutes. However, she still may need to go to the clinic for intravenous glucose.

4. **Give her a small, high-protein meal like meat baby food when she's feeling better and can eat.**

Avoiding toxic table scraps

Even though your intentions may be kind, your dog isn't a barking garbage disposal, so don't treat him like one. Table scraps are okay here or there. But a few table scraps can fill your Pom's little belly — make sure they're nutritious. And remember: When he finds out how good your food is, you can expect him to want more.

Strangely, people are able to eat certain foods that appear to have toxic effects on dogs. This effect is magnified in small dogs. Avoid these human foods:

- ✔ **Alcohol:** Can get a small dog drunk with just small amounts and can be deadly in larger amounts.

- ✔ **Chocolate:** Contains *theobromine* (a mild stimulant related to caffeine), which can cause death in dogs because they metabolize it more slowly than humans do. Baking chocolate is especially toxic. As little as half an ounce can be life-threatening to a 4-pound Pom.

- ✔ **Macadamia nuts:** Cause some dogs to get very ill; scientists don't understand the cause. (The choking hazard is also an obvious warning sign.)

- ✔ **Onion:** Destroys red blood cells in dogs. Eating an entire onion can be fatal to a Pom.

- ✔ **Peach pits and other fruit pits and seeds:** Contain cyanide.

- ✔ **Raisins and grapes:** Have been associated with kidney failure and extreme sudden toxicity in some dogs.

- ✔ **Raw dough:** Can expand inside the warm environment of the gut, causing impaction.

- ✔ **Xylitol, an artificial sweetener in some chewing gums:** Can cause a sharp drop in a dog's blood sugar, resulting in depression, loss of coordination, and seizures (see the preceding section for more on this dangerous situation).

Boning Up on Nutrition

Feeding a tiny dog entails some considerations that you may not have to think about for a large dog.

- ✔ **Pint-sized Poms have tiny tummies.** You may be able to feed a big dog a handful of potato chips and cookies before a meal, but try that with a Pom and her stomach's going to be too full of junk to fit in any nutritious food.

> ✔ **Little dogs need more calories per pound of body weight compared to big dogs, so their food needs to be jam-packed with essential nutrients and energy.** Study the ingredients and nutritional analyses on commercial dog foods. You don't have to be a nutritionist, but understanding some basics can help you make decisions. *Note:* The dry foods that target the wee ones usually cram in more calories per gram than the foods for their larger counterparts do.

The nutrition guidelines in this section are for healthy dogs. Dogs with health problems have special nutrient requirements or restrictions, as I describe in Chapter 10.

Nutrients come in two basic varieties: those that provide energy (calories) and those that don't. Both types are vital.

The energy providers

Although you usually think of nutrients as providing energy, that's just one of their jobs (see the next section for more info), and even foods that provide energy have several different functions.

Carbohydrates

Carbohydrates make up the bulk of ingredients in most commercial dog foods, and the most digestible carbs are in starches and sugars. But dogs can only utilize nutrients from *cooked* carbs; even then, they utilize the carbs to different degrees, depending on the source. The following list ranks the sources of carbs from best to worst:

1. Rice

2. Potatoes and corn

3. Wheat, oats, and beans

Active dogs have a hard time maintaining weight and condition when their diet is too high in carbs The more-poorly digested carbs (numbers 2 and 3 in the list) are especially guilty of causing diarrhea and flatulence. If this sounds — or smells — like your Pom, don't blame the dog! Just change her food to one with higher protein or better-quality carbohydrates.

Dogs need particular enzymes to digest the carbs from dairy products and soybeans. But when they're not regularly eating these foods, that enzyme activity can be low. So, if you intend to give dairy products and soybeans to your Pom, slowly work up to higher levels of these foods. Need more convincing? When enzyme activity is low, the carbs end up fermented by colonic bacteria, which produces — you guessed it — diarrhea and flatulence.

Protein

Protein contains various amino acids that provide the building blocks for bone, muscle, coat, and antibodies. Eggs have the highest quality and most digestible proteins, followed by milk, fish, beef, and chicken (the latter two are tied).

Puppies need higher levels of protein than do adult dogs, and old dogs need even higher levels than puppies.

Keep these points in mind:

✔ Your Pom requires very little food, so consider buying foods that include high-quality protein.

Because meat and other animal-derived protein sources are expensive compared to plant-derived sources, commercial food companies tend to use minimal amounts of animal protein and often use less wholesome sources, such as meat and bone meal or animal by-product meal.

✔ Many people add meat or even eggs to their dog's commercial food, which is probably a good idea. *Note:* No supplement should add up to more than 10 percent of the total diet.

Always cook the eggs because raw egg whites contain a substance that makes biotin unavailable. By cooking the whites or by serving them along with cooked yolks (which are so high in biotin that they offset the deficit), you don't risk a biotin deficiency.

✔ A variety of meats ensures the best sampling of essential amino acids, but proteins from plants aren't as beneficial (although soybeans are almost as high in amino acids as chicken). In addition, most proteins from plants are more difficult to digest and have insufficient levels of some specific amino acids.

Fat

Fat provides energy, contributes to good taste, and aids in the transport of fat-soluble vitamins. But too much fat can cause diarrhea, obesity, and a reduced appetite for more nutritious foods. In contrast, diets deficient in essential fatty acids cause skin problems, inability to reproduce, and slowed growth.

To provide a good balance of fat in your Pom's diet, include rich sources of fatty acids, such as egg yolks and vegetable oils, and aim for a diet with at least 5 percent fat dry matter (the amount of nutrients in the food minus the water content). To figure this percentage out in nondry foods, see the formula later in "Reading the label and between the lines."

The non-energy providers

Nutrients also provide substances that are essential to life, even though they may not fuel the body directly. For example, you may not think of water and fiber as nutrients, but they, along with vitamins and minerals, are critical components of a good diet.

Water

Water is the single most important nutrient. Although your Pom (and all of us, for that matter!) can skip other nutrients for a day or even a week with little noticeable consequence, your Pom needs water every day. Water dissolves and transports other nutrients, helps regulate body temperature, and helps lubricate joints. Like all animals, your Pom's body consists mostly of water. If he gets dehydrated, he can become very ill.

Although water is a pretty simple dish to serve, your dog will appreciate your thoughtfulness in serving it. Follow these suggestions and revel in your little friend's contentedness:

- ✔ Consider using filtered or bottled water. After all, how much can a Pom drink!

- ✔ Keep the water bowl full at all times. Just because the water's running right through her and perhaps wetting the carpets is no excuse to hold out.

- ✔ Change the water every day; wash the bowl each time.

- ✔ Add some ice to her water on a warm day. Your Pom appreciates the gesture — just like you do.

Vitamins and minerals

Dogs require the following vitamins in their diet: A, D, E, B1, B2, B12, niacin, pyridoxine, pantothenic acid, folic acid, and choline.

Minerals help build tissues and organs, and they're part of many body fluids and enzymes. Deficiencies or excesses can cause anemia, poor growth, a strange appetite, fractures, convulsions, vomiting, weakness, heart problems, and many other disorders.

Most dog foods have vitamins in their optimal percentages, so supplementing with vitamin tablets is rarely necessary. And supplementing your dog's diet with minerals, especially calcium, is not a good idea.

Fiber

Fiber (like beet pulp, rice bran, or various gums) affects the absorption of other nutrients including carbs, proteins, fats, and some vitamins and minerals. Although fiber is common in weight-loss diets to give the dog a full feeling, its effectiveness is controversial; some research suggests that it doesn't really help dogs lose weight or even feel less hungry.

Fiber does increase stool volume and encourages more frequent defecation. So, if your Pom's poop is as big as he is, check the fiber content of his food — it could be you're using a diet food with more fiber than standard foods, or that you're using a cheap food that's mixed in a bunch of peanut hulls to save money. Look for a fiber content of about 4 percent for dry foods and 1 percent for wet foods.

Perusing the Pet-Food Aisle

What is it about the pet-food aisle that transforms confident connoisseurs into confused consumers? It's probably all those labels shouting out to proclaim *high protein, low fat, hypoallergenic, small breed, large breed, puppy,* and *geriatric.* You just want to grab a bag and go, but there are too many choices. Don't worry — all you have to do is narrow them down, and I help you do just that in this section. Start by deciding the form of food and then move on to comparing labels.

Comparing bags, cans, and pouches

Commercial foods come in dry (bagged), canned (wet), and semi-moist (pouch) varieties. Differences among them are as follows:

- **Dry (bagged):** Pomeranians, like most tiny dogs, can develop dental problems, but chewing hard foods may help avert them. The typical kibble, however, simply crumbles when the dog bites into it. Specially formulated dental foods maintain their shape long enough to scrape against the tooth surface. *Note:* After dental problems develop, the teeth may be too sensitive to chew any hard food. See Chapter 9 for more information about dental problems.

- **Canned (wet):** Most Pomeranian owners use canned food in their dog's diet, either mixing it with dry food or making it the entire meal. However, a diet of just canned food isn't advisable because it provides no chewing action. Canned foods also tend to be higher in fat, which adds to their texture, so they may not be good for dieting dogs.

Some veterinarians recommend feeding canned foods and other supplements first, then finishing the meal with dry feeds for better cleaning action from chewing. Some dogs with dental problems (missing, loose, or sensitive teeth) may only be able to eat soft foods; these dogs, of course, need veterinary attention first and foremost.

✔ **Pouches (semimoist):** These foods are high in sugar and lack the better attributes of dry and canned food. The high sugar content makes them particularly unsuited for tiny Pomeranians or Pom puppies because the sugar can create a rebound situation that leads to hypoglycemia (check out "Watching out for low blood sugar" earlier in this chapter for this dangerous condition).

However, semimoist foods may be handy to keep around in case a dog's showing signs of hypoglycemia and needs a sugar fix. Some wet foods now come in pouches, too.

When buying dry food (which I highly recommend), keep these tips in mind:

✔ **Dry foods formulated for small dogs are definitely a good idea.** Many of the standard dry foods are too large for tiny Pom mouths. In addition, small dogs require more calories in relation to body weight than large dogs do (see this chapter's earlier section "Boning Up on Nutrition").

✔ **Buy the little bags.** The food loses it nutritional value, can become rancid, and can hatch little bugs and moths (yuck!) when it sits around too long. Don't stock up on it.

✔ **Poms eat so little food that you can afford to buy the best.**

Reading the label and between the lines

Ignore the picture on the food package of the cute dog doing a back flip for the juicy hunks of meat pouring into his bowl. Your dog will probably just stand there, and the food won't look anything like the picture.

Instead, look for the statement that declares the food to be complete and balanced according to feeding trials. Some foods are declared healthy simply because of their ingredients. But because dogs may metabolize some ingredients better than others, the better food companies go the extra mile to test several generations with that food alone.

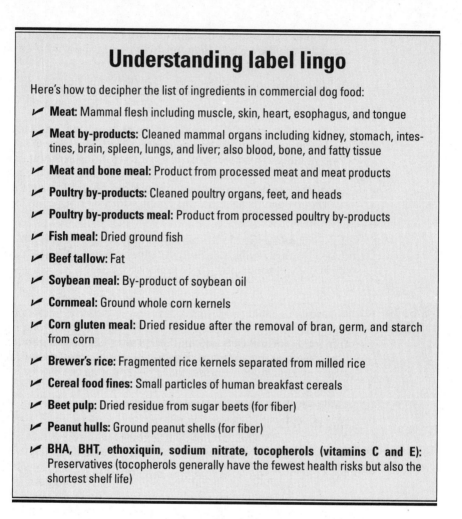

Understanding label lingo

Here's how to decipher the list of ingredients in commercial dog food:

- **Meat:** Mammal flesh including muscle, skin, heart, esophagus, and tongue

- **Meat by-products:** Cleaned mammal organs including kidney, stomach, intestines, brain, spleen, lungs, and liver; also blood, bone, and fatty tissue

- **Meat and bone meal:** Product from processed meat and meat products

- **Poultry by-products:** Cleaned poultry organs, feet, and heads

- **Poultry by-products meal:** Product from processed poultry by-products

- **Fish meal:** Dried ground fish

- **Beef tallow:** Fat

- **Soybean meal:** By-product of soybean oil

- **Cornmeal:** Ground whole corn kernels

- **Corn gluten meal:** Dried residue after the removal of bran, germ, and starch from corn

- **Brewer's rice:** Fragmented rice kernels separated from milled rice

- **Cereal food fines:** Small particles of human breakfast cereals

- **Beet pulp:** Dried residue from sugar beets (for fiber)

- **Peanut hulls:** Ground peanut shells (for fiber)

- **BHA, BHT, ethoxiquin, sodium nitrate, tocopherols (vitamins C and E):** Preservatives (tocopherols generally have the fewest health risks but also the shortest shelf life)

Know what your dog is really eating

When buying food for your Pom, be aware that what you see isn't necessarily what your Pom gets. Marketing buffs have found a way to mask not-so-great food qualities in an enticing description. Hmm, imagine that.

Look at the name of the food and consider its real meaning. Buyer, beware!

- A commercial food labeled *beef flavored* may not even contain beef *if* feeding trials show a dog recognizes the food as beef.

- A food labeled *with beef* may contain as little as 3 percent beef.

✔ A *beef dinner* or *entrée* need not contain beef as its major ingredient, but beef products must make up at least 10 percent of the total product.

✔ Only a product that contains at least 70 percent beef can be labeled simply *beef* without any fancy modifiers. (The same is true for other types of meat.)

After checking out the marketing copy, study the label (it lists ingredients in descending order according to their amount). You want a product that has at least three animal-derived ingredients in the first six ingredients. But pay attention to words such as *meal* and *by-products.*

✔ **Animal meat *meal*** is unfit for human consumption because it can come from dead and even slightly decomposed animals. True, your dog may think a can of sun-roasted road kill is ambrosia from heaven, but that doesn't mean you should buy it for him.

✔ **Meat *by-products*** tend to be perfectly good parts of animals. They may turn your stomach, but your dog finds them delectable. They're perfectly safe and nutritious, just not something you usually serve your human family — unless they're visiting and you're ready for them to leave. Spleen, anyone?

Weighing the nutritional value of dry versus wet versus semimoist foods

The first time you read labels, you notice that the dry foods seem jam-packed with nutrition compared to the canned or semimoist foods. And they are — kind of, sort of. Canned (wet) foods, especially, have so much water that it makes their nutritive content look low. So technically, if you really want to compare dry and wet foods, you have to first factor out the moisture contents and then compare them on their *dry matter.*

Here's how to equate nutrients in foods with different moisture contents:

1. **Subtract the listed moisture content from each food.**

   For example, if a food contains 75 percent water, then 25 percent of the food is dry matter.

2. **Divide the remaining number (the food's dry matter) into each listed nutrient percentage.**

   In the example for Step 1, if the food listed its protein content as 10 percent, then divide 10 percent by 25 percent to get 40 percent protein based on dry food matter.

Making your own?

Many owners have decided that, if they can cook for themselves and survive, they can cook for their dogs, too. (Or not cook, in the case of raw diets.) Raw-diet proponents point out that you never see a wolf cooking his catch over a campfire, so why should a dog eat cooked food? Several dog books now list *bones and raw food* (or BARF) diet ingredients. Unfortunately, many people who go this route forego the books' wisdom and adopt a watered-down version of the diets. For example, they choose a diet that's exclusively raw chicken wings, which is neither natural nor balanced.

Critics of raw feeding point out that you should just toss your dog an intact carcass, complete with fur, head, and guts if you really want to go au natural. After all, they argue, buying chicken parts from the grocery store isn't exactly the way wolves do it in the wild either. Nevertheless, even true BARFists don't care to plunk a dead bunny in a bowl. The kids react badly.

The few controlled studies on the nutritional value of common raw diets show that most of these diets lack important nutrients. Many of the diets contain salmonella and E. coli. Although dogs are more resistant to illness from these bacteria than people are, dogs aren't immune, and dog studies have implicated raw feeding in several serious cases of food poisoning.

Some owners prefer to cook their dog's food. This cooking actually makes some nutrients more available and certainly lessens the chance of food poisoning. A Pomeranian owner can easily make a week's supply of food all at one time and freeze it. A few appropriate recipes are available in *Dog Health & Nutrition For Dummies* (Wiley).

3. **Compare the protein content of the nondry to the dry food.**

    You may be surprised to see that the seemingly puny percentage of protein in the canned or semimoist food is really quite high. Of course, you're still paying for a lot of water!

Deciding How Much, How Often

Pomeranians have been called the hummingbirds of the dog world because of their high metabolism. They have to eat more food more often than larger dog breeds. So just how often and how much does your Pom need to eat? This section tells all.

Starting and sticking to a feeding routine

How often your dog eats depends in part on his age. Because tiny dogs, especially tiny puppies, are prone to hypoglycemia (refer to the earlier section "Watching out for low blood sugar"), you need to feed your Pom puppy lots of small meals. In fact, many breeders advocate *free-feeding* (leaving a bowl of dry food down at all times) until the age of 6 months. If you prefer to feed separate meals, follow the guidelines in Table 8-1.

Table 8-1	Feeding Schedule by Age
Age	*Frequency of Feeding*
0–3 months old	At least five times a day
3–6 months old	Four times a day
6–12 months old	Three times a day
1 year and older	Twice a day

Although commercial dog foods often display recommended feeding amounts on their bags or cans, consider those amounts as only a starting point. How much to feed your Pom depends on her size, her activity level, her individual metabolism, and the surrounding temperature.

Your dog is still the best gauge of how many calories he needs. You should be able to feel his ribs slightly, and he shouldn't have a roll of fat over his shoulders or rump. Just like you, he should have an hourglass figure. Keeping track of his body shape is a lot easier than computing calories!

Dieting your pudgy Pom

Poms can get away with hiding all sorts of weight problems under their lush coats, so you need to get in there and feel your dog's body beneath the coat. In doing a chub check, consider the following guidelines:

> ✔ You should be able to feel your Pom's ribs slightly when you run your hands along the ribcage.

✔ You should also be able to feel a waistline from above and from the side.

✔ Your Pom shouldn't have a dimple in front of the tail or a fat roll on the withers.

Keep track of his healthy weight. Remember, a gain of just 1 pound is significant in a dog that should only weigh 6 or so pounds! It's the same as a 120-pound person gaining 20 pounds!

If your fat Pom is simply fat from overeating, you need to dish out some tough love. You can try feeding smaller portions of a lower-calorie food. Commercially available diet foods supply about 15 percent fewer calories compared to standard foods. Protein levels should remain moderate to high, at least 25 percent calculated on a dry-matter basis (see "Reading the label and between the lines" earlier in this chapter to see how to calculate this) to avoid muscle loss when dieting.

If your dog eats a *prescription* (special diet) canned food but seems tired of it, try refrigerating the food so it holds its shape. Then cut the chilled food into thin slices, place the slices on a cookie sheet, and bake at a moderate temperature (350 degrees) until they're crisp — or the smoke alarm goes off. Voila! Prescription dog treats!

Who can resist those pleading Pom peepers when it comes to treats? Substitute baby carrot sticks, broccoli, pea pods, or rice cakes for fattening treats. Mix some green beans in her dinner. Keep her away when you're preparing or eating human meals, and, instead of feeding her your leftovers, make a habit of taking her for a walk.

Sometimes a dog that looks fat actually has a medical problem such as heart disease, Cushing's disease, hypothyroidism, or the early stages of diabetes. A bloated belly in a puppy may signal internal parasites. And a dog with an enlarged abdomen is especially suspect. For these reasons, always get a health check before subjecting your little guy to a diet — which may be the last thing a sick dog needs. Your veterinarian can also supply you with healthy diet dog food.

Enticing your picky Pom

Older puppies often go through a poor appetite stage between 9 and 12 months of age. Stress can also cause a reduction in appetite. But, if you can feel every rib, if the bones in the spine are sticking up like a dinosaur's, or if the hipbones remind you of an old cow, your Pom is way too thin. You need to have your veterinarian examine your skinny Pomeranian. Unexplained weight loss can be caused by heart disease, cancer, and any number of endocrine problems. If she checks out normal, try one of these strategies to beef her up:

✔ Feed her more meals of a higher-calorie food.

✔ Add canned food, ground beef, or a small amount of chicken fat.

✔ Heat the food to increase its appeal.

✔ Add a late-night snack; many dogs seem to have their best appetites late at night.

Sick dogs often lose their appetites, yet eating can be critical for them. And eating anything is usually better than eating nothing, even if it's not ideal for their condition. The following are a few suggestions that just may do the trick:

✔ Feed the reluctant eater meat baby food.

✔ Keep the food cold for nauseous dogs (don't warm it).

✔ Put baby food in a syringe (no needles!) for extreme cases and squirt a tiny bit in his mouth to get him started.

✔ Give him canned goat's milk or a high-calorie drink for humans through a syringe.

Of course, sometimes your picky Pom is just being persnickety. He's learned to play the starving-dog you-can't-honestly-expect-me-to-eat-dog-food routine in order to get you to dish your own dinner into his bowl.

Don't fall for it. Let him stare at his full bowl while you finish eating your dinner, put the leftovers away, and go about your business. If he's truly skinny or sick, of course, you have to give in. But if he's the typical plotting Pom, you may have to wait him out. After he's eaten his food, then you can give him some table scraps as a treat.

Feeding to Feel Better: Special Diets for Diseases

Most dog foods are formulated for typical dogs with typical health. But for some dogs with some health problems, these foods aren't the best diet. For these dogs, the right diet literally becomes a life-or-death situation. Take heart: With certain foods, you can make your sick dog feel much better and live much longer.

You can get foods specially formulated for various conditions from your veterinarian. Some dogs tire of these foods, especially if they started eating the new food when they didn't feel well. The reason for this rejection is that the dog can actually associate the new food with feeling nauseous; as a result, she mistakenly develops an aversion to that food.

Try not to introduce the new food when your dog is really sick. If your Pom does decide he hates the commercially available food, your veterinarian can supply special diets that you can prepare at home. By understanding which ingredients you must avoid with a particular illness, you may be able to include some treats in the diet as well.

Pomeranians are big dogs in little bodies, and they're just as likely to feel the call of the wild.

Choosing just one Pom may seem impossible! But don't worry: Whichever one you choose will end up being the friend of a lifetime.

Pomeranians, like all dogs, enjoy stretching their legs in the great outdoors. Just make sure that any time you let your Pom off her leash she's away from traffic, big dogs, deep holes, rushing water, or predators.

This sabled cream puppy is an elegant addition to any home, but don't let that patented innocent Pom face fool you. As soon as he can he's attacking that plant!

You can't go wrong choosing from a litter from a responsible breeder — the breeder can help you go beyond a pretty face to find your perfect match.

This black and tan hurdles a jump in an agility trial.

Pomeranians make good companions for gentle, responsible children.

Orange Pomeranians are the most popular color.

Pomeranian purses, complete with mesh windows for ventilation and viewing, make outings with your Pom a pleasure. Just be sure to get one big enough to fit the whole dog in!

Good grooming shows with clear eyes free of discharge, clean teeth, and a tangle-free coat.

Always keep plenty of fresh water available. But somebody needs to tell that Pom it's for drinking, not playing!

Like all dogs, Pomeranians relish the chance to explore the great outdoors. Because of their size, it's safest for them to do so on a leash.

Pomeranians are spitz dogs in miniature, with small prick ears, a stand-off coat, and a foxy expression.

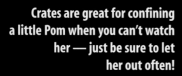

Crates are great for confining a little Pom when you can't watch her — just be sure to let her out often!

Pomeranians are eager to do things with their people and will often stare, bark, and otherwise cajole them into putting down their work and doing something more productive, like playing.

Practice obedience lessons in all sorts of places. You never know when or where you'll need your Pom to sit or stay.

Black and tan Pomeranians, which are black with varying degrees of tan on their eyebrows, cheeks, upper neck, lower legs, feet, and under the base of the tail, are comparatively uncommon but especially eye-catching.

It's never too early to start training your Pom by using gentle, reward-based methods. Even a 3-month-old puppy, like this one, can learn to sit and stay — but only for short periods!

Chapter 9

Primping Your Pom

. . . .

In This Chapter

▶ Caring for hair 101

▶ Gently managing eye problems

▶ Knowing the ins and outs of ear care

▶ Taking the bite out of dental problems

▶ Mastering the art of Pom pedicures

▶ Leaving it to a pro: Groomers

. . . .

Can you imagine having a child and not bothering to brush her hair, give her a bath, or brush her teeth? Nobody would want to be around her, she'd feel awful about herself, and people would talk about you — and not in a good way. Taking good care of your dog makes sense for all the same reasons — not to mention that a clean dog is more enticing than a stinky one for you to hold, cuddle, and love.

This chapter covers all the steps for keeping your Pom gorgeous (or handsome as the case may be). Necessities such as caring for the hair, eyes, ears, teeth, and nails are clearly laid out for you. I even throw in some tips to take your Pom from ordinary (like that could ever be the case!) to extraordinary in a few quick moves.

Perfecting the Pom-Padour

One of the pleasures of sharing your life with a Pomeranian is being able to show him off in public. Few people can resist raving over a Pomeranian pom-pom. But if your dog looks more like a tiny tumbleweed, get out the grooming box and give your dog a new 'do.

As I mention in Chapter 5, a grooming table is a luxury you'll love, but if you want to spare the expense, simply place a towel in your lap and groom your dog there. Make sure both of you have a comfortable place for the grooming project. Otherwise neither of you will want to stay long.

Brushing the puff

The Pomeranian's long, puffy coat is a combination of a long, coarse *guard* coat (the coat you mostly see) and a dense, wooly undercoat that allows the guard hairs to stand off the body. You can easily drag a brush over the outer guard coat to make your Pom look quite presentable, but the undercoat, if left unbrushed, weaves itself into an impenetrable mat of feltlike hair. So, to provide a good Pomeranian grooming, direct most of your attention to the undercoat, the part you don't really see.

Knowing how often to brush

In an ideal world, you'd brush your dog every day, perhaps while watching a favorite television show or just as a scheduled relaxation time. Your world may not be ideal, but don't despair; you can achieve excellent results by brushing every other day. However, waiting longer than that can create problems.

Shed hair has to go somewhere. It can get tangled in the other coat to form frightening mats, or it can ball together into tumbleweeds that bounce down your hallways, or it can cling to everything from your furniture to your clothes. The only other choice is for your brush and comb to catch it, which explains the need for daily grooming during shedding season. Brushing your dog every day cuts down on the amount of hair that decorates your home and clothing.

Getting the technique down

When you're ready to brush, have your Pom lie down and relax. At first, when you're teaching your puppy to let you groom her, just groom tiny areas, maybe her neck in the morning, her belly at noon, her legs in the evening, and her back at night. Each time, hand out treats like a politician hands out promises. With more experience, you can expand the areas you brush in one sitting, ask her to change position from one side to the other, and even have her stand for a while. Just keep doling out the treats!

Professional groomers, and especially show-Pom groomers, can't imagine brushing a Pomeranian coat without first misting the coat using a spritzer bottle of water (or water with just the slightest bit of conditioner — see Chapter 5 for more on grooming supplies). The goal isn't to wet the hair but to make the air around it humid. Brushing a dry coat in dry air causes static electricity, which in turn causes coat breakage.

If you're trying to grow a long coat, avoid brushing it when it's dirty because the hair can break. If you must brush it when dirty, be very careful, and brush as little as you can get away with; wash him immediately, and then brush him again when clean. Never wash a matted coat (see the section "Rats, those maddening mats!" later in this chapter).

In order to brush the undercoat, follow these steps:

1. **Part the hair with your hands so you can see the skin; then spritz the air above it so the mist falls on the coat.**

2. **Use a bristle brush or a pin brush and gently brush from the skin out (see Figure 9-1).**

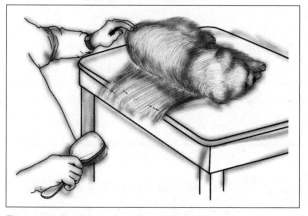

Figure 9-1: Brushing out the coat in layers.

3. **Make the next part close enough to the first so that you don't miss any hair between parts.**

4. **Repeat Steps 1 to 3 in every area that has long hair.**

5. **Using your fingers and then a comb, make sure you didn't miss any tangles or mats on his body.**

If your Pom has a lot of undercoat or is shedding, whip out the *slicker brush,* a wicked-looking brush and — keep in mind — a wicked-*acting* brush. If you drag it through the coat with a heavy hand and stiff wrist, you're likely to pull out a lot more coat than you planned. Instead, use it gently with a loose wrist, working on small sections at a time.

Shedding misconceptions

A Pomeranian in shedding season looks just like a dandelion in a strong wind. Because shedding is controlled in part by changes in light, most natural shedding occurs as the days get longer. But because modern dogs live in our homes with year-round artificial lighting, they shed somewhat all year. However, they still tend to have more intense shedding periods in the spring and, for some reason, fall. *Note:* Females also shed following their seasons and especially after whelping puppies (they go practically bald!). During those periods of intense shedding, your house may look like it's in a snow flurry.

Puppies shed parts of their coat at different ages:

- At about 14 weeks of age, the face starts looking slick; this stage lasts about three weeks.

- Around 4 to 5 months of age, its hair starts falling out in a stripe down the back. The shedding continues until an adult coat replaces the puppy coat.

  Because the puppy tends to shed unevenly and can look so scraggly, you may start to think your puppy's a mixed breed or has caught some terrible coat disease. Don't worry. Unless bare skin is showing, this is the normal puppy shed.

- About 9 or 10 months of age, your naked Pom blossoms into a powder puff.

Rats, those maddening mats!

Mats happen! Hair that's dirty, ignored, chewed, scratched, or in a friction area is likely to mat. Areas with soft, fine hair are even more vulnerable, and the armpits, between the hind legs, and behind and below the ears usually mat first.

Deal with isolated mats by brushing or cutting. But be aware that your dog may end up looking moth-eaten if you keep cutting out mats. Always try to get rid of the mats first by brushing.

Brushing away mats

When you find a big mat, you doubt whether it can turn into pretty hair again. But like all big jobs, you just have to break it into smaller jobs. You may need to tackle it in several sections, mostly to give your dog a break. And while you're persevering, repeat over and over, "I could have prevented this with a few minutes of grooming."

Now get started. Use a slicker brush to lightly brush the outer surface of the mat, working your way in. Always brush the hair out of the mat, not the mat out of the hair.

Try working cornstarch into the mat to help you pull it apart. Or soak the mat in a hair-detangler liquid (human or pet products work fine). Don't use cornstarch *and* detangler because you'll coat the mat in a muddy paste.

If you've previously missed brushing down to the skin, your Pom probably has extensive areas of matting. The result is known as *felting* because the undercoat actually binds itself into such large areas of feltlike material that you can't even find the skin.

Don't try to de-mat a felted dog. It's far too painful for the dog, and this is no time for you to experiment. Instead, take her to a professional groomer who will shave her. The skin under a felted coat is very likely damaged, so your Pom may have large areas of irritated or even raw skin. For this reason, you may have to sign a release before a professional groomer agrees to tackle the job.

Cutting out mats

If you have a big mat attached by only a few hairs, you can snip it out. But when a big mat is attached close to the skin by a lot of hair, you may end up cutting your dog. To avoid this problem, try wriggling a comb between the mat and skin so the comb acts as a shield for the skin when you come at it with the scissors. Even better, use a small, rechargeable electric clipper that is almost silent. It's safer to use than scissors, and most dogs don't object. After the cut, use thinning shears on the area to avoid an unattractive straight-line cut.

You can also try cutting the mat lengthwise into several smaller mats, and then work on each of the small mats. You can wedge a comb between the mat and the skin to avoid cutting skin. A mat-breaking tool combs and cuts at the same time, breaking large mats into small ones.

Bathing beauties

A clean coat smells and feels better. And because dirt and oil form the foundation of mats, a clean coat's also less apt to develop them. Most groomers advocate washing a Pomeranian at least once a month.

Bathe your Pom only when you have time to dry her thoroughly. Never let her run around in the cold with even a damp coat. Her small size makes her susceptible to chilling, and her thick coat takes a long time to dry on its own. Even in warm weather, her coat is so thick that her skin stays moist, providing, unfortunately, a great environment for flourishing skin problems.

Some Pom owners stick cotton balls in their dogs' ears to try to prevent water from getting in them, but this trick usually just leads to ears with sopping-wet cotton balls in them. A better idea: Just be careful around the ears. If water does get in them, use a drying agent, such as drops for swimmer's ear. (The Pom's upright ears usually allow plenty of drying without such aids.) Don't put powder in them because it can turn into a muddy paste.

Brush your Pom thoroughly before you bathe him. Your aim is to remove as much loose hair as possible because wet hair tends to mat. Loosen the dead hair by sprinkling it with baby powder before brushing. Then when you bathe your Pom, you also remove the powder.

Bathing a tiny Pom in a big bathtub is possible, but it's hard on your back. It's easier to bathe your little dog in a sink with a hand sprayer. Take these precautions:

✔ Place a nonslip pad in the bottom (a towel works too).

✔ Put a strainer over the drain so it doesn't get clogged with hair.

✔ Make sure your Pom can't accidentally bump a handle and turn the hot water up without you noticing.

Many male Pomeranians have bad aim and manage to get urine on a front leg when urinating. Rather than giving your Pom a full bath each time he prances in the door with a pee-leg, keep a spray bottle of rinse-free shampoo and a washcloth close at hand.

Picking the right shampoo (and conditioner)

Put down your people-shampoo bottle and step away from the Pom! Your Pomeranian's skin has a pH of 7.0, and your people shampoo is formulated for a pH of 5.5. Using a shampoo made for more acidic hair can eventually dry the Pom's hair and skin.

You can't judge a shampoo by its suds. Sometimes more suds simply mean more residue. Because shampoo interacts with your water's hardness, no single brand is best for all Pomeranians. Keep in mind these special shampoo needs:

✔ Color-enhancing shampoos can make whites brighter, oranges more vibrant, and blacks deeper.

✔ Texturizing shampoos can add body to an overly limp coat.

✔ Oatmeal-based shampoos can help soothe itchy skin.

- ✔ Tar-based shampoos can help cut greasy scaling.
- ✔ Antimicrobial shampoos can help heal damaged skin.
- ✔ Rinse-free shampoos can spot-clean your Pom without rinsing.
- ✔ Flea shampoos can kill fleas, but most nonflea shampoos also kill them.

As for conditioners, you want one that maintains body so your Pom stays poofy. Adding too much conditioner just makes the coat hang.

Washing your soggy princess

When you bathe your little love muffin, follow a protocol to make sure you get her as clean as a whistle (and keep yourself clean and dry in the process). These steps can guide you:

1. **Wet the dog down to the skin with warm water, starting just behind the head and working from front to back. Save the head for last. Use a sponge for her face.**

   Holding her ears and holding the nozzle very close to her skin may cut down on how often she shakes water all over you.

2. **Gently massage shampoo all over her body, making sure it reaches down to the skin.**

   If you mix one part shampoo to ten parts water, it's easier to apply, lasts longer (saving you a little money!), and still gets your Pom clean.

3. **Rinse until the water runs clear, this time starting with the face and working back and down to the feet and tail.**

4. **Shampoo and rinse again as an optional step.**

   This is the best way to get your dog really clean.

Shampoo left in the coat can cause dry skin and itching. As an optional step, you can use a doggie conditioner to help alleviate dry skin, but again, you must rinse it thoroughly. Experiment with various types because some can leave your Pom's hair too limp. Remember, a little goes a long way.

A Pom's eyes don't need special attention; just be careful when bathing and rinsing around them. You can use tearless or soap-free shampoo made for dogs, but eye ointments tend to trap irritants and prevent the dog's tears from cleansing the eyes.

Drying your doused dog

Quick! Close the door! When you've finished rinsing, put your Pom in a safe place, step back, and let him shake. His next plan will be to run amok like a crazed animal escaped from the zoo. (That's why you shut the door!) But don't let him run on slick surfaces where he can slip and hurt himself. If you let him do this outside, he'll just end up looking like a mud ball and you'll have to start over.

When he's finished shaking and you have him under control, use your hands to squeeze the excess water from his coat. Next, towel-dry him, taking care not to rub so vigorously that you create tangles.

 The best way to dry your Pomeranian is with a blow dryer, preferably using a no-heat forced-air dryer. *Note:* Your own blow dryer relies on blowing heated air to dry your hair. A forced-air dryer blows unheated air at high velocity. It dries faster and with less chance of burning your dog's skin, but it does cost more. If you do use a hot-air dryer, set it at the lowest possible temperature and be very careful that you don't overheat the skin or hair.

For best results, follow these steps to dry your Pom:

1. **Give her an overall drying until the coat is damp rather than wet.**

   You can use a towel for this step.

2. **Have her lie down so you can focus on more thorough drying efforts; part the hair just as you did when brushing (see the earlier section "Getting the technique down") so the blow dryer's air reaches to the skin.**

   Continue with this step until all the hair is almost dry.

3. **Dry her the rest of the way, starting at the rear and blowing the hair forward, brushing slightly so the hair fans out.**

   The hair shouldn't have any parts in it when you're done.

4. **Comb through the hair with a coarse, then medium-toothed comb for the final touch.**

 Some owners put their wet Pom in a crate and aim a fixed hot-air blow dryer at her. Do not do this! Countless dogs have been killed because their owners too often forget them — the hapless dogs can't escape the heat. This is a dangerous way to save you a little effort.

Trimming those tresses

The truth is that you don't need to trim your Pom unless you want him to look like a show dog. Even then, the Pomeranian standard only allows for "trimming for neatness and a clean outline." Grooming a show Pomeranian means judicious trimming well ahead of a show so that the shaped coat grows back looking entirely natural. Of course, you may opt for a cute clip to beat the summer heat or just to cut down on grooming.

Ears

Neaten up the ears so that scraggly hair doesn't frame them. If you want that show dog look, you can round the tips, which naturally grow to a point. Consider the following suggestions:

1. **The easiest way to trim is by running your thumb up the inside of the ear to the very end of the ear leather (the skin) and a tiny bit beyond (for safety).**

2. **Use small scissors to cut around your thumb for a rounded look. Don't miss!**

If you do accidentally slip, be forewarned that ears bleed a lot! Use styptic powder to stop the bleeding. Severe cuts may have you heading to the veterinarian for sutures. If this happens, maybe leave this step to a groomer next time.

The ears normally poke up from the rest of the coat, but if the rest of the coat is too long, the ears may be invisible. You can ignore this detail or you can use thinning shears to shorten the coat in that area.

Feet

You can also tidy the feet so they almost form little columns, but with the feet clearly visible. Here are some suggestions:

- Trim the feet by cutting in a circle around the bottom of the foot (the pads); then flip the foot up and trim all the hair so it's flush with the foot.

- Cut down on mud and dirt that your Pom tracks in your house by trimming

  - Behind the front foot up to the stop pad (the rounded knob behind the wrist, technically called the *meta-carpal pad*)

  - Behind the rear foot up to the *hock* (the first joint)

Rear

Trimming around the anus lessens the chance of feces getting caught in the coat. Two suggestions are as follows:

- ✔ Using your thinning shears, carefully cut in the direction of hair growth all around the anus.
- ✔ Raise the tail so it's over the back, and then trim away excess hair at the base of the tail.

Note: If you're trimming for a show look, the entire rear of the dog is almost flat. But this is a job for an experienced show groomer!

Clipping the coat for function or style

The time may come when you just don't want to fool with all that coat. In this case, clipping your Pom is a far better alternative than letting him mat. If you do decide on a clip job, use a professional. Your dog will look better, and there's no chance that you'll mangle her or her fur.

If you're just clipping your dog in order to keep her cool in summer, try combing out the undercoat as much as possible instead. This thick undercoat (not the longer guard hairs) traps body heat. Combing it out may be enough to keep your Pom feeling as cool as he looks.

Professional groomers can suggest a variety of cute haircuts that simplify your grooming time. For example, the *lion cut* leaves the front half of the body fairly long and natural, but the rear half, from the last rib back, is short.

You can also have your dog cut short all over. This shaved do takes about a year to grow back to its former length. Some groomers caution, however, that cutting the hair too short can actually damage the hair follicle so it never grows back right again.

Cleaning Your Pom's Peepers

All Poms have some eye tearing or crusty eye goo, so tear-staining is pretty common, especially on light-colored Poms. Staining is not caused by eating certain foods. The orange stain contains an iron substance that's excreted in tears, saliva, and urine, which explains an orange area that she may get around her lips or any area she licks a lot. Exposure to sunlight makes it worse. To minimize the problem, do the following:

- ✔ Wipe the stain daily with a moist tissue.
- ✔ Give antibiotics in low doses to block the staining. (You can get these meds from the vet.)

In addition, some people advocate

- ✔ Giving only distilled water
- ✔ Giving vitamin C
- ✔ Using eye-moisturizing drops

As a first step, however, your veterinarian should check her for an eyelid or lash problem that could be irritating her eye or blocking a tear duct. Sometimes a simple surgery can fix the problem.

If your dog has severe staining, especially if he's a light color, you can apply a homemade stain remover taking these steps:

1. **Mix one part hydrogen peroxide, one part cornstarch, and one part milk of magnesia.**

2. **Apply the mixture very carefully to the stained area with a cotton swab, making sure it doesn't get in the eye.**

3. **Let the area dry; then, holding the eye closed, carefully brush the mixture off using a small, soft toothbrush.**

4. **Repeat Steps 2 and 3 for optimal results.**

This procedure is something you'd do for special occasions or when the stain just gets too bad. Otherwise, the mixture eventually dries the hair.

Clearing the Hearing: Getting the Wax Out

Peer down into your dog's ears every week. A little bit of wax is normal, even desirable, because it serves a protective function. Overzealous cleaning (digging down with cotton swabs and scratching the delicate lining) can actually contribute to ear problems by creating a foothold for bacteria.

If you see dark gunk, use an ear-cleaning solution from your veterinarian or simple mineral oil (although it's a little messy). To use the solution:

1. **Squirt the ear flush solution quickly into the ear.**

   The slower the liquid goes in, the more it tickles.

2. **Gently massage the liquid around the base of the ear (see Figure 9-2).**

3. **Let go and stand back while your dog shakes.**

4. **Repeat Steps 1 through 3.**

Carefully swab out the ear, taking care not to pack debris down the canal or irritate the ear lining. If the ear is especially dirty, it may need veterinary attention (see Chapter 11).

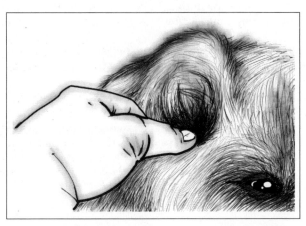

Figure 9-2: Massaging your Pom's ear to make cleaning easier.

Brushing Up on Tooth Care

Fact: Little mouths tend to have big dental problems. To give your Pom's teeth the best care, you need to know the most common problems and how to solve them. You also want to maintain good dental practices for your Pom.

Caring for the pearly whites

You wouldn't think of going days, weeks, months, or even years without brushing your teeth. Nor would you expect to eat a hard cracker in place of brushing your teeth. Poms are the same. If you let food remain along the gum line, it feeds bacteria that produce *plaque,* a gluelike substance. When minerals from food, water, and saliva collect on the plaque, it turns to a cementlike compound commonly known as *tartar* (but veterinarians like to call it *calculus*). The plaque spreads rootward, causing irreversible periodontal disease with tissue, bone, and tooth loss. The bacteria gains an inlet to the bloodstream, where it can cause kidney and heart valve infections.

Although many Poms start losing their adult teeth at a very early age, you can help save your dog's teeth by being vigilant about her dental care — beginning in puppyhood — as you teach your Pom to enjoy getting her teeth brushed. You can use a soft-bristle toothbrush and meat-flavored doggy toothpaste.

Because dogs don't spit, the foaming agents in human toothpaste can make them feel sick when they swallow it, and the high sodium content of baking powder is unhealthy for dogs. Besides, how many people toothpastes are meat-flavored? Make a habit of brushing your Pom's teeth a little once a day. Many veterinarians believe that regular tooth brushing may be the number-one health preventative you can do for your Pom.

Hard, crunchy foods can help reduce plaque, but they don't take the place of brushing. If tartar accumulates, your Pomeranian may need a thorough cleaning under anesthesia. Check the teeth, especially the upper ones at the back of the mouth. If they have a line of tartar around the gums, or if the gums are rimmed in red at the gum line, they need cleaning (see Figure 9-3).

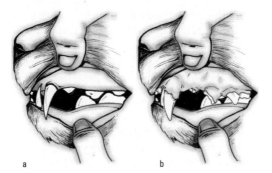

a   b

Figure 9-3: Healthy teeth and gums (a) versus unhealthy teeth and gums (b).

Inspecting your Pom for dental problems

In the correct Pomeranian bite, the top incisors (the little front teeth) fit just in front of the bottom ones. However, a Pom's teeth are comparatively large for their mouth and can be crowded or have somewhat shallow roots. Crowded teeth can affect the bite, which in turn affects dental health.

In a related problem, Pomeranians normally shed their baby teeth between 4 and 7 months of age, but some of these teeth (particularly the canines) tend to stick around. As a result, the permanent teeth grow in alongside them and may be displaced. This situation is okay for a few days. If it persists for a week or more, ask your veterinarian whether the baby tooth needs to go so it doesn't permanently affect the bite.

Likewise, some toy dogs never get all of their permanent teeth. So, before having baby teeth pulled for any reason:

- ✔ Have your veterinarian make sure (usually with an X-ray) that a permanent tooth is ready to take its place.

- ✔ Be sure that a permanent tooth isn't mistaken for a baby tooth. Pom teeth can be so small that sometimes it's hard to tell the difference!

Giving Your Pom a Pedicure

For Poms, having their nails *just so* is about more than beauty. Nails that grow too long can get pulled from the nail bed if they get caught in carpet loops. And *dew claws* (those rudimentary thumbs on the wrists) are especially prone to getting caught and ripped out. As they grow back, these claws can even loop back into the leg. Regular nails that are overly long can push against the ground with every step, splaying apart the toes and causing discomfort.

Ideally, cut your Pom's nails every other week but at least once a month. Unfortunately, some dogs think they're losing their toes as well as their nails. To convince your Pom that this ordeal is worthwhile, heap on the treats after you cut each nail. If you use this reward from the time he's a puppy and avoid cutting the *quick,* your Pom will be wishing he had more toes.

Follow these guidelines for a painless pedicure:

✔ Use sharp, small nail clippers; even those for cats work well with Poms. A nail file also works to shorten these tiny nails. Dull clippers crush the nail and hurt.

✔ Hold your Pom upside down in your lap (okay, *try* to hold him that way!), and look at his nails (see Figure 9-4).

- If they're light colored, you can see a pink core inside them. That's the *quick* — the part you don't want to cut (see Figure 9-5).

- If he has dark nails, look for where the nail suddenly gets fatter. Stay below that point.

- If you look from the underside, you can see where the tip of the nail is somewhat hollow. That's the safest place to cut without cutting too far.

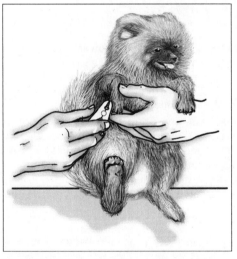

Figure 9-4: How to carefully cut a Pom's nails.

Occasionally you cut too far. It happens. The short nail stings and bleeds, and you run around in a panic trying to make it better. Instead of panicking, place your pup somewhere off your white carpets and press some styptic powder (best choice) on the nail. Then beg his forgiveness with even more treats. In a pinch, forage in your pantry for some flour or a wet tea bag to press over the nail in place of styptic powder. And beg his forgiveness with even more treats.

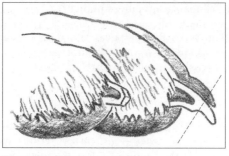

Figure 9-5: Where to cut a Pom's nails.

Just not up to it? Take your dog to the veterinarian or a groomer for a nail trim. Most dogs become amazingly cooperative in a strange place with a strange person. The charge is usually fairly nominal, maybe $5 to $10.

A Spa Day at Pom Springs

Many Pom owners prefer to have a professional primp their precious pup rather than do it themselves. An experienced groomer can have your dog looking her best with a visit about every six weeks. You still need to brush her several times a week, however.

Professional groomers have often graduated from dog-grooming schools or apprenticed under experienced groomers. Many attend grooming seminars and a few are even certified by professional grooming associations. Although groomers may have their own shops or work at veterinary clinics or pet supply stores, some work from home or have mobile grooming vans that come to your front door.

Ask for a tour of the facilities before even making an appointment. They don't have to be fancy, but check out the following:

 ✔ Each dog needs a clean cage or run that separates her from the other dogs. The groomer should sanitize the cage for each dog and clean the clipper and scissor blades with a sterilizing solution between dogs. Otherwise bacteria and even parasites can transfer via the cage and tools from one dog to another.

 ✔ Reliable groomers never leave dogs unsupervised on grooming tables, in tubs, or inside closed cages with dryers. Dogs left alone in these circumstances can meet with serious accidents. Look for such situations on your tour, and ask the groomer whether they use drying cages. If dogs are left unattended, look for another shop.

✔ Professional groomers don't use drugs to sedate your dog for grooming, although they may use a muzzle. These people are trained to handle dogs (even old and lame ones) safely and comfortably, but always advise them if you have special concerns about your dog. If your Pom isn't manageable, seek a groomer who works in a veterinary clinic, where a mild sedative can be given under veterinary supervision.

The groomer trims the nails, cleans the ears, brushes out the coat, removes any mats, and bathes and dries the dog. During the bath, the groomer may empty the anal sacs. Emptying the sacs is only done when the dog needs it, so discuss this step with your groomer ahead of time. Depending on your wishes, the groomer may also clip or trim your Pom.

One important advantage of an experienced groomer is that she may spot an abnormality that you overlooked. For example, alert groomers are often the first to notice infected anal sacs, skin disease, parasites, dental problems, and eye or ear problems.

The cost for professional grooming varies greatly. Groomers who work from their homes are less expensive than those with fancy shops. Those in big cities are more expensive than those in small towns. And of course, those with more experience and expertise can charge more. Expect to pay from $30 to $70, with higher costs for dogs that are matted or need clipping. Most groomers allow you to drop your dog off in the morning and pick her up after work.

A good, professional groomer will have your Pom looking gorgeous *and* looking forward to her next day at the spa!

Chapter 10

Maintaining Your Pom's Health and Happiness

- -

In This Chapter

▶ Setting the course: Regular checkups and vaccinations

▶ Standing guard on your dog's health

▶ Dealing with worms and pests

▶ Making life simple for you and your Pom: Castration and spaying

▶ Easing your Pom into senior-citizenship

- -

*Y*ou are your dog's single most important healthcare worker because you're the one who sees to her everyday health and makes vital decisions about her care. When to vaccinate? What about worms? What's the hurry with spaying and castration? How can you keep your dog healthy, and how do you know when he's not? All of a sudden you have to play healthcare professional. Fortunately, you have help.

Visiting the Vet: Checkups and Vaccinations

Now is the time to get to know your Pomeranian's other major caretaker, his veterinarian. Don't wait until you have an emergency because you may have trouble getting an appointment if you're not already a client. Instead, establish a relationship when your dog is healthy.

The annual rendezvous

Your Pom should have an annual checkup — at least. Dogs age so rapidly compared to humans that an annual one is like a seven-year checkup for you. Especially when she's older (say, 7 years on up) she may need more frequent checkups. So don't procrastinate. Besides taking your puppy's weight, the vet normally covers the following bases:

- ✔ Checks the knees
- ✔ Listens to her heart
- ✔ Checks the eyes, ears, and teeth
- ✔ May gently palpate her internal organs to check for enlargements or tumors

Note: You may have the option of blood or urine tests. These tests can provide valuable early warnings of several serious disorders and are usually a good idea. However, tests can add up in cost, so discuss those fees beforehand. For example, a basic CBC (complete blood count, which checks for anemia and infection-fighting cells) might cost $20 to $40; one that also includes various typical blood chemistry values may run $70 to $90. If your dog is ill, and your vet suggests these tests, get them. If he's not ill, discuss whether you really need them just for baseline results.

Understanding vaccinations

Not so long ago, veterinarians generally believed that the more vaccinations, the better. But no longer. Now veterinarians and researchers advocate giving dogs only the vaccinations they need, only when they need them. Makes sense, right? But what vaccinations does your dog need and when?

The two main types

Vaccinations fall into two categories:

- ✔ **Core vaccines:** Advisable for all dogs for rabies, distemper, parvovirus, and hepatitis (see Table 10-1)
- ✔ **Noncore vaccines:** Advisable only for some dogs for leptospirosis, coronavirus, tracheobronchitis, Lyme disease, and giardia

Your veterinarian can advise you whether your dog's lifestyle and environment make him a candidate for any of these noncore vaccines. For example, leptospirosis is a concern for dogs that walk in wildlife areas. Lyme disease is a concern for dogs in certain areas of the country. Most boarding kennels require a recent (within 6 months) tracheobronchitis (kennel cough) vaccination and core vaccinations.

The whens and whats of vaccinations

Your puppy receives her early immunity through antibodies in her mother's *colostrum* (the first 24 hours of milk flow following birth). As long as the pup still has that immunity, vaccinations don't do her any good. But by the time she's several weeks old, that initial immunity begins to fade and she becomes more vulnerable to communicable diseases. Fortunately, her immune system also becomes more responsive to vaccinations.

If all puppies lost their initial immunity at the same age and rate, vaccinations would be easy. But because immunity diminishes at different times in different dogs, you need to give a series of vaccinations starting around 6 weeks of age so you can vaccinate at just the right time (after vaccinations become effective and before she's unprotected).

During this time of uncertainty, keep your pup away from places where unvaccinated dogs may congregate. Some deadly viruses, such as parvovirus, can remain in the soil for six months after an infected dog has shed the virus in its feces there.

Table 10-1	Core Vaccinations and Frequency		
Age	*Shot*	*Purpose*	*Other*
6 weeks	A series of injections over the course of a varying number of weeks	Protect puppies from distemper, parvovirus, and hepatitis	
16 weeks	Rabies	Protect against rabies	
1 year after puppy shot series and then every 1–3 years	Rabies booster	Protect against rabies	Frequency depends on local law
Every 6 months	Booster for kennel cough, if appropriate	Prevent kennel cough	This is optional
Every 3 years after puppy's first year	Boosters for core vaccines	Prevent distemper, parvovirus, and hepatitis	

Don't hedge your bets on herd immunity

Some proponents of natural rearing condemn vaccinations; they prefer using home-opathic *nosodes* (medicine prepared from the diseased part or discharge of something, which supposedly works as well as a vaccination). These people point to their dogs' good health as proof that nosodes work. However, their good fortune is probably the result of *herd immunity,* that is, as long as most other dogs are vaccinated, the unvaccinated dogs rarely come in contact with the infectious agents.

No controlled study has ever supported the effectiveness of nosodes. Vaccinations aren't without a downside, but they're essential components of your dog's healthy future.

Some owners elect to test a dog's blood *titers* (test to check a dog's level of immune defenses) to various diseases to see whether he needs a booster. A high titer generally indicates protection, but a low titer doesn't mean the dog isn't protected.

Dealing with bad reactions

Occasionally a dog has a bad reaction to a vaccination. This problem occurs most often in toy dogs, which, of course, include Pomeranians. The dog may seem tired and sore for the next day or two. On rare occasions, the dog may get hives or vomit. Call your veterinarian if your pup has either of these symptoms.

In order to quickly counter a bad reaction (or to avoid one entirely), take the following precautions:

- ✔ **Give your Pom an antihistamine before she gets her shots.** Many Pom breeders suggest this. Ask your veterinarian beforehand about the proper type and dose of antihistamine.

- ✔ **Ask your veterinarian to skip the leptospirosis vaccine.** Leptospirosis, while a serious disease, is most often encountered in areas where wild animals urinate. This vaccine has been associated with the most adverse reactions in young dogs. You can probably put it off until later.

- ✔ **Hang around the veterinary clinic for about 20 minutes following vaccinations.** This wait time allows your dog quick access to treatment if she experiences a reaction.

- ✔ **Be sure to remind your veterinarian on subsequent visits about any adverse reactions your dog has had to vaccinations.**

Some toy dog owners believe their dogs may have bad reactions because vaccinations aren't given by weight. Your 5-pound Pom gets the same amount as a 105-pound Pyrenees. But weight has nothing to do with it. A virus infects a small dog the same way it infects a large dog — by acting on his immune system. So a vaccine has to act on the immune system the same way. Don't be tempted to vaccinate your dog yourself so you can lessen the dosage.

Playing Doctor: The Do-It-Yourself Checkup

You plan to take your dog to the veterinarian for an annual checkup, but that doesn't mean you just close your eyes to her health the rest of the year. Set aside five minutes a week — you need to groom her that often anyway — to do a quick home health-check.

Start with some overall considerations:

- ✔ **Has her behavior changed?** Sudden changes could mean she's in pain or has some sort of neurological problem. She needs to be seen by the vet this week.

- ✔ **Does she act listless, weak, or confused?** These can be signs of pain, fever, anemia, neurological problems, or general illness. She needs to go to the vet today. Check her temperature and gum color to report to the vet when you make the call.

- ✔ **Is she limping?** This could indicate knee problems (patellar luxation) or injury. If it's not too bad, give it a day, then go to the vet if she's still limping.

- ✔ **Is she coughing, wheezing, or gagging?** She could have kennel cough, congestive heart failure, or tracheal collapse. If she's having difficulty breathing, she needs to see the vet today.

- ✔ **Is she urinating or drinking more than usual?** She could have diabetes, kidney failure, or a urinary tract infection. She needs to see the vet this week.

- ✔ **Has her appetite changed?** She could have any number of problems. Take her temperature, check her over, and if she still has a poor appetite in a couple of days, take her to the vet.

- ✔ **Has she lost or gained weight?** She could have cancer, heart disease, kidney disease, Cushing's syndrome, or any number of problems. Get her checked by the vet this week.

- ✔ **Are her stools normal?** If diarrhea continues for another day, call the vet and ask if you should bring her in.

Next, give her body a once-over:

- ✔ **Are her bones and muscles fairly symmetrical on both sides?** Any asymmetry could indicate muscle wasting, tumors, or broken bones. Take her to the vet this week.

- ✔ **Do you feel new bumps or masses?** First, don't freak out. Dogs are good at growing noncancerous bumps. But have it checked out this week.

- ✔ **Does she act like anything hurts?** Depending on the problem, she could have a urinary tract infection, slipped disk, or who knows? Take her to the vet!

- ✔ **Is her skin clear, without crusting or hair loss?** It's not an emergency, but skin conditions could be caused by parasites or infections. Take her to the vet soon.

Now start at the front and work back:

- ✔ **Are her gums pink, as they should be?** Pale gums indicate anemia or internal bleeding, gray gums indicate poor circulation, and gums with little red blotches indicate a potentially serious blood-clotting problem. All of these are potential emergencies. See the vet now!

- ✔ **Are her teeth clean and secure?** Dirty, loose teeth can cause pain and additional disease. She may need an appointment for a teeth cleaning under anesthesia.

- ✔ **Are her eyes clear and without significant discharge?** A bit of clear discharge is normal, but goopy, green discharge means irritation or infection. See the vet the next day.

- ✔ **Are her ears clean?** A little dirt is fine, but if they're clogged with debris, she may have an infection or mites. Your veterinarian can diagnose the problem and prescribe a cure. Go in the next day or so.

- ✔ **Are her nails short and without splits?** If not, cut them! If they're split, you can tape them. If you can't handle nail care yourself, have your vet do it this week.

- ✔ **Are her feet without cuts or foreign objects?** Treat cuts like you would your own, by cleaning and gobbing on antibiotic goop. Spray a bitter-tasting spray (your vet sells this) on it to keep her from licking it, or wrap a bandage around it. If it's deep, your vet may need to clean or suture it.

- ✔ **Is her at-rest pulse between 70 and 120 beats per minute?** See Chapter 11 to find out how to check your dog's pulse. If it's outside this range, recheck it when she's calmer (if it's too fast) or call your vet.

✔ **Is her temperature around 101 to 102 degrees Fahrenheit?**
Don't freak out if it's a degree higher or lower. But, if it's down
to 98 or up to 103 degrees, call the veterinarian. If it's below 98
or above 105 degrees, it's an emergency. Call the emergency
veterinarian and warm or cool your dog in the meantime.

To check your dog's temperature, hold her still with one hand,
lift her tail high and forward with the other, and have a helper
insert a lubricated rectal thermometer about an inch into her
rectum. If you're on your own, use the same hand to hold her
and lift her tail. The digital models are easiest to use and beep
when they're ready; otherwise, leave the thermometer in
place for about a minute.

Avoiding the Worm Farm: Preventive Measures

A cornucopia of little bloodsuckers can live inside your dog. We
commonly refer to them as *worms* whether they look like worms or
not. Some are deadly, some are just nuisances, but you should aim
to prevent them all!

Heartworms

Heartworms are deadly parasites carried by mosquitoes. If your
Pom has any chance of being bitten by a mosquito, she needs to be
on preventive heartworm medication.

Your veterinarian can advise you when to start giving your pup the
medication; the recommendations vary by location. Most veterinarians prefer to start dogs on preventive medication before
they're 4 months old. Dogs over 6 months of age need a simple
blood test to check for heartworms before beginning heartworm
prevention. The once-a-month preventive, which works by target-
ing heartworms at a particular life phase, is safe and effective.
Treatment is available for heartworms, but prevention is far
cheaper, easier, and safer.

Intestinal parasites

Most pups have worms at some point because some types of worms
lie dormant and protected in the dam. When a dog is pregnant and
experiences hormonal changes, the worms become active and
infect the puppies as fetuses, or through her milk. Puppies also can
pick up worms from the environment. The breeder should have

checked and (if necessary) dewormed your pup before sending him home with you, but it doesn't hurt to check your Pom again on his first checkup and periodically after that (the eggs don't always show up in tests).

Your dog can also pick up worms from the ground where other dogs congregate. The best prevention at home is to clean up feces immediately, but purging a yard of some kinds of worms can be difficult.

There's one kind of worm that's easy to spot: the tapeworm. You can see flat segments wiggling around on your dog's fresh stool (don't get too enthralled studying them or your neighbors will definitely think you're weird), or they may look like dry rice stuck around your dog's butt. Tapeworms are different from other intestinal worms in that your dog picks them up mostly by eating fleas. Think your dog wouldn't eat fleas? She sure would, when she's nibbling at something biting her. Your veterinarian can prescribe medication to rid her of the tapeworms, but the best prevention is to keep the fleas off.

Two other common intestinal parasites aren't worms but *protozoans* (single-celled organisms). Dogs and especially puppies pick them up in the environment, so avoiding them is difficult.

- **Giardia** is fairly common in both puppies and dogs. Although many dogs have no symptoms, some dogs with giardia tend to have loose, light-colored stools. Giardia is diagnosed with a stool sample and can be treated with medicine from your veterinarian.

- **Coccidia** may or may not cause overt symptoms, and it's diagnosed with a stool sample. Over-the-counter dewormer treatments are not effective.

Preventing Bugs: Fleas, Ticks, and Mites

Depending on your location and the season, at some point fleas and ticks will try to make your dog's body their breakfast — and lunch and dinner. It's best to keep some long-acting flea repellant, such as the ones that are stored in the skin and wick out over the course of a month or two, on your dog even before flea season.

If you're in a tick-infested area, you need to apply some hands-on care by meticulously feeling and examining your Pom's body down to the skin, paying special attention to the ears, neck, and between the toes.

For more on fleas, ticks, mites, and your dog, check out Chapter 11.

Castrating and Spaying

Pomeranians begin to reach sexual maturity at about 6 months of age. The male's testicles begin to grow in size, and his mind turns to thoughts of the fairer sex. The female doesn't give you any clues until one day you're shocked to see her bloody vaginal discharge. If you have both a male and female, prepare for the worst three weeks of your life.

Knowing what to expect

At first, caring for your she-dog in heat doesn't seem so bad. She's messy, but you can keep her confined or have her wear those little bitch's britches for dogs in heat. Of course, she needs to urinate more often when she's in season just so she can advertise her beautiful scent, and of course, she does it in those pretty little britches, so you'd better buy several sets. The males are sort of interested, but not much. In fact, you may start thinking your girl lacks sex appeal. This is the phase meant to lull you into complacency.

Somewhere in the second or third week, her scent changes. Males find her the most alluring creature to ever walk the earth, and they howl, dig, whine, and travel great distances to woo her. Your chaste little girl is suddenly acting like a harlot, and you're counting the days until your personal time in purgatory ends. Great news! In six months, you can expect it to happen all over again.

Lowering the sexual zest

You can nip (or snip) the promiscuity of your Pom in the bud by castrating your male or spaying your female. But the advantage to doing this before your dog reaches sexual maturity depends on the sex of the dog:

- ✔ **Male:** When a male reaches sexual maturity, he starts to lift his leg when urinating in order to mark objects in his territory, which include your furniture. He may also become more aggressive toward other dogs. The longer he practices these behaviors, the more likely they'll persist after neutering.

✔ **Female:** The advantage to spaying a female before her first season is medical rather than behavioral. Spaying before her first heat season drastically reduces her chance of breast cancer later in life. Spaying before her second season helps, too, but not as much, and after that season, spaying has little benefit against breast cancer. Spaying at any time eliminates the possibility of *pyometra,* a potentially fatal infection of the uterus that's common in dogs.

The best age to castrate or spay is around 5 or 6 months. This timing gives your Pomeranian a chance to grow, making surgery a little easier. Because toy dogs often retain baby teeth alongside their permanent teeth, the surgery also provides an opportunity for the veterinarian to remove those teeth.

Addressing thoughts of breeding

Breeding tiny dogs is not for the inexperienced and, in fact, has several disadvantages:

✔ A Caesarean delivery is likely.

✔ Serious postnatal complications such as *eclampsia* (a potentially fatal condition of the dam) are likely.

✔ Litters are small, so don't count on raking in the bucks by selling lots of puppies.

✔ The requirements of a good breeder, which I discuss in Chapter 3, are stringent. Ask yourself these questions:

   • Can you meet the requirements?

   • Have you had the necessary health clearances performed on the potential sire and dam?

   • Has she proven herself in an objective competition to be of better-than-average quality?

Unless you're adamant about wanting to breed your Pom, you're safe to go forward with the castration or spaying.

Good Pomeranian breeders screen for hereditary defects, prove their dogs in some form of competition, educate themselves, and stand by their puppies for a lifetime. They often require that buyers neuter or spay their dogs (either by giving a partial refund when they do, withholding full ownership until they do, or registering the dog with a Limited Registration, so any puppies from it can't be registered) because they know too well the problems that poor dog breeding can create.

Giving Your Pom a Chip on His Shoulder

One preventive veterinary measure you'll want to take is preventing your Pom from becoming lost. Besides taking all the normal precautions, such as not letting him roam, keeping your fence secure, and having him wear a license, there's one measure your veterinarian can help with: a microchip.

A microchip is about the size of a grain of rice and is inserted just above the shoulders, beneath the dog's skin, with an injection. Now, it takes a big needle to inject something this size, so I advise waiting until you have your dog spayed or castrated so she won't feel it. Otherwise she'll probably wince and may yip, but she'll get over it.

The microchip transmits a number when a special reader is passed over it. This number can then be traced to you. Animal shelters check dogs for microchips when they come in and have reunited many lost pets with their families because of them.

Keeping Your Senior Pom Healthy

With the help of good care, good genes, and good luck, your Pomeranian will be with you for many years. He'll mature gradually from perky pup to competent companion, getting better all the time. But one day, maybe when he's anywhere from 8 to 12 years old, you'll notice that he's matured into a senior citizen, a stage that many Pomeranian owners contend is nonetheless the best time of all. But a Pom pensioner needs you to take special precautions to help him stay healthy and happy.

Eating and the elderly Pom

Older Poms need several small meals a day. If your grand Pom has tooth loss or other dental problems, you may need to feed her mushy foods. Both physical activity and metabolic rates slow in older dogs, so they tend to need fewer calories. And just like with humans, excessive weight can place a burden on the heart and joints. However, because very old dogs tend to lose weight, at some point you may find you're trying to keep your dog's weight on, not off.

Most older dogs don't require a special diet unless they have a special medical condition (see Chapter 11). Moderate amounts of high-quality protein, such as those found in dog foods formulated for seniors, are especially important for seniors.

Coping with senior sensory problems

Older dogs, like older people, may experience sensory or cognitive losses. Fortunately, dogs deal well with these changes — better than most people do.

Vision loss

As your dog ages, you'll start to notice a slight haziness in the pupils (black part) of his eyes. That change is normal and doesn't affect vision that much. However, if the pupils become very gray or even white, he probably has cataracts.

A canine ophthalmologist can remove the lens and even replace it with an artificial lens, just like people get. Two concerns that your veterinarian will evaluate first are

✔ Is he healthy enough for surgery?

✔ Is the retina of his eye still functioning?

Cataract surgery is expensive — anywhere from $1,000 to (gulp) $5,000 — and entails a fair amount of aftercare, but it can make a world of difference for your dog.

Not all vision problems can be fixed, and you may not notice his vision is deteriorating until he's almost blind. To help your senior Pom get around safely, take the following precautions:

✔ Block dangerous places (stairways and pools).

✔ Don't move your furniture unnecessarily.

✔ Place sound and scent beacons (such as playing radios, ticking clocks, perfumed cloths, or stinky shoes that never move) around the house and yard so he can hear and smell where he is.

✔ Make pathways that he can feel with his paws (carpet runners inside and gravel walks outside).

Many blind dogs live very happy lives.

Hearing loss

Older dogs also tend to lose their hearing. The ability to hear high-pitched sounds usually goes first, so if you notice your dog isn't responding to your call, try lowering the tone of your voice.

Unfortunately, dogs and hearing aids don't mix, so your best bet is to help her understand new ways to communicate. For example, a dog can easily understand your simple hand signals, and she can respond to a flashing porch light when you want her to come inside. Also, be sure to pet your dog a lot; otherwise she'll wonder why you quit talking to her.

Cognitive loss

If you find your older Pom walking around aimlessly, pacing back and forth, or standing in a corner looking like she's stuck, she may be suffering from cognitive dysfunction. Basically, she's not thinking as clearly as she once did. Your veterinarian can prescribe a drug (selegiline hydrochloride is the fancy name, but it goes by Anipryl) that may help her get back to being her old self. It doesn't work for all dogs and may take weeks or longer to see a difference, but in those dogs that it works for, owners report almost miraculous improvements — just like her old self!

You can also help by involving her in activities and small mental challenges, either through games or by teaching her new tricks. If she enjoys the same games she did when she was younger (like short games of tag or fetch), great! Just be sure not to overdo them. She may prefer less strenuous activities, though. For example, hide treats around the room and challenge her to find them. Or take her for rides in the car; even though she may not be as demanding as she used to be, she probably still enjoys getting out and going places with you. Research has shown that these activities help ward off cognitive impairment.

Senior health concerns

Just as you start feeling more aches and pains as you age, so does your Pom. And unfortunately, it's not just the bones and joints that go in older people or dogs. The heart, kidneys, and other organs may not function like they used to, and cancer is more likely to threaten health. This is a time when preventive health care really can be a life saver.

Your older Pomeranian needs a veterinary checkup twice a year. Although blood work was optional when she was younger, it's a necessity now. Standard blood work can tell you whether she's suffering from anemia, has elevated white blood cells (indicating infection), or has too few platelets (indicating a clotting disorder). Other tests can tell you whether she has kidney failure, diabetes, liver failure, or other major problems.

Check out the following list of more common ailments and note how you can best respond to them:

- ✔ **Arthritis:** Pomeranians stay perky even into their senior years, but you shouldn't push the physical activities. Even if your Pom is used to jumping on and off furniture, encourage him to use doggy steps or a ramp (see Chapter 5). Older dogs tend to have arthritic changes that can be made worse by such stresses. The same is true for exercise; you don't want your older Pom to just lie around, but give him a soft bed when he does. You can help your arthritic dog by walking him a short distance (say, around the block, or less if it's a big block) one or more times a day.

  Also, ask your veterinarian about drugs such as carprofen that may help alleviate some of the symptoms of arthritis or even improve the joint. Glucosamine stimulates the production of collagen and may help rejuvenate cartilage. Chondroitin sulfate helps to protect cartilage from destructive enzymes. These medications are available from your veterinarian or most drug or health-food stores.

- ✔ **B.O.:** Older dogs often have a stronger body odor than they did when younger. Search for its source. The most likely sources are the teeth, ear infections, or even kidney disease.

- ✔ **Body temperature:** Older dogs are more susceptible to both chilling and overheating, so be sure you keep an eye on whether he's curled up and shivering or spread out and panting.

- ✔ **Dry skin:** Dogs lose moisture in their skin as they age, making them itchy. Regular brushing can stimulate oil production. Also consider using a moisturizing conditioner when you bathe your dog.

- ✔ **Digestion problems:** Vomiting or diarrhea can dehydrate and debilitate an old dog quickly. They can also signal some serious problems such as kidney or liver failure. When he was younger, you may have waited a day or so before you took your dog to the veterinarian. Now that he's older, don't take a wait-and-see approach. Get him to the clinic today.

- ✔ **Immune system deficiency:** Because the immune system is less effective in older dogs, shielding him from infectious disease with vaccinations is now doubly important. However, if he's turned into a homebody, the vaccination regimen may no longer be necessary. This decision remains controversial among veterinarians in the field. Ask your veterinarian about the latest guidelines.

✔ **Tooth problems:** Tooth problems are very common in older Pomeranians. Bad breath, lip licking, reluctance to chew, and avoidance of hands near his mouth are all signs that your dog needs veterinary dental attention. Pulling loose teeth and cleaning the remaining teeth can help your dog feel much better.

In addition to the typical ailments that dogs of any age suffer, older dogs are far more vulnerable to a number of serious disorders. For example, heart disease, kidney disease, cancer, diabetes, and Cushing's syndrome (which occurs when the adrenal glands make too much cortisol, causing a pot-bellied appearance, among other symptoms) are all much more common in older dogs. Symptoms of these disorders include

✔ Abdominal distension

✔ Appetite changes

✔ Coughing

✔ Diarrhea

✔ Increased thirst and urination

✔ Nasal discharge

✔ Weight loss

Many of these disorders can be treated successfully, especially if caught early (see Chapter 11). For this reason, don't ignore these signs, especially in your older Pom. Old age, combined with small body size, mean Poms are somewhat vulnerable when ill. If you see any of these symptoms, get your Pom to the vet within the week; the sooner the better.

Chapter 11

Doctoring Your Dog

*L*iving with a pet for many years means dealing with illness — both minor and more serious, short-term and long-term. Unfortunately, because their life spans are so much shorter than ours, dogs tend to rush through the stages of life, rushing also into these illnesses at an advanced pace. But here's the good news: When you're able to extend their lives by even a short time in people terms, you're actually extending it a long time for them.

In this chapter I show you how to recognize problems and address many of them on your own. I also point out when to turn a problem over to the veterinarian so you can extend your dog's life *and* quality of life with the best care possible.

Saving Your Dog's Skin

The best coat-care in the world can't overcome skin problems. Itchy skin or skin that's inflamed, greasy, or smelly, as well as skin with sores can all make your dog uncomfortable and her hair look lousy. Knowing a bit about different skin-related issues can help you identify and solve your dog's skin problem.

Debugging your dog

Many people think a toy dog's only job historically was to sit in people's laps and look cute. But that concept's only half right. Many toy breeds actually had a very important job — they were to sit in people's laps, look cute, *and* attract fleas off the people.

Chances are you didn't add a Pomeranian to your household for this reason. In fact, the roles have completely reversed *and* expanded: Now you're getting fleas, ticks, and mites off your dog!

Making fleas flee

Fleas are little brownish bugs that scurry under your dog's coat next to the skin. They can move pretty fast after you part the fur because they're flattened and very narrow. They also leave behind poop that looks like black dirt and turns red if you get it wet. Fleas make your dog itch, both when they bite and afterward, because their saliva often causes allergic widespread reactions for days afterward. They also transmit tapeworms. After they get into a home or environment, fleas hang around, sometimes for months, waiting for a warm, fuzzy host to stroll by.

Fighting fleas — the scourge of dogdom — had been a losing battle until recently. Not so long ago you had to soak your dog, your house, and your yard in so many poisons that it made Chernobyl seem like a nature preserve. The time and expense added up until some owners finally gave up.

Today the situation's improved. Newer products available from your veterinarian have a higher initial purchase price but are cheaper in the long run because they work from the get-go and need reapplication only once a month or so.

Most of these products are available only from your veterinarian, although some discount products try to sound like they're just as effective. Look for a product with one of the following ingredients:

- **Nitenpyram:** If your Pom is covered in fleas, reach for this oral medication that has the fleas kicking the bucket within two minutes. Every flea is dead within four hours. The drawback? Nitenpyram has almost no residual activity, so it's mostly a quick fix for heavily infested dogs.

- **Selamectin:** Want something that does it all? This chemical takes care of fleas, ear mites, and several internal parasites for one month and acts as a heartworm preventive. But if your dog doesn't need all this, don't go overboard. Opt for just what he does need.

- **Imidacloprid:** Only bothered by fleas? Apply this spot-on chemical between your Pom's shoulder blades. It distributes itself all over the dog's body within a day and kills fleas for a month. Your dog can get wet, but repeated baths will wash the product off.

✔ **Fipronil:** Are ticks also a concern? This chemical collects in the hair follicles and wicks out over time. It kills fleas for up to three months and ticks for a shorter time, and it's resistant to bathing. It's sold as a spray or as a *spot-on,* a liquid applied to the back.

✔ **Permethrin:** If fleas aren't a big problem for your dog (for example, you're on a trip and just found one or two fleas), this short-term, very safe spray may be your answer. But don't rely on it for anything more than a quick fix.

✔ **Lufenuron, methoprene, or fenoxycarb:** Have a flea problem that's spread to the house or yard? These chemicals render fleas sterile. It doesn't kill them though, so you'll need something else for that. You can also spray your home and yard with poisons, but sterilizing the fleas is generally safer for you and your dog.

Your best bet? Use a combination of products. Fleas are building up immunity to some of these chemicals. By alternating between two or more of them with every application, you catch the few fleas that were immune to the previous chemical. And don't scrimp on products! Use them frequently enough (once a month, in general) and heavily enough to make sure there are no survivors!

The later section "Alleviating allergies" contains additional information about fleas with regards to your dog's *allergic* reaction to them.

Getting ticks unstuck

Ticks are fairly small parasites — some are smaller than the head of a match, some a bit larger, especially once they're puffed up with your dog's blood. They live off the blood of mammals, and they can stick to your dog's skin for long periods of time if you don't get them off. They're harder to kill than fleas, but at least they hold still.

The most common way to get rid of ticks on your dog is to remove them one by one. Feel all over your Pom's body, but especially around the ears, neck, and between the toes for the telltale bumps. Then use a tissue to grasp the tick as close to the dog's skin as possible, and pull it gently out — don't jerk it. Even if you leave part of it, it won't hurt your dog.

Another way to kill ticks is with chemicals. Products containing *amitraz* (usually found in tick collars) or *fipronil* (usually found in sprays or spot-on applications) kill ticks. However, they don't kill the ticks immediately, so chemicals are typically reserved as back-ups. Your hands are still your best tool.

Ticks are a particularly serious concern because they can transmit several diseases such as Lyme disease, erhlichiosis, Rocky Mountain spotted fever, and babesiosis. A vaccination is available for Lyme disease, but it's not advisable for dogs that don't live in Lyme endemic areas. Your veterinarian can order blood tests if any of these conditions are suspected — for example, if you live in an area where one of these diseases is common, if your dog is suddenly lethargic, or if he has intermittent lameness.

Taking the bite out of mites

Mites are tiny bloodsuckers that can make your dog's hair fall out. I detail the three different types of animal mites in Table 11-1.

Alleviating allergies

When people have allergies, they tend to sneeze. But when dogs have allergies, they tend to itch. The most common allergens for dogs are flea saliva, pollens, dust mites, and food. A veterinary dermatology specialist can perform *intradermal* (skin) testing with common allergens but not food allergens. If the culprit is identified, a series of injections can often help the dog overcome the allergic reaction. A good clue: If your dog is biting at her skin, especially her front feet, scratching at her ears, or rubbing her rump on your furniture frequently, take her to the vet to see whether something else could be the cause and to get temporary relief.

Flea allergies

Flea allergy dermatitis, or FAD, is the most common of all skin problems. With FAD, a dog is allergic to flea saliva, so not only does the dog suffer from the normal itchiness due to these small critters walking around on his skin, but he also suffers because the saliva acts as a skin irritant. So the poor pooch reacts the only way he can — by biting or chewing at his skin to make the irritation stop.

In a flea-allergic dog, the saliva from just one flea bite can send the dog chewing not just around the bite but all over, especially on the rump, legs, and paws. And this chewing often leads to crusted bumps in these areas. The solution is simple: Get rid of every flea! (See the section "Debugging your dog" earlier in this chapter.)

Airborne allergies

Inhaled allergens are similar to those that affect humans — pollen, dust mites, and molds. Your dog may have a skin allergy if you see him frequently scratching or chewing at his face, ears, feet, forelegs, armpits, and abdomen. Because the feet are so often affected, many

Table 11-1 **Animal Mites to Watch Out For**

Type	Disease	Symptoms	Treatment	Notes
Cheyletiella mites	Walking dandruff	Mild itching and dandruff, especially along the back; mites move under the dandruff scales, so dandruff appears to move	Repeated antiparasitic shampoos, or dips in amitraz, or high-dosage heartworm preventive drugs such as ivermectin	Contagious; every dog in a household needs treatment; spread by direct contact and bedding; some breeds, including Poms, are more prone
Demodex mites	Demodectic mange	Hairless spots, most often on the face, feet, and front legs; may be red but are not itchy	Repeated dips in amitraz or high-dosage heartworm preventive drugs such as ivermectin	Noncontagious but often difficult to treat; a few small patches in a puppy usually go away, but many patches or a generalized condition require treatment
Sarcoptic mites	Sarcoptic mange	Intensely itchy small bumpsand crusts on the ear tips, abdomen, elbows, and hocks	Repeated dips in amitraz or high-dosage heartworm preventive drugs such as ivermectin	Extremely contagious, even to people; all animals in household should be treated

people assume the problem is grass or carpet allergies, but that's seldom the case. It's just that allergies from anything anywhere tend to make the feet itchy.

Common short-term treatments include allergy pills or steroid medication. Bathing in cool bath water with anti-itch shampoos from your veterinarian may help. Long-term treatments including moving to another state or getting allergy tests and injections. Moving may be the less expensive option.

Food allergies

Food allergies can produce diarrhea or itchy skin and ears. Your veterinarian can prescribe an *elimination diet* (a diet consisting of novel proteins your dog hasn't eaten before, such as those from venison, duck, or rabbit). No, you don't have to get out the gun. These proteins are available in dry and canned foods from your veterinarian. You keep the dog on the diet for at least a month, withholding treats or anything else that may contain a food allergen.

If the dog's symptoms clear up, then you can add back ingredients he has been exposed to one at a time. If and when you see a return of the allergy symptoms, you know which one causes the problem. You may have to keep your dog on a special diet for the rest of his life.

If his condition doesn't clear up, he may need to try another novel diet or a hypoallergenic diet that has a special protein molecule size. Some dogs' food allergies never clear up, though.

Cooling hot spots

Hot spots, more technically known as *pyotraumatic dermatitis,* are red, itchy, painful, moist spots that seem to arise overnight. Usually something has irritated the skin, perhaps a flea bite, and the dog scratches and chews the spot. The skin gets irritated and moist, allowing first infection and then worse symptoms to set in.

If your Pom has hot spots, clip the hair away, prevent the dog from chewing or scratching, and apply a treatment that both dries the skin and kills the bacteria. (For the best results, use antibiotic powder, which you can get over the counter for people, or even bacteria-fighting mouthwash on the skin.) You may also need to give your dog an oral antihistamine to stop the itching, or your vet can prescribe steroids. (See the sidebar "Easing the itch" for more ideas.)

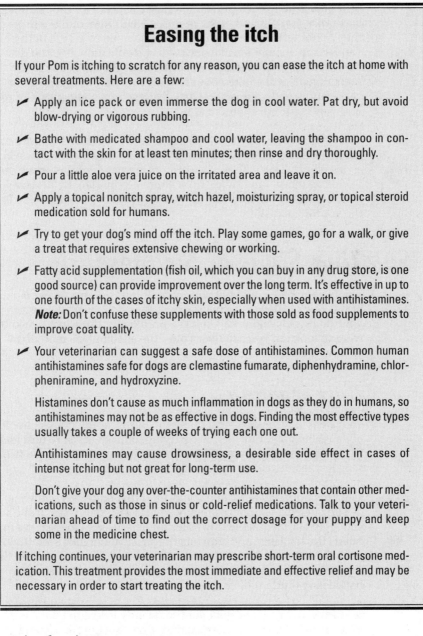

Easing the itch

If your Pom is itching to scratch for any reason, you can ease the itch at home with several treatments. Here are a few:

✔ Apply an ice pack or even immerse the dog in cool water. Pat dry, but avoid blow-drying or vigorous rubbing.

✔ Bathe with medicated shampoo and cool water, leaving the shampoo in contact with the skin for at least ten minutes; then rinse and dry thoroughly.

✔ Pour a little aloe vera juice on the irritated area and leave it on.

✔ Apply a topical nonitch spray, witch hazel, moisturizing spray, or topical steroid medication sold for humans.

✔ Try to get your dog's mind off the itch. Play some games, go for a walk, or give a treat that requires extensive chewing or working.

✔ Fatty acid supplementation (fish oil, which you can buy in any drug store, is one good source) can provide improvement over the long term. It's effective in up to one fourth of the cases of itchy skin, especially when used with antihistamines. *Note:* Don't confuse these supplements with those sold as food supplements to improve coat quality.

✔ Your veterinarian can suggest a safe dose of antihistamines. Common human antihistamines safe for dogs are clemastine fumarate, diphenhydramine, chlorpheniramine, and hydroxyzine.

Histamines don't cause as much inflammation in dogs as they do in humans, so antihistamines may not be as effective in dogs. Finding the most effective types usually takes a couple of weeks of trying each one out.

Antihistamines may cause drowsiness, a desirable side effect in cases of intense itching but not great for long-term use.

Don't give your dog any over-the-counter antihistamines that contain other medications, such as those in sinus or cold-relief medications. Talk to your veterinarian ahead of time to find out the correct dosage for your puppy and keep some in the medicine chest.

If itching continues, your veterinarian may prescribe short-term oral cortisone medication. This treatment provides the most immediate and effective relief and may be necessary in order to start treating the itch.

Global Deworming

If you see small, flat, white segments in your dog's stool, she may have tapeworms. Because she gets them from eating a flea, the best prevention is flea prevention (see Chapter 10). Tapeworms may gross you out and make your dog's butt itch, but as worms go, they're not terribly devastating. Still, you need to get rid of them. Tapeworms require special deworming medication, but you don't need to rush to the vet. Just describe what they look like to the receptionist, or if you're not sure what they are, bring one in for verification, and your vet will usually hand you some pills. Get rid of the fleas too while you're at it.

You may be tempted to pick up some over-the-counter deworming medicine at the grocery store and just blast those worms away every month. Don't! These dewormers are neither as effective nor as safe as those you can get from your veterinarian. By performing a fecal check, your veterinarian can provide the best medicine for the specific parasite.

Spotting Signs of Sickness

If only your Pom could tell you where it hurts — or *whether* it hurts. Few challenges are as frustrating as determining whether your dog's sick, and if so, what the problem is. But when you know what to look for, you discover your Pom's telling you more than you ever imagined.

Butt scooting

Your Pom may look comical doing the butt-scootin' boogie, but it's no laughing matter for her. She's trying to make her sore butt feel better by relieving some of the pressure in her anal sacs, the two sacs just inside and on either side of her anus.

The sacs normally contain a sticky fluid that squeezes out when the dog defecates or occasionally squirts out, skunk-like, if she's suddenly alarmed. If the tiny holes in the sacs get clogged, the fluid builds up, thickens, and expands the sacs balloon-like until they push through the skin to the outside and then burst. To add to the problems, the sacs become inflamed and infected. Talk about a bad-feeling butt!

Besides scooting, your Pom may constantly lick at her anus in an attempt to soothe it. Your veterinarian can unclog the sac and express the fluid as a routine matter so your Pom feels better almost immediately.

Two additional problems may cause scooting:

- ✔ **Tapeworms wriggling around the anus.** (See the previous section "Global Deworming" for the remedy.)
- ✔ **Lower-back problems.** If the anal sacs are okay and no tapeworms are present, have your veterinarian check your Pom's spine.

Coughing

Everybody coughs once in a while. But if your Pom's coughing every day or in long bouts, that's not normal. Your veterinarian can do some simple tests to pinpoint the problem.

Especially in younger dogs, coughing may indicate an infectious disease. *Kennel cough* is a group of highly contagious airborne diseases caused by several different agents, but most often by *Bordetella,* a type of bacteria. Kennel cough is characterized by a gagging cough that starts about a week after exposure.

Your veterinarian can inoculate your Pom against kennel cough, usually with nose drops, but protection doesn't last more than a few months and may not cover every possible infectious agent. Nonetheless, the inoculation is a good idea if you plan to board your dog or if he suffers from *tracheal collapse* or other breathing problems. (See the later section "Pondering Pom Predispositions" for more on tracheal collapse.)

Coughing can also be a sign of congestive heart failure, tracheal collapse, or even lung cancer. Because these are life-threatening conditions, your veterinarian should check out any coughing that persists more than a couple of days.

Diarrhea

Your little squirt can get a case of the squirts for lots of reasons: Nerves or a change in food or water can cause short-term problems; intestinal parasites, sensitivity to certain foods, and illnesses can cause more long-lasting diarrhea.

A little bit of blood in diarrhea is not the cause for concern in dogs that it is in humans. Intestinal parasites such as *giardia* or *coccidia* (see Chapter 10) can cause blood in the stool. Nonetheless, if it continues for more than a day, or if it's in copious amounts, you need a veterinarian's opinion. A Pomeranian has so few reserves that a bout of diarrhea can seriously dehydrate her. She may need to go to the veterinarian for intravenous fluids.

Take these steps to stop diarrhea:

1. **Restrict food for a meal or two, feeding just a partial meal.**

2. **Offer a bland diet consisting of rice (or tapioca or cooked macaroni) along with tofu (or nonfatty chicken) for several days when you start to feed her again.**

   You want to give the intestinal tract time to heal, and it can't do that with fatty food encouraging more diarrhea.

Ear gunk

Pomeranians are blessed with healthy ears in part due to their prick-ear design that lets air circulate within them. Nonetheless, like all dogs, their ear canal has an initial vertical segment that abruptly turns inward at a sharp angle. That sharp angle can restrict some air flow, which encourages moisture, which in turn nurtures bacteria and yeast. Although certain types of bacteria are normal and harmless in the ear canal, others can grow unchecked, causing the ear canal's surface to react to their byproducts by secreting oils and becoming inflamed.

Other factors contribute to ear problems:

✔ Allergies are the most common cause of ear problems in dogs overall. See the section "Alleviating allergies" to determine if this might be the problem, and what you can do to stop the itch.

✔ *Seborrhea* causes itchiness and contributes to a heavy accumulation of ear wax. Other parts of the dog may have greasy skin and hair. Your vet may be able to diagnose and treat this.

✔ Parasites, such as ear mites, can also cause intense itching of the ears. Your veterinarian can diagnose the presence of parasites easily and can prescribe much more effective medication for ear mites than you can buy over the counter.

Signs of ear problems can include

✔ Head shaking

✔ Head tilt

✔ Scratching at the ear

✔ Rubbing the ear

✔ Smelly ear

✔ Dark buildup within the ear

A veterinarian should examine all ear problems for the following reasons:

- ✔ The same symptoms can result from various causes that require different treatments.

- ✔ A perforated ear drum due to chronic problems requires medication that's different from the medication for an intact ear.

- ✔ If the ear is filled with wax and debris, it needs to be cleaned so that antibiotic medication can reach the lining of the canal. But if the ear is painful or the ear drum is perforated, the dog must be sedated to clean the ear.

In most cases the veterinarian sends you home with an ear flush solution in addition to antibiotic medication. The solution loosens wax and debris (so the medication can reach the ear's surface) and has a drying agent so it doesn't leave the ear wet — find out how to use it in Chapter 9. To apply the medication, first clean the ear with the solution, and then squeeze the medicated ointment or drops into the canal, again gently massaging the base of the ear to disperse the medicine.

Tears and eye goop

No doubt you look at those pretty Pom peepers more than any other part of your dog. So while you're at it, keep an eye out for eye problems such as squinting, tearing, or mucous discharge. These signs can indicate lid problems, foreign bodies, tear drainage problems, or dry eyes.

Watery tearing is the least worrisome eye problem. Dogs frequently have blocked tear ducts that cause tears that normally drain from the eye socket to overflow onto the cheek. Your veterinarian can do a simple test to see whether the duct's blocked, and in some cases she can flush it out.

But the duct in many toy dogs is simply too small and your pup may just have to live with it. You can combat the staining below her eyes by wiping the tears often with an over-the-counter eye wipe specifically for tear staining. Turn to Chapter 9 for additional solutions.

If the tearing is chronic, if the eye shows any other signs of discomfort, or if the discharge is thick rather than watery, then a veterinarian needs to check your dog. Your Pom may have

- ✔ An infection, which can be treated with antibiotic drops.

- ✔ An irritation to his cornea, which may also be treatable, or a lid problem that needs attention.

✔ Dry eye syndrome, or *keratoconjunctivitis sicca* (KCS). The dog doesn't produce a normal amount of tears, so the cornea (the outer clear coat of the eye) dries out and looks dull. The eye may have a thick discharge, and the dog may blink, squint, and rub at his eyes. Your veterinarian can diagnose the condition with a simple tear test and prescribe several treatment options.

Limping

Your Pom may not be expected to run the Iditarod, but he does need to run around your house on all four legs. All dogs can stub a toe and end up a little gimpy now and then. But if your dog is favoring one leg and not using it, examine the leg for broken bones, tenderly feeling down the leg's length and comparing every bone, including those of the foot, with that of the leg on the other side. A broken bone, of course, needs veterinary attention.

You can treat less serious injuries at home. Follow these suggestions:

✔ Ice packs help minimize swelling if applied immediately after an injury, but moist heat is better for older injuries.

✔ Complete rest, even if it means locking your Pom in a crate, is the best medicine for most cases of lameness. Rest him well past the time he appears to be cured.

✔ Let him resume exercise gradually and on a leash.

✔ If three days go by with no improvement, you need to get a veterinary opinion.

Aside from injury, an all too common cause of rear-leg lameness is *patellar luxation* (see the later section "Pondering Pom Predispositions" for more on this problem) or sometimes, *Legg-Calve-Perthes* (destruction of the head of the femur [thigh] bone that may start at 3 to 4 months of age. Treatment is absolute rest or surgery to remove the femur head.) Neither is an emergency, but the sooner your veterinarian diagnoses them the better because they only get worse with time.

Listlessness

When your Pomeranian pistol suddenly prefers to stay in bed rather than play, take time to study her. Is she bored, tired, or really sick? Poms can be misleading because they can push aside their feelings of malaise and show up waggy-tailed for a favorite activity such as a walk or ride if you tempt them enough. Of course, dogs gradually slow down as they mature and age, but a relatively sudden change in activity level is cause for a trip to the veterinarian. Look for these clues:

- A sick dog often lies in a curled or hunched up position rather than sprawled out. This is a go-to-vet-today situation.

- A dog with a high fever is usually lethargic. Take the temperature (see Chapter 10), call the vet if it's over 103 degrees, and go to the emergency vet if it's over 105. Cool the dog with wet towels in either case.

- A dog with anemia or circulatory problems may seem weak. Call the vet right away if the gums are white or gray.

- A dog having a *hypoglycemic* episode (low blood sugar; see Chapter 8) may sleep (even when you try to rouse her) or stagger and appear uncoordinated. Rub corn syrup on the gums and go to the emergency vet right away.

- An uncomfortable dog may walk around restlessly, dig at the ground, lie down, and then get right back up. This dog needs to see the vet as soon as possible.

- A dog with abdominal pain often stands with her rear in the air and the front flat to the ground, as though stretching. If this continues more than an hour, see the vet promptly.

- A dog having a hard time breathing is often reluctant to lie down; if she does, she lies on her stomach with head up and nose pointed upward. This is an emergency vet situation.

- A dog in pain may shiver, pant, or both. See the vet right away if it continues.

Loss of appetite

If your Pomeranian sticks his pointy nose up at dinner occasionally, don't think it's cause to rush to the veterinarian. But if he's been a hearty eater and then gradually leaves more and more in his bowl, he needs to be checked out. By the same token, if he suddenly stops eating and misses more than a meal or two, something's probably not right. Take into consideration, though, that dogs eat less during hot weather.

Because of the dangers of hypoglycemia (see Chapter 8), you're wiser to overreact than to wait and see, especially with tiny, thin, young, or older Poms.

A spoonful of sugar or blatant trickery: Giving your Pom medicine

Medicine that sits in the bottle or splatters all over the floor doesn't do your Pom (or your wallet) much good. But managing to get pills and liquid medicine where they need to go can be frustrating if not downright impossible.

For pills, try one of these options:

- **The stick-it-down-the-throat option:** Gently open the mouth, place the pill as far back as possible (aided by a tiny shove with your index finger), close the mouth, and gently rub the throat. You also can buy a *piller,* a small plunger that takes the place of your finger. If your pup is used to you opening her mouth and handing her a treat from puppyhood, this should be a snap.

- **The hide-it-in-food option:** Unless medical reasons prevent this method, hide the pill in a bit of peanut butter or liverwurst. If your Pom's suspicious and filter-feeds her way through the food, add these steps:

1. Make three balls of food.

2. Feed her the first one to convince her that the food's safe to eat.

3. Feed her the second one that holds the pill.

4. Excitedly show her the third ball before she finishes the second one so she wants to eat the second one, plus pill, in a hurry.

5. Give her the third ball.

Liquid medicine is tougher to administer than pills. You need to pull out one cheek so it makes a little pocket, squirt the stuff in, and hope for the best. (And giving a little treat as a reward never hurts.)

Urination changes

You may notice that your dog has accidents or needs to go out more often than normal. This clue means you need to pay close attention to her. Several disorders can cause changes in urination, and the types of changes vary widely. Your veterinarian can often pinpoint the problem with a simple urinalysis.

- **Urinating small amounts** suddenly and often, especially in females, may indicate a urinary tract infection. The dog may also cry out when urinating. Antibiotics can cure this uncomfortable condition, and cranberry tablets can help prevent this condition in Poms that are prone to it.

- **Dribbling urine during sleep** most commonly occurs in spayed females. Drugs often treat it successfully.

✔ **Cloudy or bloody urine** can indicate infection of the prostate or bladder. The dog may also strain to urinate. These infections can be extremely painful and require antibiotic treatment. Left untreated, they can reach the kidneys and cause even more serious problems. Castration is usually the treatment of choice for males with repeated prostate problems.

✔ **Painful urination,** often with blood in the urine, can indicate urinary stones, especially in males. These stones can be diagnosed with a radiograph and often controlled with diet. Surgery may be necessary initially to resolve the problem, however.

✔ **Increased urination and increased thirst** can indicate diabetes or kidney disease. Diabetes can be diagnosed with a urine test and controlled through diet and insulin injections. I cover ailments common in older dogs, including kidney disease, in Chapter 10.

✔ **Inability to urinate** is an condition that requires immediate veterinary attention.

Vomiting

Every dog owner has been awakened by the "urp, urp, urp" of precious Patty puking all over the best carpet in the house. Dogs seem to vomit almost as a recreational activity.

Vomiting is a concern when it

✔ Continues for more than three upheavals at a time

✔ Contains more than a tiny bit of blood

✔ Contains a substance resembling coffee grounds (it's partially digested blood)

✔ Contains anything resembling fecal material (unless your dog eats feces)

✔ Accompanies any other symptoms of illness such as lethargy or diarrhea

✔ Has no results (the dog repeatedly tries to vomit but nothing comes up)

All these instances merit a call to the veterinarian.

Sometimes dogs vomit early in the morning simply because their stomachs are empty. Feeding your dog a late-night snack can fix the problem. In another scenario, dogs often vomit after they eat grass. Nobody knows exactly why they do this, but it seldom means your dog is sick.

Two different breeds of medicine

Just as with human medicine, complementary and alternative therapies may help your sick dog. *Complementary therapies* are out-of-mainstream veterinary medicines that accompany mainstream therapies; *alternative therapies* replace mainstream therapies. Many veterinaries use both traditional and nontraditional therapies in their practices.

Popular complementary and alternative therapies include acupuncture, aromatherapy, Bach flower therapy (for emotional harmony), botanical medicine, chiropractic, homeopathy, magnetic therapy, massage therapy, nutraceutical (natural foods) therapy, nutritional therapy, and physical therapy.

For more information, visit AltVetMed, the most comprehensive source for alternative veterinary medicine on the Web, at www.altvetmed.org.

Pondering Pom Predispositions

Like all breeds, Pomeranians descend from a comparatively small group of founding fathers and mothers that were eventually interbred so that today's Poms are all related to one another. So the entire population forms what geneticists call a *closed breeding population.* Unfortunately, every dog (Poms too) averages six deleterious (bad) recessive genes. As Pom descendents started to interbreed, chances naturally increased for both a father and a mother to carry the same bad genes. As a result, their progeny inherited two copies of that gene and inevitably exhibited the undesirable trait.

So every breed of dog has passed its own menu of hereditary headaches down through generations. Breeders try to avoid pairing parents who may carry the same recessives genes — and with the advent of DNA testing, that solution's becoming more and more effective. But genetic problems are still a long way from disappearing. Meanwhile, be on the lookout for the Pomeranian predispositions covered in this section.

Alopecia X: Hair loss

Pomeranians have one hair trait that they'd rather do without: a condition called *alopecia X.* Common to many of the spitz breeds, the condition goes by several other names: *black skin disease, castration responsive alopecia,* and *growth hormone responsive alopecia.* Because the condition is much more common in males than females, researchers speculate that it's gender-linked.

The trait seems to have two forms:

- **Early onset form:** A puppy grows a luxurious puppy coat, sheds it, and no adult coat ever replaces it.

- **Late onset form:** A Pom with a normal adult coat loses guard hairs, which leaves the fuzzy undercoat and gives the dog a puppy-coat look. Eventually the undercoat goes, too. The bald skin turns dark, but the dog doesn't seem uncomfortable or itchy.

Because this hair loss occurs in several other disorders, your veterinarian will test your Pom's blood, urine, and skin to rule out hypothyroidism, Cushing's disease, and other conditions.

For some reason, spaying or castrating resolves the condition in many dogs, so that's the first step if your Pom hasn't been fixed. The dog often grows a full coat within months of the surgery, although the coat isn't always permanent.

If neutering your dog doesn't work, the next step is melatonin (hormone) tablets, which help 50 percent of dogs within three months. If the hair does grow, you can eventually taper the dosage, but he'll probably need to stay on some dosage forever.

Ask your veterinarian about the pros and cons of other options such as therapy with adrenal sex hormones, methyltestosterone, lysodren, growth hormones, prednisone, and cimetidine, which have varying degrees of success. Some of these have undesirable side effects, so they aren't generally first choices.

Alopecia X is mostly a cosmetic condition; at some point you may find it's better to simply accept it than to administer drugs that adversely affect your Pom's health. For more information, go to `pcoc.net/black-skin-disease.htm`.

Entropion: Eyelid problems

With entropion, an eyelid (usually the bottom one) rolls inward toward the eye. The lashes irritate the cornea, causing tearing, squinting, and perhaps sensitivity to light. If the cornea continues to be irritated, it can actually develop ulcers and scars that impair vision. Entropion is hereditary, although the exact genetic mechanism is unknown.

The condition is often first noted in puppyhood, but some pups outgrow the disorder as the face structure changes. For this reason, veterinarians don't perform surgery on pups but may temporarily tack the lid to help alleviate any discomfort. If the lid still rolls

Help find a cure

You can help the future health of Pomeranians by contributing to health research, either with money or samples. For example, at the time of this writing, the Canine Health Foundation is sponsoring research into alopecia X in Pomeranians. Monetary contributions from individuals are needed to supplement the funding, however. In addition, researchers need blood samples from Pomeranians, both normal and affected, in order to find the gene or genes responsible. Go to `pcoc.net/black-skin-disease.htm` to find out how to contribute or participate.

Remember to consider other canine health projects through the AKC Canine Health Foundation (`www.akcchf.org`) and the Morris Animal Foundation (`www.morris animalfoundation.org`).

inward after the dog's matured, major surgery can resolve the problem. Because it's better to undercorrect than overcorrect, more than one surgery may be necessary.

Hydrocephalus: Water on the brain

Small dogs with a tendency toward domed heads, such as Poms, seem to be predisposed to *hydrocephalus,* or water on the brain.

The brain is normally bathed in cerebrospinal fluid, which is constantly produced, circulated, and reabsorbed. In some dogs, either too much fluid is produced or too little is reabsorbed, so the fluid accumulates around the brain, pushing the soft bones of the puppy's skull outward and giving the appearance of a big, round, head. After the skull hardens with maturity, it can't expand, so the excess pressure pushes in on the brain.

A Pom puppy with hydrocephalus generally has the following symptoms:

- An abnormally round skull at 12 weeks old
- An open *fontanel* (soft spot)
- Eyes that diverge so that each is directed outward (the opposite of cross-eyed)
- Seizures or blindness
- Presses her head into walls
- Is extremely difficult to housetrain

Your veterinarian can take radiographs. A definite diagnosis usually requires more sophisticated scans from specialists.

Poms with mild hydrocephalus can live long and full lives, but may be somewhat mentally retarded. In most cases, though, the condition gradually worsens throughout puppyhood. Drugs can temporarily decrease pressure and swelling, but they're not usually a lifelong fix.

For a more permanent fix (needed in all but the mildest cases), a specialist places a small tube in the brain to drain the excess fluid to another part of the body. The shunt must be replaced as the puppy grows, and complications often occur. Because of the difficulties treating hydrocephalus, euthanasia is often recommended.

Open fontanel: Soft spot

Just as with a human baby, a canine infant is born with the bony plates of the skull somewhat soft and separated. These bones usually harden and gradually fuse together over two to three months. In some Poms, the plates never fuse and a soft spot, the fontanel, remains throughout life.

Because the skull's function is to protect the brain, obviously a soft spot is a worry. A hit on the head in just the wrong place can mean brain damage. Affected dogs don't know they should be more careful, and most Poms with open fontanels are never bothered by them — except by their owners' fretting. No treatment is available.

Patellar luxation: Bad knees

Have you seen a dog that takes a few steps, then holds one hind leg up and forward, skips a step or two, and then take a few more steps? At first this may look like a jaunty little jig, but more likely it's a challenging condition called *patellar luxation.*

This common problem involves the patella (kneecap) of one or both rear legs. Normally, the patella slides up and down in a small groove of the femur (thigh bone) as the leg bends and the knee moves. But if the groove is too shallow or the tendon of the quadriceps muscle has too much rotational pull, the patella can ride over the side of the groove.

Because the luxated (out-of-place) muscle has to relax before the patella can pop back into place, the dog often hops for a few steps with the leg straight until the patella pops back. This popping hurts (your dog may yelp) and wears down the ridge, causing the condition to worsen.

In small dogs, signs of patellar luxation appear as early as 8 weeks of age but usually are apparent by 6 months; the patella tends to slip toward the inside, giving a bowlegged look. Early diagnosis is helpful in slowing the progress, but treatment depends on the severity of the condition. Table 11-2 presents the levels of patellar luxation.

Table 11-2   The Four Grades of Patellar Luxation

Grade	Characteristics	Patella Movement	Surgical Recommendation
1	Dog occasionally skips, keeping one hind leg up and straight for a step or two	Can be pushed out of position by hand but easily returns to correct position	Surgery may be unnecessary
2	Dog often holds affected leg up and straight when moving	May not slide back into position by itself	Surgery
3	Dog uses affected leg infrequently	Usually out of position; slips back out almost as soon as it's replaced	Surgery
4	Dog never puts weight on the leg	Always out of position and can't be replaced manually	Surgery

Cases that appear in puppyhood usually develop into grade 3 or 4 in adulthood. Cases that first appear in young adults usually develop into grade 2 or 3. Cases that first appear in older adults are usually grade 1 or 2.

Surgery to tighten any stretched tissues and reconstruct the groove or realign the muscle can improve the condition. A young dog with grade 1 or 2, or any age dog with grade 3 or 4, is a candidate. Surgery may not make the leg perfect, but it will enable your Pom to run and walk relatively free of pain. An orthopedic specialist has the best chance of successfully treating the condition.

Glucosamine supplements may help to build cartilage and may be helpful for grade 1 cases, but they aren't much help in more serious cases.

The Orthopedic Foundation for Animals maintains a registry for dogs that have been screened for patellar luxation. Although only a limited number have been evaluated, Pomeranians have the unfortunate distinction of having the highest percentage (48 percent) of the condition of any breed. Most veterinarians believe the condition is hereditary in Poms.

Patent ductus arteriosus: Heart defect

Patent ductus arteriosus (just call it *PDA*) occurs when a blood vessel (the ductus arteriosus) fails to close after birth. The function of this blood vessel is to bypass the nonfunctioning lungs during fetal life. So when it stays *patent* (open and working) after birth, the vessel sends blood that's supposed to go to the rest of the body to the lungs instead.

Most puppies with PDA seem completely normal except for a heart murmur. Your veterinarian can hear the murmur, but a veterinary cardiologist usually makes an exact diagnosis. PDA can lead to heart failure. Although drugs can control the signs of heart failure, the best treatment is early surgery, preferably by 5 months of age (before permanent damage can occur). Without surgery, life expectancy is about two years. With surgery, the dog should be able to live a full life.

PDA is the most common hereditary heart problem in dogs, and it's particularly prevalent in Pomeranians, especially females.

Tracheal collapse: Breathing problems

Tracheal collapse is most common in toy breeds. The trachea, or windpipe, consists of a series of cartilage rings. In some Poms, the cartilage isn't as rigid as it should be, so some of the rings collapse, flattening the trachea and obstructing breathing. If the collapse is in the neck area, the dog has trouble inhaling. If the collapse is in the chest area, the dog has trouble exhaling.

Several factors (like obesity, respiratory infection, enlarged heart, endotracheal intubation, or inhalation of irritants or allergens) can make a tracheal collapse episode more likely. Coughing, which is a major symptom, can also make the condition worse.

Poms and anesthesia

Anesthesia, though not without risks, is far safer today than several years ago, when injectible barbiturate anesthesia was popular. Newer inhalant anesthesias (like isoflurane and sevofluran) and newer induction agents (like propofol) are far safer than traditional agents.

Risks can also be reduced by a presurgical health check that includes blood testing and by careful monitoring during surgery. Because of a Pom's tiny trachea, the veterinarian must be extremely careful when placing the tube. Your best veterinarian is one experienced with surgery on tiny dogs.

Affected dogs often cough with a harsh, goose-like honk, especially when they're excited, when pressure is put on the throat, or when they're eating or drinking. In severe cases, the dog can't get enough air, causing him to faint and get a bluish cast to the tongue.

The best way to diagnose the condition is with an endoscope, which usually means going to an internal medicine specialist, but your own veterinarian may be able to take a series of radiographs (X-rays) to diagnose the condition. The trachea changes its dimensions as the dog breathes in and out, so a single radiograph often misses the critical time of change.

In severe cases, the best option may be implanted prosthetic supports. A specialist who has experience in this type of surgery must perform this procedure because it's complex. The nature of the surgery means that it isn't always successful.

In less-severe cases of tracheal collapse, the following adjustments may help:

- ✔ Reducing weight
- ✔ Using a harness rather than a collar
- ✔ Humidifying the air
- ✔ Avoiding irritants such as cigarette smoke
- ✔ Avoiding any situation that may lead to overheating, stress, heavy panting, or coughing
- ✔ Taking glucosamine and vitamin C supplements to strengthen cartilage
- ✔ Using bronchodilators (this practice is controversial)

Dealing with Emergencies

If you face an emergency with your Pom, remember to stay calm. Your calm voice is the best medicine at first.

If your dog appears to be severely injured, start with the ABCs of first aid (I explain them in this section). Then call your veterinarian or go to the emergency clinic — and drive carefully! What would happen to your sick dog if you had an accident and ended up going to the hospital yourself?

A is for airway

Small dogs can choke on dog treats, small balls, rawhide, bones, toys, and other items around the house and yard. A choking dog may paw frantically at his mouth, try to retch, or make heaving chest motions — but he can't breathe.

Open his mouth and either pull his tongue forward or push down on the back of the tongue. Then look and gently feel for any obstructions. If you can see an obstruction, try to gently reach two fingers in and extract it. But if this doesn't work, use the Heimlich maneuver.

1. **Hold him against your chest, head up, and facing away from you.**

2. **Place your fist just beneath the end of his sternum (chest bone).**

3. **Grasp that fist with your other hand and give five rapid thrusts inward and upward.**

4. **Check the airway and repeat Steps 1 through 3 if needed.**

5. **If he's unconscious, give artificial respiration (see the next section).**

B is for breathing

Is he breathing? Is his chest rising and falling? If not, check for obstructions (see the previous section). If no obstruction is present, perform artificial resuscitation.

1. **Place him down on his side.**

2. **Open the mouth, clear away any mucus, and pull the tongue forward. Seal your mouth over the dog's nose and mouth.**

3. **Blow gently into the nose for two seconds, then release.**

   Use gentle puffs. Pomeranians have very small lungs. Blow just enough to see the chest rise. If the chest doesn't rise, blow harder, make a tighter seal around the lips, or check again for an obstruction.

4. **Repeat Step 3 at the rate of one breath every five seconds, stopping after one minute to monitor breathing and pulse.**

5. **Repeat Steps 3 and 4 until he's breathing on his own.**

6. **When he does resume breathing, get him to the vet.**

C is for circulation

Check your dog's pulse by placing your fingers on his femoral artery (inside the thigh, near where the rear leg meets the abdomen — see Figure 11-1) or on his left chest just behind the elbow. Also check the tongue and gum color. If they're bluish or if the gums are pale, he's not getting enough oxygen but may still be breathing. In this case, evaluate him for shock.

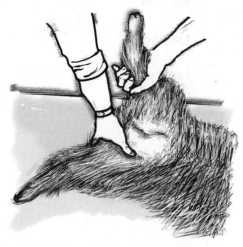

Figure 11-1: Where to take a Pom's pulse.

If you're sure his heart isn't beating, begin cardiopulmonary resuscitation (CPR):

1. **Place him on his right side on a table or floor.**

2. **Place your fingertips (one hand on top of the other) on his left chest about 1 inch up from and behind the elbow.**

3. **Press down and quickly release at the rate of one compression per second.**

4. **After every 10 to 15 compressions, stop to give two breaths through the nose (see the previous section). If you have a helper, you can continue while your helper gives breaths every 3 to 4 compressions.**

5. **Continue with Steps 2 through 4 until you feel a pulse. Then get him to the vet.**

Chapter 12

Traveling with a Pom Pilot (Or Leaving Him in Others' Care)

*M*ost everyone likes a road trip, especially dogs. And all dogs seem to be entranced by the automobile more than any other product of modern technology. Pomeranians are no exception. Utter the magic word "Goforaride," and your Pom turns into a whirling dervish of excitement.

With some planning, you may find that having your Pom as a travel mate is the best idea you ever had. After all, he never complains about getting lost or about your taste in radio stations. And he gives you a good excuse to stretch your legs and take little nature side trips.

Without planning, though, traveling with a dog can be a hassle. You can find yourself turned away from motel after motel or paying expensive pet fees. You may not be able to take him to many of the attractions on your list, and in warm weather, you may have to skip shopping altogether because it's too hot to leave him in the car. You may also start to describe your sightseeing as *drive-bys,* as in "I drove by this" and "I drove by that."

Unfortunately you can even lose a friend if you stay at her house with a Pom that suddenly forgets his housetraining, as dogs too often do when away from their comfort zone. And on really long trips, your Pom may drive you crazy with whining and scratching, the canine equivalent of "Are we there yet?"

Because I care about your sanity (and your dog's!), in this chapter I help you pack the important stuff and navigate the sometimes-frustrating motel experience. I also tell you all you need to know to travel safely and happily with your Pom, whether on asphalt or up in the clouds.

Packing for Your Pomeranian

Everybody on your excursion will surely have a suitcase. And before you load up and head out, make sure your dog does, too. Even though she doesn't need five pairs of shoes and an armload of clothes *just in case,* she does need her own essentials. Be sure to pack the following items:

✔ Basic grooming equipment

✔ Bed

✔ Bottled water or water from home (strange water can sometimes cause diarrhea)

✔ Bowls for food and water

✔ Bug spray or flea spray

✔ Chewies and interactive toys to pass the time

✔ Flashlight for late-night walks

✔ Food (if you use cans, get the pop tops or bring a can opener)

✔ Identification tags

✔ Medications including antidiarrheal medication and possibly his monthly heartworm preventive; also, motion-sickness pills if your dog suffers from that malady

✔ Paper towels, moist towelettes, and rinse-free shampoo for that carsick thing

✔ Plastic baggies or other poop-disposal tools

✔ Rabies certificate (some places require them)

✔ Recent color photo in case he gets lost

✔ Short and long leashes

✔ Towels (figure on one or two a day, including one to place over his bedding in the crate in case he gets carsick)

✔ Travel crate or (second choice) doggy seatbelt

Hitting the Road

"Let's go!" Those words will have your Pom running to the car, bouncing with excitement, and barking at you to open the door. It's no secret that the automobile is the Pom's favorite mode of transportation. You can keep your easy rider loving it for years to come by keeping him safe, ride after ride.

Practicing safety first

In the good old days you could simply throw your dog and your kid in the backseat and tool down the road. Now your child has to ride in a car seat or with a seatbelt because these restraints happen to save lives.

Take the same care to ensure your Pom's safety, whether traveling cross-country or just to the store. Although using a crate may seem to take some of the fun away, traveling within a secured crate (either attached to a seat belt or to some solid part of the car) has saved many canine lives. Besides, you don't need a dog jumping on your lap or checking out the driver's seat floor while you're driving.

What about a seat belt? You can buy a doggy seatbelt that is pretty much like a harness attached to an existing seat belt (see Figure 12-1). It's probably not quite as safe as a crate, but it's better than a flying Pom. And it does let him ride in the front seat and look out the window.

This seems unnecessary to mention, but just in case: Never let your Pomeranian ride in the back of a pickup truck! And don't let him hang out the window! If you wouldn't let a toddler do it, don't let your Pom do it either.

Although the thought is unpleasant, preparation for a problem is key. What if you had an accident and couldn't speak for your injured dog? As an extra safety measure, place emergency information on the side of the crate that says something like "In case of emergency, take this dog to a veterinarian, then contact the following persons: [Insert contact info]. Payment of all expenses incurred is guaranteed." Include a list of any medications or health problems your dog may have.

Of course, your dog should be wearing identification as well, and not just your home phone number. After all, you're not home. If you're on vacation, add the contact number of somebody back home or the number where you can be reached. (Obviously, this last number is in case your Pom gets lost.)

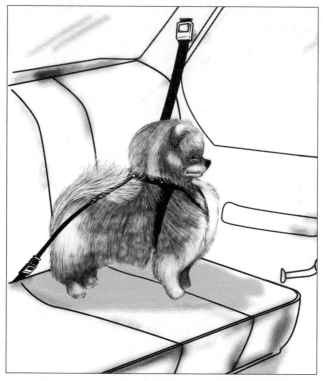

Figure 12-1: A doggy seatbelt lets your Pom enjoy the ride safely.

Keeping your Pom cool and comfy

Your Pom can't reach the control knobs for heat and air in the car, so you have to keep an eye on him to make sure he's comfy. Unless you're in snow country, that's pretty easy. Just keep your car as warm as you like it, and he'll like it, too. If you have to leave him in the car for a short while, consider bringing along a hot water bottle to put in his crate or at least cover the crate with a blanket.

Despite all the warnings about leaving dogs in cars in summer heat, many dogs die every year from just that. Cars take a very short time to heat up, reaching more than 100 degrees in minutes when it's mild outside and reaching 160 degrees in minutes when it's warm to hot out.

In hot weather, keep the crate where the air conditioning can reach it. A fan that plugs into your car battery is cheap and can direct air onto your Pom. Keep him out of direct sunshine, and consider bringing a cooler with an ice pack so you can place the pack beside him in the crate.

But you can't rely on any such measures on a hot day. Even if you can keep your car running with the air conditioner on, don't trust it. The price of mechanical failure is too high. You may just have to choose between leaving your dog at home and going shopping.

Flying the Friendly Skies

Small dogs, including Poms, have many advantages when it comes to travel. In a car, they take up less space than the average suitcase. In an airplane, they can ride with you in the passenger section instead of the baggage compartment. The only qualifiers are that

- ✔ You must make reservations well in advance because most airlines allow only one or two dogs per flight to ride in the passenger section.

- ✔ The dog must ride in a wide, low crate that can fit under the seat in front of you.

- ✔ She must stay in the crate throughout the flight.

Few times do the words "I told you to do that before we left home!" have as much meaning as when your dog suddenly has to go at 40,000 feet. This is one time you may want to go easy on the water before you leave. The same goes for food. Place an absorbent puppy housetraining pad in the crate; if the situation becomes desperate, you can take the dog and the pad to the plane's restroom, disposing of the pad as you would a baby's diaper.

The following items can make the trip more endurable, even enjoyable, for your pup, you, and the other passengers:

- ✔ A few treats or a chew to help the time pass (although you don't want to give out too much food)

- ✔ Ice cubes from the beverage cart

- ✔ Paper towels and extra bedding just in case she has an accident in her crate

Minding Your Motel Manners

It's time to stop for the evening. You're tired, your dog's restless. You pull into another motel . . . another sign proclaims *NO PETS*. Time to face the music: Too many motels have been subjected to the inconsiderate ways of too many dog owners. These owners let their dogs pee on the carpet, shed on the bed, and poop on the grass where people walk. The problem costs the motels money to clean up, and it costs them the goodwill (and future business) of guests who grow tired of stepping in dog doo-doo or hearing dogs bark all night.

Fortunately, many motels still leave their doors open to well-mannered pets. You can go online and visit several Web sites that list pet-friendly lodgings. Here's a quick list of some good sites:

- ✔ www.fidofriendly.com
- ✔ www.dogfriendly.com
- ✔ www.canineauto.com
- ✔ www.petswelcome.com

To keep pets welcome, follow these rules:

- ✔ Never leave your dog unattended in the room. He may feel deserted and try to dig his way out the door, or he may simply bark the whole time.

Heading for doggy destinations

Your dog won't hesitate to erupt with ecstasy at even the most mundane trips, whether it's a trip to the gas station or a move across the country. She'll even like going with you on your vacations. But what about taking her on a trip that's all about her?

Is your Pomeranian a cosmopolitan canine? Several high-end hotels now cater to their canine clientele. Some luxury hotels in big cities offer dog-spoiling services such as special treats, menus, toys, and even walking and grooming services. Some rural lodges offer fenced acreage, beaches, or short hiking trails. Expect to pay more than your run-of-the-mill place that caters to humans, anywhere from $100 to $300 a night.

Is your dog more the back-to-nature type? How about camp? Dog camps are big these days. No, your dog doesn't make leather wallets or lanyards, but she can pick up a variety of skills and tricks, play games, go hiking, and just plain have a yapping good time. The best part is that you don't just drop your dog off — you go there with her! It's fun for you, too, and you can make new friends who also like to share activities with their dogs. Dog camps average about $100 a day.

Plan to study the offerings of each camp because different camps specialize in different types of activities. For example, a camp specializing in chasing an artificial rabbit or weight pulling may not be the best choice for a Pomeranian. In addition, any camp where all the dogs run loose together just isn't safe for a tiny dog. Ask whether they have special sessions for small dogs.

✔ Bring his crate (or at least his own dog bed) into the room with you. If he likes to get on people beds, bring a sheet or roll down the bedspread so he doesn't get hair on it.

✔ If he has an accident on the carpet, don't try to hide it. Clean what you can and tell the management. Leave a big tip for housecleaning.

✔ Instead of washing food bowls in the sink (food clogs the drain), use disposable paper bowls.

✔ Clean up any dog poop your dog deposits on motel property.

✔ Be considerate of others. Don't let him bark! Don't rev him up with games that make him bark. Instead, distract or correct him if he tries to bark at the sound of other guests walking past the room.

Don't try to sneak your dog into a motel room. It's a recipe for a miserable night, and you can be sure your Pom will suddenly find a hundred reasons to bark as you desperately try to shush him.

Leaving Your Dog Behind When You Must Go

Sometimes leaving your dog behind when you go out of town is the smartest choice you can make — as long as you make smart choices about where you leave him.

Taking your dog to a boarding place

If your dog has no issues being away from home, a boarding kennel is usually your best choice for care while you're away. They're generally safest because there is no chance of escape, and somebody is there in case your dog gets sick, or in case of fire, earthquake, or UFO attack.

The ideal kennel has the following features:

✔ Is approved by the American Boarding Kennel Association

✔ Has climate-controlled accommodations

✔ Has private runs for each dog that don't allow dogs to poke parts of themselves into adjacent runs

✔ Disinfects each run prior to a new boarder

If your pet takes a trip without you . . .

Nobody expects to lose a dog, but it can happen to even the most conscientious caretaker. A door is left open, a hole appears in a fence, or the dog escapes from a car window. Most lost dogs are found, but the sooner you organize search efforts, the better your chances of being reunited with your Pom.

Begin your search by going to the place your dog is most likely to go and to the most dangerous place for your dog to go (usually a roadway) and call for your dog. Be careful that your calling doesn't lure your dog across a road.

If you haven't found your dog after a couple of hours, spend your time getting the word out:

✔ Ask area delivery people, children, and neighbors whether they've seen a dog matching the description of yours.

✔ Call area veterinarians to see whether someone's brought in an injured small dog.

✔ Call area shelters. Even if they say no such dog has been brought in, visit them by the following day. And keep checking.

✔ Call the nonemergency phone number for the local police agencies and ask that patrolling officers be on the lookout for the dog.

✔ By the end of the first day, make large posters and saturate the area; place them on the cars of anyone in your search team. Some large pet supply stores sell rolls of plastic fill-in-the-blank lost-dog posters.

   Describe your dog well. (A photo is always the best descriptor.) Most people don't know every breed, so don't just state *Pomeranian*. Describe it as something they may be more familiar with, like "looks like a Chihuahua with puffy hair."

   Don't describe everything about your dog. Keep some identifying markers secret so that you can ask people who claim to have found your dog to identify as proof.

✔ After a few days, make mailer postcards for delivery in a larger target area (like a 2-to-5-mile radius from the place your dog was lost) and to veterinary clinics and animal shelters. Note that some national organizations like Sherlock Bones (www.sherlockbones.com;800-942-6637) can help you prepare posters and preaddressed mailers (depending on your location) and deliver them to you by overnight mail for a fee.

✔ If your dog is lost while away from home, take something familiar (like his crate, bed, or your clothing with your scent on it) to where he last saw you. Many dogs return to the place they were last with their owner. If possible, keep your car parked with a door open where the dog last saw it.

Don't give up hope. Many dogs have been found days, weeks, and sometimes even months after they've been lost. But the less time that elapses before you mobilize your search, the greater your chances are of recovery. This is one time it pays to be an alarmist and one of many times it pays to be prepared. And remember, it always pays to microchip your dog! (See Chapter 10.)

✔ Has a caretaker on the grounds 24 hours a day

✔ Requires proof of current immunizations and an incoming check for fleas

✔ Allows you to bring your dog's toys and bedding

✔ Provides a raised surface area so dogs don't have to sleep on the floor

Ask to see the facilities. It won't smell like Grandma's kitchen, but it shouldn't make you lose your lunch.

Your veterinary hospital may also provide boarding services. If so, it's your best choice for a dog that has ongoing health problems. These facilities usually aren't as spacious as regular boarding kennels, but space isn't necessarily a big deal for a little Pom. Veterinary hospitals and boarding kennels may have comparable runs and prices and both may offer grooming. But if you want luxury perks like playtime, television, and walks, you need to find a luxury boarding kennel.

Some individuals offer in-home boarding for a limited number of dogs. The dogs essentially live as the person's dog during that time. This arrangement provides a comfortable environment for your dog, but keep these two cautions in mind:

✔ Make sure the home is safe for such a small dog.

✔ Make sure the individual doesn't board large dogs that can run loose at the same time as your Pom.

Hiring a pet sitter

If your Pom is a little uneasy around other dogs or in strange places, consider having a pet sitter come in to take care of her in your home. Keep in mind, though, that having the kid down the street take on this important responsibility is seldom a good idea. What if the dog gets out? What if your pup or the sitter gets sick? An inexperienced pet sitter — just like an inexperienced babysitter — doesn't know what to do in times of need. That's why you should opt for bonded, experienced pet sitters.

The main drawback is that pet sitters usually visit only a couple of times a day. Unless your Pom is paper trained or litter-box trained or you have a doggy door leading to a secure kennel, two visits aren't really enough. Another concern is for Poms susceptible to hypoglycemia, who need more frequent feedings. Small dogs, especially those with medical problems, need supervision throughout the day.

To find a responsible pet sitter, check out

- www.petsit.com
- www.petsitters.org
- www.petdogandcatservices.com

Part IV
Training Your Pom
with TLC

The 5th Wave   By Rich Tennant

"Okay, this is getting ridiculous! Either teach
your dog not to run away, or name him
something other than 'Fire.'"

In this part . . .

*P*oms may be little, but they still need to be trained. Little dogs can be as much a nuisance as big dogs, and you don't want your friends thinking your dog is a spoiled little brat that they need to avoid.

Besides, training makes life pleasant for both of you — no more urine-soaked carpets, no more run-away dog, no more jumping on your new white pants. And training makes your Pom safer. You need your dog to come when called, to stop when doing something dangerous, and to refrain from biting or other bad behaviors that can label your dog a public menace.

The best part of training, though, is that it's fun, and training with rewards strengthens the bond between you and your dog. When you try the positive reward based methods I show you, you may find your Pom reminding you that it's time for her class.

What fun you're going to have showing off your little genius!

Chapter 13

Saving the Carpets: Housetraining

● ●

In This Chapter

▶ Setting the stage: The when and where of housetraining

▶ Managing the *gotta-go* schedule

▶ Defining the den

▶ Ready, set, go!

▶ When training comes up short: Special challenges

● ●

*B*abies don't come potty trained. Neither do puppies. Toy dog puppies, in particular, seem to take a little longer to housetrain — but at least their messes are miniature!

As you soap up yet another Pomeranian puddle, don't despair. By following some simple guidelines, you really can housetrain your Pom puppy. And if your adult Pom has problems, maybe she wasn't trained well to start with. You can go back to basics and train her as though she's a puppy. This chapter guides you in all you need to know — from getting started with the training to solving potty-behavior dilemmas.

Deciding When and Where to Housetrain Your Pom Pup

The best time to introduce housetraining is when your puppy is between 7 and 9 weeks of age. Younger puppies either don't have the physical control to comply or can't comprehend what crazy idea you're driving at.

After 9 weeks of age, puppies often try to go on the surface they were using between 7 and 9 weeks. For example, if somebody thought it was a good idea to throw a scatter rug in the pen for them to use, it's likely they'll use any scatter rug or big rug in your house as their preferred potty surface. This is one reason to raise puppies with access to grass or the surface they'll use as adults.

Every time your puppy goes on grass, the routine reinforces grass as the appropriate place. The same is true if you want her to go on cement (for city dogs) or even on doggy litter. Unfortunately, it's equally true for rugs, newspapers, and other places you *don't* want your dog to use for the rest of her life.

Newspapers? I highly recommend that you steer clear of them as potty-training surfaces unless you have some desire to use them as your ultimate potty surface. The problem is that urine-soaked newspapers smell worse than just plain urine. And if you have a habit of placing your newspaper on the floor, you guessed it — you may find the paper soaked when you pick it up to read!

First, make up your own mind about where you ultimately want him to go. Will he mostly be going in the yard? On the curb? In an indoor potty? Practice early on with any of these options you plan to use later. Fortunately, the training concept is the same.

Of course, your puppy won't know where you want her to go, but she instinctively knows where she *should* go — away from her own *den* (in human terms, her crate or X-pen; more on these later). Little puppies instinctively totter away from their nesting area to relieve themselves. The problem is that they don't go far because they consider their den to be so small. So although she may be careful to avoid her own bed or even her crate, she may deposit her gifts right smack in the middle of *your* den and think she's done just fine.

Your goal, then, is to help her expand her definition of *den* so she instinctively has no desire to make a deposit any place in your home. You can broaden her limited viewpoint in three ways:

- **Keep her confined unless she has just pottied.** You can use baby gates or exercise pens to confine her in a small area just around the crate. As she grows older and goes longer without soiling that small area, you can gradually expand her confinement area, now her den.

- **Expand the area of your home she considers her den.** A common problem as you give your puppy more freedom is that you may find surprises in parts of the house you seldom visit.

  The guest room is a favorite spot for such deposits, which of course makes a wonderful impression on your guests. Your first inclination may be to mumble something about that sneaky little brat pretending to be housetrained but just doing it where you don't see. But that's not the problem. She has simply failed to identify these distant or unused areas of your home as her den area because the two of you haven't spent any time there. She thinks they're the great world beyond the den, and remember, to a dog, the world is her potty.

To adjust her thinking, take a few steps backward by restricting her freedom. Then make sure you play or hang out together in every room of your house to enforce the idea that this is home turf.

✔ **Get rid of the scent.** Dogs are programmed to potty where they can smell they've pottied before, so clean up an accident with a special enzymatic cleaner (available from pet supply stores).

Creating a Schedule (And Sticking to It)

To prevent your puppy from choosing the wrong location to potty, you have to get her to the right place *before* she has to go. The problem is that young puppies have poor bladder and bowel control, and even adult Poms have their limits.

To avoid accidents, remember the two *S* words: *Schedule* and *Signs*. Later in this chapter (see the section "Housetraining in Action") I help you identify when your Pom needs to pee — for those times it's not completely obvious — but in this section I give you an overview of the schedule you need to keep.

Dogs thrive on schedules, and keeping to a schedule is essential for housetraining. There's even a physiological reason for this: a dog's (and even a person's) gut becomes unconsciously tuned to certain rhythms. The bowel that empties itself at a certain time of day wants to do it at that time every day, whether you remember to let your dog out or not.

The bowel is also stimulated to empty itself by triggers that occur after eating (usually about 15 minutes after eating a meal), so be sure you have your pup in the right place at the right time. For the same reason, don't feed your puppy a big meal as you pop him into his crate for the night or before you rush out of the house. Allow plenty of potty time — 15 to 30 minutes or so — between feeding and confinement.

When your pup wakes up, he immediately has to urinate. By keeping him on a regular wake-sleep cycle, you can also train him to urinate on a somewhat more regular cycle (although this is less reliable than relieving his bowels on schedule).

A general guide is that a Pomeranian puppy can hold his urine for as many hours as he is months old. So a 2-month-old pup can wait for two hours, or a 4-month-old for four hours, up to about 6 months of age. But every dog is different. If you find your dog urinates on average once an hour, take him out once every 45 minutes. Always take him out before his regularly scheduled program of pee or poop.

Using a Crate, Pen, or Doggy Door When You're Away from Home

You can't expect to watch your pup 24 hours a day — no one has that kind of time! So, when you can't watch him, confine him, just like you'd put a toddler in a crib or playpen rather than letting him just meander around your house alone.

Allowing a crate to teach him to hold it

One of the handiest items in your housetraining arsenal is a crate, which your dog will come to think of as her den. You'll want to first teach her to enjoy her crate, and I explain how to do that in Chapter 7.

Here's why a crate helps in housetraining: In puppy world, a crate is the equivalent of a crib. Puppies naturally avoid soiling their bed (the smart critters *know* they don't want to sit in it!), so being in the crate encourages them to hold off going for a short while. This natural response makes the crate your best bet when you can't watch him, even if you're just in another part of the house.

To use the crate, place the puppy in it for short periods, never longer than he can hold himself — never more hours than he is months old, and never more than six hours, period. Let him out when you can watch him. As soon as you open the door, take him to his potty area. *Note:* You may have to carry him to get there more quickly and avoid accidents.

If your puppy is having accidents in his crate, you can probably chalk it up to one or more of the following reasons:

- ✔ **The crate is too large.** The crate should be only big enough for him to stand up, turn around, and lie down in. If it's larger, he can step to one side, relieve himself, and curl up on the other side. No Great Dane–sized crates for housetraining a Pom!

- ✔ **You're leaving her in the crate too long.** This move is not only cruel but also stupid. By forcing him to go in his crate, you're telling him:

  - Don't bother trying to hold it.

  - The crate is in fact an acceptable place to potty.

  You're undoing every bit of housetraining and setting yourself up for a lifetime of cleaning out the crate and washing off the dog every time you leave him crated. Yuck!

- ✔ **Your puppy is experiencing separation anxiety or crate anxiety.** You can identify a dog with these problems because he'll usually also be panting and drooling in the crate, along with possibly peeing and pooping. In this case, deal with the anxiety problems first (see Chapter 15) or try using an exercise pen setup, which I cover in the next section.

Letting her housetrain herself in an exercise pen

Perhaps you need to crate your pup for longer than she can hold it. Or maybe the weather's too cold or too wet — your dog just stands there on three feet, staring at you incredulously when you try to get her to run out into the elements. Then again, maybe you live on the 20th floor and the elevator stops on every floor while your poor Pom tries to cross her legs. Maybe she's had surgery, is incontinent, or just plain can't hold it until you come home. If you face any of these situations, your best bet is to set up a small indoor-exercise pen (see Chapter 5). This will allow her to step away from her crate and into an indoor potty arrangement.

To potty train your Pom by confining her to a pen, you need a crate and a litter box or indoor potty. Place her crate (with the door open) in one corner and a litter box or indoor potty (see the following section) in the other. This setup gives her access to a proper surface and allows her to practically housetrain herself.

Using a grassy litter box

"But aren't litter boxes for cats?" you may rightly ask. *Au contraire* — litter boxes work for small dogs, too. Here's the plan:

1. **Buy a cat litter box or an even larger flat pan.**

   An ideal box has fairly high sides but a low entrance area so your puppy doesn't have to jump to get in it.

2. **Buy some sod squares and place them inside the box or on the pan.**

   Purchase these squares at a home supply store.

3. **Place the box or pan where the puppy can reach it inside.**

   Now your puppy has an indoor grassy area, and she's learning to do her duty on the proper surface. This routine makes training her to go outside that much easier. When the sod gets sodden (you'll smell it!), replace it and plant it in the yard.

You can also simply use dog litter, available at major pet supply stores. It's absorbent, has deodorizing properties, and is attractive to dogs. Dog litter is a good choice if you plan to use a litter box on a long-term basis because it's hard to keep grass growing inside and eventually you run out of places to plant the old sod outdoors — especially if you live in an apartment!

Using other indoor options

A variety of fancier indoor plumbing options are available for Poms who demand the very best. Well, maybe not *plumbing* options, more like *potty* options. They include the following:

- ✔ **Disposable absorbent pads scented to attract puppies:** The pads absorb moisture and have a waterproof barrier. Their drawback? Some dogs, especially puppies, like to shred them. Be sure to get the tie-down variety so your dog doesn't surf across the floor on them. They're also great for trips.

- ✔ **Washable pads:** These pads have a waterproof barrier, an absorbent middle layer, and a moisture-proof top layer to keep the outside surface dry. They're less expensive in the long run than disposable ones but not as practical for trips or short-term solutions.

- ✔ **Indoor yards of artificial turf placed over a grate:** With this setup, liquids drain into a disposal pan so your dog has a somewhat more natural surface to go on. You must empty the pan regularly and hose down and deodorize the turf. One thing to note is that artificial sod may not be as attractive to some dogs that are used to going on real grass, so make sure it's working for your dog.

✔ **Indoor yards of real sod:** This is, of course, the ultimate in bringing the outdoors to your dog. You have to water the grass, although some have an underground dirtless system, so you just place water in a reservoir. Still, you need to hose it down with deodorizing spray and replace the grass every few months. These systems do better on an outdoor patio but work well indoors with more frequent grass replacement.

Costs for indoor potty systems range from about $15 for a box of pads to $300 for a fancy turf system that cleans itself. Check a pet supply store or search "indoor potty" on the Internet.

Installing a doggy door

If you have a house with a yard and don't want to go the indoor-potty route, you may be able to use a doggy door. All sorts of doors are available at pet supply stores, ranging in price from $50 to $150; just be sure you get one light enough for your Pom puppy to push through. The easiest doors to install are those that work with your sliding glass door because they just slide into place, without requiring you to cut a hole in the door or wall.

The doggy door option also assumes a couple of factors:

✔ The door leads outside to an absolutely escape-proof kennel, preferably with a top that prevents predators from getting in. (The top prevents wild animals, including birds of prey, from regarding your Pom pup as a potential snack. The top is also secure from passersby who may try to steal a cute puppy.)

✔ Inside, the doggy-door is one side of a pen. The smaller you can make the indoor area, the more it will be like your pup's *den* (see the earlier section "Deciding When and Where to Housetrain Your Pom Pup" for a discussion on this important area). If possible, fill most of the area with your pup's crate, removing the door or propping it open sturdily.

Young puppies catch on to the concept of doggy doors very quickly. You can help her through the first few times, luring her with treats and holding the flap partially open. Gradually require her to push the flap open herself, and soon she'll be letting herself in and out!

Housetraining in Action

After you know the basics, it's time to walk the walk and stop the yuck. There's only one thing missing: your puppy! In this section I show you how to know when she's gotta go and how to shape her into a potty-trained pee-meister.

Recognizing when she's gotta go

You can't rely on the clock to tell you when a potty break's imminent, so watch your dog for signs of impending peeing or pooping.

Playing and exercising mean she's also drinking more water, but young puppies don't give you too much of a clue that they're about to become walking geysers. Here are a few signs to watch for:

- ✔ She walks quickly in circles.
- ✔ When playing, she stops, then walks a few steps forward, then stops again.

  You have to be fast to catch her when she has to go, so a safer bet is not to start indoor games unless she's just urinated in the proper place.

Puppies give you much more warning when they're going to poop. When you see these two signs, get your Pom to her potty area right away:

- ✔ They usually start sniffing and circling.
- ✔ Very young puppies often whine.

When in doubt, take her out!

Instilling confidence by sticking around for the potty party

Good parents don't just shove a toddler into a bathroom and lock the door behind him, expecting to achieve good results. He'd be crying to get out or looking for some sort of mischief to get into, but he definitely wouldn't be getting potty trained!

The same is true of your puppy. You can't just push him outside and then let him back in five minutes later and think you've done your part. Especially if the weather's bad, he's likely to spend that time huddled against the door. Then when you let him back in, he wets the floor. "Bad dog!" you exclaim. No — bad trainer!

You need to go outside with him every time as long as he's still training, no matter how bad the weather or how big your rush. And as soon as he goes, you need to be ready to praise and reward him for his astounding feat.

Even if you have a yard, be sure to practice with the dog on a leash sometimes. Few moments are more frustrating than taking a trip with a dog and suddenly discovering she doesn't think she's supposed to potty while on a leash.

Rewarding potty performance

Sure, you can housetrain a dog without using rewards. But the simple fact is that rewards make the job faster and easier. These are the basics:

1. **Go outside with her to the specific place you've chosen as the potty area.**

   If you've been using sod squares inside (see the earlier section "Using a grassy litter box"), plant one with her urine scent on it as a scent signpost for her because dogs are hardwired to mark the same territory more than once.

2. **Ignore her if she tries to play.**

   She's not out there for playtime.

3. **After she potties, tell her what a good girl she is and give her a reward from the stash of treats in your pocket.**

   You can move to another area of the yard and play so that playtime is yet another reward for pottying in the right place.

4. **When she gets the hang of going in the right place, add a cue (like "Hurry up") as soon as she's definitely going to go (unless you happen to say that phrase a lot around the house!). Reward her as usual afterward.**

   Soon she'll associate the cue with the action, and you'll have a dog that can eliminate on cue! "Spend a penny" is popular with people who want to sound old fashioned and also not accidentally give the cue to potty in the wrong place.

Overcoming Housetraining Challenges

Housetraining is the single most difficult training task most people have to face with any dog, and toy dogs in particular. The reasons for this problem can vary. Many people raise toy dogs inside until the dogs have formed bad ideas about the proper potty surface. New owners tend to let their puppies have too much freedom. (After all, how hard is it to clean up little puppy messes?) Then again, it doesn't help that toy dogs simply take longer than big dogs to gain control over their bladders and bowels.

Whatever the case, don't give up. Even if your dog takes longer to housetrain than your friend's dog, it will happen. However, if you seem to make no progress, or if your dog is backsliding, you may need to back up and start at square one, reverting to no unsupervised freedom. Yes, it sees like a lot of work, but it's really very little compared to cleaning up for the next decade. And good training is certainly better than banishing your dog to the laundry room.

Reacting constructively to accidents

You'll probably find some puddles and poops inside that you never saw your Pom deposit. Dragging her to the scene of the crime, pointing, and rubbing her nose in it only tells her that every once in a while, for no apparent reason, you lose your mind and turn on her. Yelling, slapping, and generally going insane doesn't get the point across any better. In fact, it's the perfect way to ruin a trusting relationship. Your dog has no idea what your problem is, because she can't relate what she did ten minutes ago to what you're going on and on about now. (For more insight about punishment and why it rarely works, see Chapter 15.)

Instead, follow up the deed with these moves of your own:

1. **Hold your temper.**
2. **Clean up the mess.**

And what to do if you catch your dog in the act, pottying inside the house? Take these positive steps:

1. **Make an abrupt noise, like "Arrgh" to get her attention.**
2. **Try to sweep her up and get her outside.**

Cleanup 101

Unless you're Super Trainer, your puppy will have accidents. A place that smells like urine or poop is a place that screams "Go here!" to your dog. To avoid repeat performances, you need to get rid of as much of that scent signal as possible. (Of course, you want to do that anyway for your own olfactory comfort!) Avoid ammonia-based cleaners, which smell like urine and can act as an inadvertent welcome sign to dogs.

To clean potty-soaked carpet:

1. **Scoop up any droppings and soak up as much liquid as possible as quickly as possible.**

   Your aim is to prevent it from reaching the carpet pad.

2. **Add a little water and again soak up as much as possible.**

   If you have a rug-cleaning machine that extracts liquid, use it.

3. **Apply an enzyme-digester odor neutralizer (a product specifically for dog accidents), and leave it on for a long time, following directions.**

   Use enough neutralizer to penetrate the pad.

   Note: Cover the area with plastic so the neutralizer doesn't dry out before it can break down the urine.

4. **Add a nice odor like a mixture of lavender oil or vanilla with baking soda to the area. Let it air out for a day, then vacuum.**

She may not be able to stop midstream, so be careful she doesn't leave a pee-pee trail all the way to the door by keeping lots of towels handy.

3. **After she's outside, ignore her until she relieves herself; then reward her as usual.**

4. **Consider it a reminder that you need to watch her more closely.**

Understanding common medical causes for potty problems

If your adult (over 1 year old) Pomeranian still isn't housetrained — or reverts back to having accidents when he's housetrained — have your veterinarian examine him to make sure a physical problem isn't the cause. Some medical reasons are as follows:

✔ Urinary tract infections cause repeated urges to urinate with little warning.

✔ Diabetes and kidney disease cause increased drinking along with increased urination.

✔ Some drugs like steroids also cause increased drinking and urination.

✔ Spayed females are more prone to urinary incontinence. Place an absorbent pad under her when she sleeps.

✔ Geriatric dogs may forget their house manners and have accidents.

✔ Internal parasites, gastrointestinal upsets, and some food allergies can cause uncontrollable diarrhea.

Dealing with involuntary emissions

Have you ever been pee-in-your-pants scared? That's one type of involuntary emission — and your dog is even more susceptible to pee that is out of her control. Even a trained dog can suffer from some type of involuntary urine emission.

Submissive urination

Picture this: You come home, bend over to greet your sweet little Pom, and what does she do? Squats and pees all over the floor! If you're living the nightmare, odds are that your Pom has a classic case of *submissive urination,* which she's doing in response to your dominant signal of bending over her.

She can't help it — and punishing her only makes the condition worse. The good news is that she'll probably outgrow the problem if you help her. Avoid these actions that make her feel submissive:

✔ Bending over her

✔ Staring at her

✔ Scolding her

✔ Intimidating her in any other manner

Instead, keep your greetings calm, get down on her level, *and* forgive and forget if she urinates. By teaching her a few tricks, you can increase her confidence and give her a way to earn rewards.

Excitement urination

Some dogs just can't help dribbling urine when they're excited. They, too, usually outgrow this *excitement urination* as they gain bladder control. The best treatment is to decrease the excitement level. To do this, greet your dog calmly and teach him to do some simple tricks in exchange for treats. Also reward him just for being calm. The goal is to train your dog by gradually conditioning him to be calm during low-excitement events, working up gradually to higher-excitement events. In addition, teach him some simple low-key tricks to distract and calm him.

Punishing a dog with excitement urination only leads to his confusion and possible submissive urination.

Tackling the not-so-involuntary emissions

Is your Pom driving you crazy with general lack of housetraining or with marking (when a sexually mature male dog lifts his leg to urinate, thus marking his territory), and you're thinking of banishing him to the laundry room, garage, or outer space? You're not alone, and thankfully, solutions are available.

Absorbing the puddle

Enter the belly band for males. A belly band is, simply stated, a band that goes around the belly with an absorbent pad strategically placed to catch any urine a male dog may aim in any direction (see Figure 13-1). Replace the pad as needed, and your home is pee free. These belly bands are available in many pet supply stores, most dog catalogs, and in any toy dog specialty catalog.

For females, a belly band won't work because the part she pees with isn't near her belly. Instead, try the panties they sell for females in heat. Place an absorbent pad in the panty and change as needed.

Whichever you use, change the pad frequently, and don't use it in place of proper housetraining efforts.

Discouraging the problem

Sometimes the smaller the dog, the more he tries to make a good mark and the higher he tries to lift his leg.

The best cure is prevention by neutering before sexual maturity. This step can't guarantee that he won't mark, but it greatly lessens the chances. If he's already sexually mature and has started marking, then neutering usually (but not always) helps alleviate the problem.

Figure 13-1: A belly band for male dogs keeps your home pee free.

If you don't want to neuter him, you may or may not be lucky, and he may or may not be a marker. If you would like to make a million dollars, invent a way to keep intact male dogs from marking.

Chapter 14

Mastering Manners and Basic Commands

. . . .

In This Chapter

▶ Communicating to your Pom

▶ Figuring out your Pom's communication system

▶ Motivating your pup to achieve

▶ Training the basic commands

▶ Adding some tricks to the repertoire

. . . .

*N*obody likes a brat. Sure, the brat's parents may think she's just so cute, but everybody else — humans *and* canines — run at the sight of her. You don't do your Pom any favors by letting her become the brat everybody avoids, and trust me, even a small dog can be a huge annoyance!

Fortunately, she doesn't need to be a scholar to become polite. A little home schooling, perhaps a short stint at a finishing school, and she's ready to hold her own in any social gathering.

But before you can train your Pomeranian, you'll need to speak her language as much as she'll need to speak yours. What you don't want here is a failure to communicate.

Talking to Your Pom

Most people use such a mishmash of signals, it's a wonder their dogs haven't attacked them in their sleep just for being so confusing. The fact that dogs still manage to figure those signals out is a testament to their patience and intelligence. But why not make it easy on your dog?

Communicating with body language

The problem with communicating with your dog through body language is that what seems right in people culture is often wrong in dog culture. So follow these guidelines:

- ✔ **Don't stare at your dog.** Dogs consider an unwavering direct stare to be a threat. It can cause a dog that's on the verge of biting to attack in protest or, more often, in self defense. Staring also can frighten a dog so she runs away or pees on herself. Rather than staring, look off to the side a bit.

- ✔ **Protect your Pom from strangers quickly approaching her.** When strange dogs meet each other, they sidle up sideways in a circular motion to check each other out. Dogs that don't display this approach send the message that they just may attack. In the same way, dogs consider humans who stride right up to be pushy and threatening. The dog may bite in self defense, try to get away, or sink to the ground. If your dog appears fearful, amble up and stop with your side facing her.

- ✔ **When other people pet your Pom, have them scratch her under the chin.** Dogs consider a pat on the head or back to be a sign of dominance. (A dominant dog would do this to a submissive one.) So if your dog is already overly submissive, try scratching her under her chin instead. It feels better to her, too.

- ✔ **If you want your dog to come, turn your back to her and call her as you walk away.** Conversely, to stop her in her tracks, you can turn toward her, make yourself look big, and take a step or two toward her. Dogs consider somebody coming toward them to be a signal to walk in the same direction and stay out of the way. (A dominant wolf leads the pack this way.) People tend to call dogs by facing them — and then wonder why the dog trots away! She's not being obstinate; in fact, she's being a perfect follower by wolf pack rules.

- ✔ **Avoid hugging your dog.** The closest dogs come to hugging is when they hump each other in play, and then the humpee generally isn't too thrilled. So when you hug your dog to make her feel more secure, she sees it as a sign of dominance and will likely try to squirm loose.

Speaking up: Using verbal skills correctly

Of course you also talk to your dog with words. If you're like most Pom owners, you babble an endless stream of words throughout the day, and your Pom cocks his head knowingly. And even though he seems to hang on to every one of your profound words, you can be sure he's actually trying to detect a magically important word — like *walk* or *eat* — among the drivel.

 Just as you need to be careful when you're talking to people, heed your speech when you're talking to your dog. Your dog pays attention to the volume, tone, and cadence of your voice in addition to the words themselves. Keep the following points in mind to maximize your verbal effectiveness:

- **Pick one word for a command and stick with it.** For example, if you want your Pom to come when called, don't use *here, come, come on, over here, here girl,* and *get your butt over here right now before I come and get you!* Pick one command (preferably not that last one), and use it consistently.

- **Pick unique command words.** Make sure the words you choose for one command don't resemble other commands or your dog's name. For example, if your dog's name is Sid, you may find that "Sit" isn't a good command cue. In such cases, many people simply train their dogs to commands in a foreign language — and showing off your bilingual dog is a lot of fun, too!

- **Be consistent with the sound as well as the word choice of each cue.** Dogs hear your cues as sounds, not as words that have one meaning no matter how you say them.

- **Teach your dog commands in a normal voice.** Your Pom's hearing is far more sensitive than yours. If he doesn't respond to you, shouting at him won't help unless he happens to be half a mile away. In fact, shouting may intimidate him.

- **Use a low-pitched voice to warn or scold your dog.** In almost every species, low-pitched sounds indicate power, aggression, and leadership; they're often used as threats. They make the recipient take notice. If your dog is getting ready to run into the road or do something wrong, lower your voice into your best gruff command mode, and say "STOP!"

- **Use a high-pitched voice to encourage your Pom to play.** High-pitched sounds make the recipient feel playful or dominant. People naturally speak to dogs, especially puppies, in the same high-pitched voice that parents around the world use with their babies. This baby talk tends to encourage both babies and dogs to interact and play.

  Because the tone is nonthreatening, it's also easy to ignore (imagine a drill sergeant calling out commands in high-pitched baby talk!). When you want your dog to stop, don't use baby talk.

✔ **Mind the cadence of your words.** People naturally change their speech rhythm to communicate the response they want. By becoming conscious of it, you can use your cadence to influence your dog's actions. Here are some examples:

- Long, drawn-out, monotone speech tends to slow or calm a dog.

- Abrupt, low-pitched commands tend to stop a dog.

- A series of repeated, short, high-pitched sounds that continue to rise in pitch tend to speed up a dog.

For example, if you want your dog to come running, you call, "Go, go, go, go, go, GO!" with short, high-pitched sounds. After he gets to you and starts to jump on you, you can say, "Ahght! No!" in a low-pitched voice. Then to calm him down, you say, "Eaaaasy, doooown" in a slow, monotone voice. Adjusting your tone and cadence adds meaning to your words.

Understanding Your Pom

It's not fair to expect your Pom to be the only one to learn a new language. She's also using body language and verbal language to communicate to you. And because she can't exactly dictate it or tap it out on the keyboard, you're duty bound as the supposedly smarter member of the team to learn what's she's saying.

Reading your Pom's body language

Take the time to watch your dog as well as other dogs; you'll discover they're speaking volumes with their body language and facial expressions.

Putting all the clues together takes a little practice, but as you get to know your Pom and her reactions, reading her body language will become second nature. Of course, you have to listen to her, too. But more on listening later in this chapter. For now, just watch.

Notice how she moves and stands around other dogs. See Table 14-1 for a variety of these movements and their meanings.

Table 14-1	Pom Body Language
Movement	*Meaning*
Leans forward	Confidence and interest
Leans forward and stands stiff-legged	Dominance or aggressive intention
Leans backwards	Fear or submission
Crouches or lowers head	Fear, anxiety, or submission
Lowers and twists head to the side, especially while crouching	Submission
Lowers front end only so elbows touch the ground and butt is in the air	Playfulness
Rolls on back	Possibly extreme submission or fear, depending on circumstances
Rolls around on back	Having a good time!
Places paw or head on another dog's back	Dominance
Slams another dog with shoulder or hip	Playful dominance
Turns head away	Submission or call for a truce
Holds head high	Possibly issuing a challenge to another dog; turn him away before he gets himself into trouble!

Translating Pom talk

Dogs do more than bark. They whine, growl, pant, hum, and howl. And all those sounds mean something different! Many new dog owners are alarmed when they hear their cute little Pomeranian growl like a saber-toothed tiger. But growling is a natural part of her vocabulary, and not all growls are created equal. The next time your Pom starts to bark or growl, don't shush her — at least not right away. Take the time to understand what she's saying. Table 14-2 translates a few common Pom sounds.

Table 14-2	Pom Sounds and Their Interpretations
Sound	**Meaning**
A single short bark or yip	A demand *(feed me, walk me, play with me,* or *do what I want!)*
A single low-pitched bark	A warning to stay away
Repeated quick barks	An intruder alert
Repeated yips	Excitement
A single soft bark	An invitation to play or a first uncertain warning
A low-pitched growl	A warning for a subordinate to go away; fine if it's directed at another dog but not if it's directed at you
A low-pitched growl with some yips mixed in	Probably a threat to an equal to stay away; not appropriate if it's directed at you
A high-pitched and undulating growl	Fear or uncertainty
Frequently repeated short, high-pitched growls	A playful growl

A repeated rough-sounding exhalation while playing is really the canine equivalent of laughter — don't mistake it for a growl!

Providing the Motivation for Training and Tricks

Want to know what makes your dog tick? In truth, it's not all that different from what motivates you. Learning for canines *and* humans is about cause and effect.

Although you really can teach an old dog new tricks, it's even easier to teach a new dog old tricks. Puppies can learn simple things like "come" at just a few weeks of age and "sit" by 7 weeks or so. The earlier your puppy learns to learn, the easier it will be to train him throughout his life.

Rewarding with treats

When you do something that pays off, you try to do it again to get that same payoff. That payoff may be money, a chance to relax, a

Training isn't wasted on the young

Young puppies are ready to accept the rules of their new world, and if those rules include doing a trick or two in exchange for a treat, that seems normal to them. Some research indicates that dogs are more receptive to reward-based training when they're puppies than at any other time in their lives.

In terms of learning ability, an 8-week-old puppy's behavior and brainwaves function at nearly adult levels. In fact, a puppy's ability to learn actually decreases slightly beyond the age of 16 weeks. This means that if you wait until your pup is older for his first lessons, he's more likely to be confused and intimidated by this bizarre new game you've devised.

You don't have to teach him to count, but a simple trick or command can get the idea of a trick for a treat across. Tricks learned at this young age tend to stick with a dog through life, though, so make that trick a handy one!

good meal, or any number of rewards. The payoff works the same way for your dog, except that it's likely to be a tasty treat, a chance to play, or — to a lesser extent — praise from you.

Are treats really a good idea? Maybe your dog should mind you simply for a kind word and a scratch under the chin. True, kind words and scratches help, but would you go to work every day if that was all you got? How long would you stay at a job if you got a gold star and a pat on the back but no paycheck? Dogs are materialistic, too.

If you need more convincing, consider the dogs and other animals that do all those amazing feats in movies, circuses, and other performances. They're exchanging tricks for treats.

For most dogs, the way to their brains is through their stomachs. But some dogs also consider the chance to chase a ball or play tug equally rewarding. Dogs place different values on different rewards, and they know what their work is worth. For example:

- ✔ They may consider a piece of kibble fair pay for a few feet of walking on a leash but not for a whole string of tricks.

- ✔ Your dog expects a bigger reward for doing something she doesn't enjoy compared to the payment for something she does enjoy.

- ✔ If your dog's behavior is slacking, maybe she doesn't approve of the pay structure. Don't be stingy when it comes to rewards!

The old school of dog training warned that if you started training your dog with treats, you'd have to give your dog treats forever or he wouldn't cooperate. They had a good point. Nobody likes a pay cut — and most dogs consider going from treats to praise to be a serious cut in pay.

When you substitute praise for tangible rewards, the dog either quits work or figures he's doing something wrong. Result? He tries to come up with some different way of doing what you've asked. You start to think he's bored, stubborn, or stupid, but really, he's disappointed and confused. Keep these guidelines in mind for managing your pup's rewards:

 ✔ Avoid spending the rest of your life as a walking treat dispenser by giving treats sometimes but giving praise all the time. So you either give praise and then treat or give praise alone.

 ✔ The way you choose to schedule rewards can have important implications for your dog's learning. Just like people, a Pom's performance depends on whether she's paid by the hour or the job. You want her to work by the job!

When you first teach her a trick, reward her every time she does it right. But after she knows it, cut back gradually, rewarding her only some of the time but still praising every time.

Like a slot machine, pay off at random times so she's always wondering whether the next time will be the jackpot. And in fact, you can add special jackpot rewards to really keep her working.

 ✔ If you train your dog before her regular meal time, she works much better for food. In fact, you can simply dole out her dinner bit by bit as rewards during training sessions. If you're in a hurry, just train for a few minutes, give a few rewards, and then give a jackpot of her entire meal.

Clicking to show your praise

Hang around a group of successful dog trainers in action and you'll start wondering what all these clicking sounds are about. They're using clicker training, which works very well with most animals, including dogs.

A click is merely a signal that tells your Pom he's doing something right. Why not just say "Good dog"? Because your dog can tune out much of what you say, but he's more likely to notice a distinctive signal. In addition,

✔ By following the click sound with a reward, your dog quickly learns that the click means "Yes, that's it!"

✔ Because the click is faster and shorter than your voice, it can more precisely mark the moment your dog is doing something right.

✔ The click tells the dog that he can end the behavior — so don't expect him to continue after you click.

✔ After he understands how to do something, you can phase out the click but not the praise and rewards.

You can buy an inexpensive clicker device from any pet supply store or use anything that makes a distinctive click sound. You can even make a cluck sound with your mouth — just make sure you don't use the same sound in situations other than training.

To train with a clicker, follow these steps:

1. **Have lots of tiny treats on hand.**

2. **Begin clicking and then give your dog a treat so she learns that a click means a treat is coming.**

   Repeat this step (at least 20 times) until she looks at your treat hand expectantly after she hears the click.

3. **Give a click instantly when your dog does what you want.**

   The faster you click, the easier it is for her to figure out what you like.

4. **Give a reward as soon as you can after the click.**

5. **Always praise and pet your Pom as part of the reward!**

No dog performs perfectly at first. You have to gradually teach her, shaping her behavior closer and closer to your expectations.

Schooling Your Pom in Manners and Obedience

When your puppy realizes that his actions are related to treats, you have a good foundation for further training. And if you have plans to enter your Pom in competitions involving obedience, agility, or even tracking, this is the best time to introduce him to some of those behaviors.

New training methods focus on rewards and positive associations. They produce happy, well-trained dogs that are eager to learn more.

With the positive methods I outline here, you just use a buckle collar (you don't tug on it), a 6-foot leash (not chain!), and maybe a 20-foot light line.

To get started on the right foot (or feet, as the case may be), keep the following suggestions in mind:

- ✔ **Train in a quiet place away from distractions.** You can gradually start practicing in other places after your dog has learned a skill very well.

- ✔ **If your dog is tired, hot, or has just eaten, hold off on the training.** You want her peppy and hungry for your fun and treats.

- ✔ **If you're impatient or angry, wait until you're in a better mood.** You won't be able to hide your frustration, and your dog will be uneasy.

- ✔ **Keep your training sessions very short.** Dogs learn best in 10- to 15-minute sessions. Quit while she's still having fun and performing well. You can train her several times a day if you want.

If you plan to clicker train (see the previous section), introduce it in your first training sessions.

Of course, most Poms have the important job of being an owner's best friend. For this responsibility, he needs to know some basic obedience, some house rules, and even the best ways to play and cuddle.

Sitting pretty

For a quick trick, teach your pup a simple sit-and-stay. This trick won't exactly amaze your friends, but at least it'll be handy.

Forget the old smash-his-rear-down-and-pull-up-on-his-collar technique. Poms have enough knee problems without you putting added stress on them, and nobody likes to be forced. The training's more effective when you get him to sit on his own. Follow these steps:

1. **Place your puppy on a raised surface, or sit on the floor with him, with one hand behind his butt to prevent him from backing up.**

Otherwise he's too likely to spend all his time trying to jump up on you.

2. **Hold a treat just above and behind his nose, right above his eyes, so he has to bend his hind legs to look up at it. Click and reward.**

3. **Repeat Step 2 several times.**

4. **Begin moving the treat farther back each time so he has to bend his legs more and eventually has to sit.**

   Don't shove his rear to the ground! Just wait and demand that he go a little farther down each time before he gets the treat. Eventually he'll automatically sit when he sees you move the treat back.

5. **Start saying "Sit" right before you show him the treat; only give him the treat when he sits after you say "Sit."**

   If you give the treat if he sits without the cue word, he'll just sit whenever he feels like it, not when you ask him. Say his name before the cue word to alert him that the next word is directed at him.

6. **Gradually fade out luring with the treat so you use just your empty hand and eventually just your command.**

   Be sure to continue rewarding him afterward, though.

He's probably wondering how he can con you out of more treats. Fortunately, you know plenty of ways, starting with standard obedience commands.

Staying put

What's the use of teaching your dog to sit if she jumps back up like the floor is electrified? By teaching a separate stay command, you can convince her to stay in any position, whether she's sitting, lying down, or standing up.

Because staying is essentially asking her to do nothing, you teach it a different way than you teach sit and most other commands:

✔ **You introduce the cue word "Stay" immediately.** Otherwise how does she know the difference between a sit, where you forgot to reward her, and this new behavior?

✔ **You don't use a clicker (see the earlier section "Clicking to show your praise).** Staying is an imprecise behavior that relies on duration, not action. Because the clicker normally signals the end of the behavior, the dog assumes she is free to get up for her reward . . . hello! I said "Stay."

So you teach stay the old-fashioned way:

1. **Say "Stay" to your sitting dog and hold your palm in a stop signal in front of his face for a few seconds.**

2. **Reward him and say "Okay!" (the release signal that says he's free to move about the cabin).**

   If your dog isn't getting the concept, have him sit on a raised surface or behind a small barrier so it's more difficult for him to come to you.

3. **Work up gradually to a longer duration of the stay.**

   If he gets up, simply put him back in position and start over, decreasing the duration you expect of him.

4. **Move to different positions around your dog (in front of, to either side, and behind), still remaining close. Repeat Steps 2 and 3.**

5. **Move farther away from him. Repeat Steps 2 and 3.**

   Give a reward, then use a release word like "Okay!" to tell him he can get up.

Lying down on the job

Having a dog that lies down quietly is a big help when you want her to stay in the room and impress your guests, or when you take her to an outdoor café that allows dogs, or anytime you need her to stay in place and out of the way.

Instead of trying to push her down to the floor until she gives up struggling (good grief!), try this kinder, gentler way:

1. **Have her sit on a raised surface. Show her a treat and move it toward the ground (see Figure 14-1).**

   You may need to gently place your other hand on her shoulders to prevent her from popping up.

2. **As soon as she lowers her front legs, click (see the section "Clicking to show your praise") and reward her.**

3. **Repeat Step 2, clicking and rewarding for going farther down until her elbows touch the surface she's sitting on.**

4. **Repeat Step 1 but without a treat in the hand you've been using to lure her. Gradually abbreviate your hand movements until you're only using a small hand signal.**

Figure 14-1: Luring a dog into a down.

5. **Add the verbal cue "Down" right before the hand signal.**

6. **Practice the down-stay just as you did the sit-stay (see the two previous sections for these commands).**

Coming when called

If your Pom learns only one command, it should be to come when called, and the best time to teach him is when he's still a puppy. No doubt he already has a good idea of the command. After all, he probably comes scampering when you call him to eat or do something else he thinks is fun.

You can use this same command to make sure he comes running every time you call. A great way to teach the command is with the help of a friend and a long hallway or other enclosed area. Here's how:

1. **Have your friend hold your dog while you back away, enticing your dog with a treat or toy.**

2. **When the dog pulls to get to you, the helper releases him so he can run to you.**

   You can even turn and run away to increase your pup's enthusiasm.

3. **The moment he reaches you, click (see the section "Clicking to show your praise") and then give him the treat or toy.**

4. **Gradually require him to let you catch him before giving him the reward.**

   Some dogs come but then dance just out of your reach while you gradually turn purple with frustration.

5. **Eventually add the cue "Come!" just before your helper releases him. Practice this several times for many sessions.**

6. **Let him meander around on his own after he's learned to come on cue. Call "Come!" and reward him as before.**

   If he doesn't come, try attaching a long, light line to him to give him a hint.

7. **Practice in lots of different places, gradually choosing places with more distractions.**

   Always keep him on a long, light line for his safety.

Always make coming to you rewarding. If you want your dog to come so you can give her a bath or put her to bed or do anything else she isn't keen about, go get her instead of calling her. If you do call her, make sure you give her a good reward before moving on to the part she doesn't like. Never call her to you to punish her. She's not stupid and will quickly learn to go the other way!

Walking the floor

Your Pom was born with feet for a reason — so he can walk on them and not be carried in your arms all the time. But many Pom owners think those four appendages are some evolutionary vestiges of extraneous structures, so they insist on carrying their dogs everywhere. My advice: Don't do it. Your Pom needs to know how to walk like a dog.

But getting your Pom to walk *with* you — without pulling or twirling, or weaving between your feet, prancing in front of you, and tripping you — doesn't come naturally. You'd like him to walk politely by your side — in other words, to heel.

The heel position is the best place to keep your Pom out of the way when walking with you. Heel position is on your left side, next to you but not crowding you, with his neck about even with your leg. If you plan to attend obedience classes or even trials, heeling will play a big part in your Pom's overall performance.

Like the other commands you want your pup to learn, heeling is most easily mastered when you take deliberate but gradual steps.

From collar to leash

Leash training is the first step toward heeling and often the pup's introduction to formal training. To begin, place a simple buckle collar around her neck, tight enough so that she can't get her bottom jaw around it, but loose enough so that you can get a finger or two between it and her neck. (It may feel funny to your pup at first, so she may scratch or bite at it.) As soon as she stops fidgeting with it, give her a treat. Then lure her so she gets used to walking with you, still off the leash. Soon — and how long will vary from one minute to one week — she'll ignore the collar and walk with you around the house or yard as you dole out treats. At this point you can attach the leash.

 If she decides somewhere along the way that she's supposed to object to this leash, she may freeze, flip over, or just lie down. Unfortunately, many traditional trainers believe you should drag the dog along as you walk, but that's not good. Instead, pick your pup up, change directions, and encourage her to walk again, step by step. Take a walk to the kitchen and hand out a jackpot reward. Then take her back and do it again. End the session while she still wants more.

From leash to short walks

Start practicing walking on a leash in your yard or house. Only when she's reliable here should you set your goals on short walks out in the real world.

Your Pom will find everything fascinating on these first walks. In fact, she may become so excited that she leaps at the end of the leash, twirling and voicing her frustration that her human anchor is preventing her from going where she pleases. You can put a stop to this by doing the following:

1. **Stand in place when she starts to tug.**

2. **Click (see the section "Clicking to show your praise") and reward her when she lets the leash go slack.**

3. **Repeat Steps 1 and 2, stopping, standing, and waiting until she stops pulling as soon as you stop walking.**

4. **Walk toward something that she wants to get to, such as a tree.**

5. **Stand in place if she pulls. When she stops pulling, go toward the goal again.**

Reaching the goal is her eventual reward, but the only way she can reach it is to stop pulling!

Pom-sized training

Training a little dog to heel has a couple of special challenges:

✔ **Problem:** Because the leash is so far above the dog, he can arc out in many directions so you have very little control over his exact position.

Solution: Try stringing the leash through a section of PVC pipe. The pipe should reach from your left hand to just above your dog's collar. Now he has very little slack in which to maneuver, and you can control his position precisely. Train him by guiding him into place, then clicking and rewarding him. Gradually guide him less, only rewarding when he assumes heel position on his own. When he consistently heels, add the cue word, "Heel!"

✔ **Problem:** Getting a treat to him in a timely manner may be difficult especially if you plan to use treats to lure him into heel position. Not everybody can bend to give a treat time after time, and you don't want to throw treats on the floor because that teaches him to sniff the floor in search of food all the time.

Solution: One solution is to attach a spoon or paper plate to the end of a stick. Slather peanut butter or squeeze cheese on the spoon or plate. Train him by holding the spoon or plate in front of him until you've lured him into heel position. Let him take a lick only when he is in that position. Eventually hold the target only in the heel position so he has to come to position on his own to get the reward. Add the cue, "Heel!" Gradually raise the stick so it isn't always there, but lower it after he's in position. Your goal is to fade the stick away altogether.

You probably can't handle the PVC leash guide and the treat stick at the same time, so you may have just figure out which works best for you.

No matter which way you choose to train, make staying in heel position a game by running and turning, clicking, and rewarding when she is able to stick to your side. Just be careful not to trip over her!

Even though your Pom should know how to walk on her own four feet in public, it's not always the best idea. If you're in a crowd, or some place where other dogs could reach her, carry her in your arms or put her in a carrying bag for her protection.

Teaching Your Pom a Bagful of Tricks

Knowing how to sit, lie down, come, heel, and stay on command are vital lessons for your Pom to learn. But they're not exactly going to astound anyone. Besides, if you've taught your dog using rewards, she's probably itching to learn more. And that's when a few dog tricks come in handy!

The number of tricks you teach is limited only by your imagination and your dog's physical abilities. But you can start with some standard favorites such as shake hands, roll over, and spin in a circle, and then see where you go from there.

What a greeting! Shaking hands

Every well-bred Pomeranian knows how to greet guests at formal affairs by offering her paw. Here's how to teach yours:

1. **Have her sit facing you.**

2. **Reach for her right paw with your right hand.**

3. **Praise and reward her if she gives you her paw naturally.**

4. **Add the cue words "How do you do?" or some such phrase. Give her your hand and reward her only when she shakes on cue.**

If she doesn't offer her paw, have her sit facing you and then do the following:

1. **Use a treat to lure her head way to the left so she's almost looking over her shoulder.**

   This step makes her right paw lift.

2. **Praise and reward her as soon as her paw goes up.**

3. **Repeat Steps 1 and 2 until she lifts her paw when the lure is close to her head and eventually at only the sight of the treat.**

4. **Add the cue words "How do you do?" or some such phrase. Give her your hand and reward her only when she shakes on cue.**

Stop, drop, and roll, dog-style

No dog trick repertoire is complete without rolling over. Fortunately, it's easy to teach.

1. **Have your Pom lie down beside you.**

2. **Show him a treat and move it over his back so he has to twist his head over his shoulder to see it. Give him the treat.**

3. **Have him twist a little more in order to get the next treat.**

4. **Keep on expecting him to twist more and more until he eventually ends up rolling onto his side.**

   You can help a bit at this point with a gentle nudge to keep him going until he's on his back.

5. **Keep moving the treat to the opposite side so he has to finish the roll and end up back on his stomach before getting the treat.**

6. **Add the cue "Roll over!" when he can do a complete roll easily.**

   Only reward him for rolling over on cue. You can keep on adding roll after roll. Just don't get him too dizzy!

Speaking when called upon

Teach a dog to bark? Is somebody insane? Don't dogs bark enough on their own? Yes, but consider the logic: When your dog learns to bark on cue, he also learns that barking on his own isn't very rewarding. Follow these steps to teach your Pom to speak:

1. **Figure out what makes him bark.**

   The best situation is if he barks at you for a treat.

2. **Click and reward him when he barks.**

3. **Introduce the cue word "Speak!" quickly for this trick.**

   You don't want to reward him for speaking out of turn!

Chapter 15

Dealing with Doggy Delinquents

. . . .

In This Chapter

▶ Understanding the limits of punishment

▶ Helping a dog overcome his fears

▶ Calming the anxious, energetic, or barking pup

▶ Working with your Pom's aggressive tendencies

▶ Dealing with nuisance behaviors

. . . .

*N*o matter how perfect your dog's parents, no matter how won-derful his puppyhood, and no matter how hard you work to socialize and train him, your dog will do something you don't like. Considering that 90 percent of all dog owners report a behavioral problem, you're lucky if your dog's bad behavior is only a nui-sance. If you're not so lucky, it's a more serious behavior that dis-rupts his or your life. Fortunately, you don't have to live with it.

In this chapter, I preview the top complaints of Pom owners and guide you through combatting each one. But — and this is a big *but* — one thing you don't get from me is advice on how to punish your Pom. Why? Because as a scientist trained in animal behavior, I strongly disagree with the use of punishment in dealing with bad behavior. After all, your dog just needs some coaxing in the right direction — a little positive reinforcement, if you will. And that's just what I help you offer for each of the predicaments in this chap-ter. First, though, I dive a bit deeper into the punishment versus positive reinforcement debate to start your training efforts on a solid foundation.

Squelching Bad Behavior: The Two Major Methods

Like you, your Pom learns from experience. She's more likely to do things that make good things happen or bad things go away and less likely to do things that make bad things happen or good things go away. That's actually the entire crux of training. The hard part is bringing this into play in real life.

Of these choices, it's easiest to make good things happen (reward) or make bad things happen (punishment). In this section, I compare the pros and cons of reward versus punishment. Here's a hint: Sparing the rod will not spoil the Pom.

Understanding the pitfalls of punishment

It's human nature to want to lash out when somebody, even a cute little Pom, destroys your belongings or does something wrong. It may make you feel better for a second while you blow off steam. But it won't help you feel better a few minutes later, and it sure won't help your dog to shape up. In fact, lashing out can undo all your other good training efforts.

I strongly advise against using punishment to shape your Pom's behavior for several reasons, among them the following:

- ✔ **Punishment doesn't tell a dog what *to do;* rather, it tells a dog what *not* to do.** Anyone who's ever tried to follow instructions of any sort can understand how frustrating this not-so-helpful type of guidance is. Eventually a dog will quit trying to figure out what you want altogether.

- ✔ **The timing of the punishment is usually too late to be effective.** In reality, a dog usually has dug several holes or barked a few thousand times before the owner decides to do something about it, but in order to be effective, the punishment needs to happen immediately after the infraction.

- ✔ **It can cause aggressive behavior.** Although severe punishment has long been the advice for dogs that show signs of aggression, in most cases, it's the worst response because it can actually *cause* aggressive behavior. Just like in humans, pain can make a dog want to strike out and direct that aggression back toward the source.

And you thought you were being clear

The key to training is communication, and too often, what you have with punishment is a failure to communicate. Pity the poor pup who has to decipher your mixed messages in the following situations:

Scenario	What You Say/Do	What Your Pom Learns
You discover your dog has urinated on the carpet.	You find him sleeping, drag him to the wet spot, and scold him while rubbing his nose in it.	Every once in awhile, when he's sound asleep, you go insane. He begins to mistrust you.
Your dog has an irritating habit of running and barking at visitors.	You tell your visitors to kick at him.	Yep, he was right: Visitors are bad. He'd better bite them next time.
Your dog growled once when you reached for his food bowl.	You yell at him and take the bowl from him to teach him a lesson.	He was right: You really did want to steal his food. Next time he may have to bite you because growling didn't work.
Your dog ignores you when you call.	When your dog does come, you snatch her, look her in the eye, and yell that when you say "Come" you mean come!	Coming to you got her punished. She won't do that again.
You come home and find your dog has made a shambles of the place.	You angrily scold him.	You're in a bad mood when you come home and should probably be avoided. Next time you come home, he slinks away, which you interpret as acting guilty because he knows he's messed up something.

✔ **It can lead to some unwanted behaviors that may be related to emotional aspects of flight-or-fight.** Examples are

- A dog that runs away when situations remind her of punishment
- A dog that's fearful of punishment so she avoids you or snaps at you because she's scared

That doesn't mean punishment never works. The problem is that it only works under specific situations, and more often than not, those guidelines aren't met when you punish your dog. For punishment to work, it ideally needs to follow these ground rules:

- ✔ It's severe enough to offset the rewards of the infraction.
- ✔ It happens immediately after the infraction.
- ✔ It happens the first time the infraction occurs.

For example, if a dog jumps up, puts his paws on a hot burner, and gets burned the first time he does it, he doesn't do it again because the circumstances follow the three ground rules.

Considering the best approach: Positive behavior training

If punishment doesn't work, then what does? You can't just let your Pom run amok, doing as she pleases. Well, not too much, anyway. Think positive: What can you do to make your dog have rewarding experiences? Doling out treats, playing with toys, or going for a walk are all things likely to turn your Pom on. And how can you make those experiences relate to her good behavior? Always be ready with a treat, toy, and special caress when your Pom makes the slightest bit of progress.

Exactly how you reward your dog's behavior will depend in part on what you're trying to get him to do — or not do.

Helping a Fearful Dog Be Brave

Dogs appear to be gregarious and brave animals in general, but in fact, many dogs have fear issues. Living in fear robs your dog (and you as his companion!) from engaging in lots of normal, fun activities and puts him at risk for panic-running, fear-biting, and high stress levels.

Fearfulness can be inborn, but it also may be the result of poor socialization or a traumatic event during puppyhood. You can address fearfulness by training, drugs, or both. The type of fear your dog exhibits determines which method(s) works best. Keep these two distinctions in mind:

- ✔ A dog with *generalized fear* is more likely to have a genetic predisposition and is less likely to benefit from training. Medication or general socialization may be the best bet in such cases.

✔ A dog with a *specific fear* is more likely to be suffering the consequences of a specific event; he's more likely to be helped through behavior modification than with medication.

Training away the fear

Dogs with a specific fear are most often afraid of strange people, strange dogs, the veterinary clinic, and loud noises. Dog trainers use one of two main training techniques to minimize the fear: desensitization and flooding. The most effective training technique to minimize fear is the desensitization method. (Because I don't advocate the flooding method, I cover it for your information in the sidebar "Freaking out your dog on purpose: Flooding.")

The best way to reduce a dog's fearfulness is to go slow and easy. Your goal is to end each session with your dog relatively nonfearful. This means either you undertake marathon sessions that last so long that your dog is finally used to the situation or you provide short sessions with milder situations where exposure to a fearful event doesn't overwhelm your dog.

To help your dog build confidence and a feeling of control, follow these general guidelines:

✔ **Gradually expose him to whatever it is he's afraid of.** For example, if he's afraid of strange dogs, start so far away from one dog that he just barely notices it. Then the next day — and only if he's calm — move a little closer.

Your dog is learning to be calm. If he's still afraid at the end of a session, you've only reinforced his fear. You've pushed him too hard, or you didn't expose him long enough. Because staying long enough might mean pitching a tent, my advice is to back off next time and go more slowly.

✔ **Prevent inappropriate responses.** Keep your dog from biting, running away, and so on out of fear. Instead, if he looks like he's going to freak out, get his attention and have him do a simple trick. Then reward him for the trick by moving away from whatever he wanted to get away from. This step gives him some control while teaching him that looking to you for leadership is the best solution.

✔ **Encourage responses incompatible with fear.** Rather than just have your dog stand there and think about how scared he is, get him to do something like relaxing, eating, playing, hunting, or walking. This way he begins to associate good events and feelings with the feared object.

Freaking out your dog on purpose: Flooding

The common alternative to desensitization is *flooding*, a practice in which you expose your dog to his fear at superhigh levels and for extended periods of time. The logic presumes that normal levels of the feared event, then, will seem like nothing in comparison. The result doesn't turn out that way, but, unfortunately, dog trainers still try this method all the time.

For example, is the dog afraid of people? A trainer that uses the flooding method would take the dog to a shopping center and hold him while everybody and anybody who goes by can pet him. The only problem is that this approach works no better than locking a person in a room with spiders. You're likely to end up with a dog really afraid of people — and shopping centers.

Flooding is ineffective for two reasons:

✔ **The dog has no control over her own well-being, and having no control increases her anxiety and fear.** In fact, when dogs are unsuccessful at escaping the situation, they often turn to the only control left to them — growling or biting in self-defense. The horrified owner then typically punishes the dog and may even decide the dog can't be trusted, so he gives up the dog.

✔ **The process depends on the dog becoming so accustomed to the feared object that she can't maintain her level of fearfulness.** In truth, that process would usually take many hours, if not days, and most people don't wait that long. Instead, they spend an hour at the shopping center for petting (*tormenting,* in the dog's view). The dog may eventually give up her attempts to escape, but her fear probably doesn't diminish much. She leaves the shopping center knowing three facts: She can't escape from these strange people; her owner won't help her; and the shopping center is a very scary place. When her owner takes her back the following week for round two, she's even more scared.

An example of this strategy is taking your dog for a walk with another person if your dog is afraid of strangers. Allowing him to focus on the walk — and have fun with the stranger — is better than just standing there while a stranger pets him.

✔ **Let him see other dogs and you behaving appropriately.** If your dog is afraid of strangers but has a doggy buddy, he may be encouraged to join in the greetings if his best doggy friend is getting petted and eating treats from a stranger.

Your dog can take cues from you as well. When he acts fearful, avoid clutching him to you, pulling on the leash, or coddling him. Instead, act jolly, like there's nothing at all to be afraid of. Have him do a trick if you really want to pet and reward him, so he earns it.

In addition to the general guidelines, these tips can help in specific situations:

- ✔ **Fear of strange people:** Select the people you want her to meet. Instruct them to stop a short way from the dog, not looking at her, not even facing her. They should ignore her while you talk or walk with them. Let them offer a treat, again without looking at the dog, and let the dog make the approaches. Remember to proceed gradually.

- ✔ **Fear of strange dogs:** Walk the dogs together, with the other dog on a leash, of course, held by his owner. Keep the other dog from getting in a position where he can chase your dog by keeping them both on leashes.

- ✔ **Fear of the veterinary clinic:** Take her for short visits to the clinic's waiting room. Just pop in and back out; then go for a ride in the car to a place she really likes.

- ✔ **Fear of thunder and other loud noises:** Fear of thunder is a difficult phobia to treat because you can't control how loud the booms are. In many cases, drug therapy is needed so the dog can experience being calm during a thunderstorm.

  For other loud noises (such as gun shots), try to drown out the bangs with loud music. For some reason, this seldom works for thunder; dogs seem to be able to sense the thunder through the music. But you can try. If loud noises are an ongoing problem, you can help your dog deal with them by gradually exposing him to louder and louder noises and rewarding him for calm behavior, just as you would for any other fearful thing.

Medicating away the fear

Prescribing drugs to dogs for behavioral problems may not seem natural. But in fact, drug therapy is often an attempt to bring a dog's chemicals that affect behavior back into normal balance. The most commonly prescribed drugs for dogs are antianxiety drugs, which may help with fear- or separation-related behaviors. They must be prescribed by a veterinarian.

The best use of drugs is in tandem with training, not in place of it. Sometimes a short regime of antianxiety drugs can help your dog be calm during training. This assistance is especially beneficial if he's too fearful to make any progress. Drugs aren't usually a long-term answer, but in conjunction with desensitization, they can help work wonders and are certainly a better alternative than letting your dog live in fear.

The field of fixing doggy behavior problems

If your dog has a serious behavior problem, especially one that has you considering giving him up or even euthanizing him (behavior problems are some of the most common reasons for these choices), your veterinarian may be a source of behavior information.

However, because veterinarians are expected to keep up-to-date in many fields covering several species, they can't be specialists in every field. So, for serious behavioral problems, a certified clinical behaviorist can be of more help. Clinical behaviorists are trained in diagnostics and treatment and have the advantage of being able to recognize and treat organic problems such as brain tumors, epilepsy, and chemical imbalances that may be responsible for behavior problems.

Professional canine behaviorists are often satirized in movies as asking dogs about their dreams or showing dogs inkblots, but in fact, these behaviorists are usually highly trained veterinarians with specialized training in behavior or animal behaviorists with PhDs. They work with animals that have behavior problems using the latest animal behavior, behavior modification, and drug knowledge. Your veterinarian can consult with one or refer you to one in your area (go to www.avma.org/education/abvs/vetspecialists.asp for a listing of diplomats of the American College of Veterinary Behaviorists).

Your dog's obedience instructor also may be a source of information. Like veterinarians, dog trainers vary widely in their levels of behavioral training. Look for a trainer who is a member of the Association of Pet Dog Trainers (www.apdt.com) and is certified through the Certification Council for Pet Dog Trainers (www.ccpdt.org).

I don't go into a lot of detail about drug therapy here, mainly because that's a job for a veterinarian, preferably one with specific training in behavior problems. Certain drugs work better for certain problems, and they know which ones. Remember, in this day and age, it's no stigma for your dog to be on doggy downers or puppy uppers!

Combating Separation Anxiety

You come back from a hard day at work, open the door, and gasp. Vandals! Your home has been ransacked by vandals! Your Pomeranian dances at your feet. The poor guy must have tried his best to stop them. He's panting and shaking, and it looks like he's drooled all over himself. You call the police and then start inspecting the damage. Funny thing — these vandals appear to have clawed and bitten everything. And that scrap of sofa stuck on your dog's tooth? Indisputable evidence. This was an inside job — the vandal is your panicked Pomeranian.

When this scenario happens time after time, it's most likely one of the most common canine behavioral problems, *separation anxiety*. A dog with separation anxiety is stressed, and in many cases, she's trying to find her owner. She only knows that her owner's gone, so she often does the following:

- ✔ Center a lot of her destruction on exits, trying to dig under doors, peel screens from windows, or chew through door frames

- ✔ Gets so upset that she urinates and defecates on the floor and then spreads it around as she paces back and forth in agitation

- ✔ Barks or howls, calling for her owner and angering the neighbors

But you don't see all this. All you see is red!

Instead of punishing her, you're better off turning around and sitting outside to cool off first. Your dog isn't doing this to spite you. Although she appears to look guilty, she's actually scared because she saw you go crazy the last time you came home after she had done this. As much as she wanted you to return, now she slinks away in fear.

Separation anxiety tends to get worse, not better, on its own. But if you can't wring her neck, how can you get through to her? Strange as it may sound, it will take *you* changing many of *your* behaviors. This is your starter kit:

- ✔ **Start with short times away.** Leave for only short periods — maybe a minute — at first. Your goal is to return before your dog has a chance to get upset. Work up to longer times gradually, repeating each level several times before moving to a longer period of absence, always using your *I'll be right back* cue (see the later bullet).

  You want her to associate the cue with feeling calm. If you must be gone longer than your dog can tolerate, don't give her the *I'll be right back* cue (see the later bullet in this list). You don't want to lie to her.

- ✔ **Downplay departures.** Make the difference between you being home or gone as subtle as possible — no long farewells and as few cues as possible that you're leaving.

Common cues are putting on your shoes, picking up the car keys, or turning off the television. Instead, rattle the keys and turn the television off at random times throughout the day when you're not going anywhere.

✔ **Use an *I'll be right back* cue.** You can also give your dog a cue that tells her you won't be gone long — spray some air freshener in the room, turn on a radio (if you don't usually have one on), or put down a special bed. Incorporate one or more of these cues into your short-time departures (see the first bullet in this list).

✔ **Return nonchalantly.** Nobody but a dog can greet you after a ten-minute absence like you've just been on a trip around the world. But for now, keep the reunion low key. Ignore her until she's calm. Even better, give her a cue to do a trick and then reward her for that to take the focus off your return.

✔ **Find a safe place.** If you need to leave your dog for a long time, play it smart and place her where she can't do much harm. You may need to crate her or place her in an exercise pen (see Chapters 5 and 13 for details).

These options don't help cure her problem — they just confine the range of destruction. And confinement isn't a long-term solution. Eventually some dogs come to associate the crate or pen with being left, and they become anxious as soon as they have to go in them.

✔ **Consider antianxiety aids — for your dog.** Antianxiety or antidepressant drugs may help dogs that are extremely stressed. Usually you must give these drugs on a continuous basis, not just when you're leaving. However, you may need to add some drugs for the treatment of panic when the dog is going to be left alone.

As with all drug therapy, this decision should be made with the guidance of a clinical behaviorist.

✔ **Consider getting a canine companion for her.** Most separation anxiety focuses on the presence or absence of people, not dogs. For the older puppy or adult dog, a person is the primary caretaker and essentially takes the place of a parent. But sometimes another dog can help alleviate separation anxiety.

Calming a Ping-Pong Pom

Pomeranians, despite their small size, are energetic dogs. They can race back and forth in your house, jump up and down at your feet, and bark at their own shadows. An active dog is fun, but is your dog hyperactive?

Most dogs labeled as hyperactive are simply active dogs without an outlet to burn off their energy. That means you need to ramp up your Pom's activity, and the exercise works best if it's both mental and physical. Here are some ideas:

✔ Throw balls for him inside the house.

✔ Take him for walks and runs.

✔ Practice some agility obstacles.

✔ Teach him some challenging tricks.

For more ideas, see Chapter 16.

After your Pom works off some of her energy, she needs to be rewarded for her calm behavior. Keep these suggestions in mind for helping her earn those rewards:

✔ Speak calmly and quietly.

✔ Ignore any pushy or overactive behavior. She must display acceptable behaviors to earn your attention.

✔ Have her sit and stay if she wants you to go play again.

✔ Reward your active dog when she's calm, even if that reward is then doing something active!

You don't want a dog that's a lump on the rug — you just want one that can follow your schedule.

✔ Show her that relaxing can be rewarding by giving her a massage as she lies down and relaxes. Soon she'll realize that sharing calm times with you can be just as pleasurable as the active times.

Quieting a Barking Nuisance

A talking Pom is cute. One that barks an alarm is handy. One that barks to alert you to the presence of oxygen in the air is a nuisance.

If you yell at your dog to make him stop barking, he thinks you're joining in the fun. Not a good plan! Instead, be calm and quiet yourself. Poms that bark when they're excited need to understand that being quiet is more rewarding than barking. Follow these steps with your noisy critter:

1. **Wait until she' quiet momentarily and then give her a treat.**

If need be, you can throw a clattering can filled with coins on the ground to stop her momentarily so she can be quiet enough to begin training. his may be easier if you have her sit and stay first (see Chapter 14 for teaching this command).

2. **Keep repeating Step 1, gradually increasing how long she must be quiet before getting a treat.**

3. **Add a cue word like "Shhhhh" as you start your timing.**

   Eventually, she figures out that the cue means she gets a treat if she's quiet.

4. **Try Step 3 when there's really something to bark about.**

You can't stop her from barking entirely, but you may get it under control.

If your Pom barks when she's alone, she may be bored or lonely. Try one or a combination of these suggestions:

✔ If she's outside, bring her in — when she's quiet — so she can share daily activities with the rest of the family. (Sometimes that means you have to stand by the door and wait for her to hush up for five seconds.)

✔ Give her something to do that's more fun than barking. It's hard to bark when you're busy chewing a bone or working the food out of a treat toy.

✔ Make sure she has plenty of exercise. It's hard to bark when you're asleep.

If your dog's barking is so bad that you live in fear of being evicted or of having your dog declared a nuisance, talk to your veterinarian about the pros and cons of surgical debarking (which usually

---

Collaring that bark

Shock collars may quell the barking momentarily, but they don't work in the long term. Citronella collars, which automatically spray a distasteful citrus scent when the dog barks, are more effective — perhaps because the scent lingers.

However, some dogs figure out that they can avoid the spray by barking and jumping backward; others just bark until it empties and then bark with wild abandon. Even if they do refrain from barking when the collar is on, many dogs figure out it's safe to bark when the collar is off.

renders the dog with a quiet, hoarse bark). This solution isn't a great choice for tiny dogs (surgery can be risky and not totally successful), but it may be the only choice in some extreme cases.

Nipping Biting in the Bud

Pom owners are often lax about curbing their pride-and-joy's aggressive behaviors. But even small dogs have the ability to inflict significant injuries. On one tragic occasion, a Pomeranian killed a human baby that the owner had left alone with the dog. That's definitely the exception, but Pom teeth can still hurt. A dog that bites is dangerous to others. She's also unpopular and at risk for euthanasia.

Dog aggression encompasses many types of behavior that result in growling, biting, or attacking. The aggression may be

✔ Play that just gets out of hand

✔ A response to pain or fear

✔ A fight with other dogs

✔ Protection of the home territory, the family, or food

✔ A protest against being controlled

✔ Without known causes

Each type must be treated differently than the others because each type has a different cause. In Pomeranians, you'll most likely encounter playful aggression, fear-related aggression, and territorial aggression. I cover playful aggression in Chapter 7.

Fear-related aggression

As strange as this may sound, a surprising number of dogs act like tough guys because they're really scared. Dogs tend to act in flight-or-fight mode — if they feel trapped, their choices are giving up or fighting back. Although most normal dogs remain quiet when frightened and will submit when cornered, some dogs figure the best defense is a good offense.

A dog who is biting out of fear demonstrates a number of telltale signs. He tends to

✔ Crouch, with tail tucked and ears back

✔ Alternately snarl and whimper or even snap in the air

✔ Bite quickly and attack briefly

To minimize your Pom's fear-related tactics in the short and long term, try a few of your own:

✔ **Immediately call your dog to you and have her act calm by sitting for a reward.** Removing the dog from the frightening situation can be a reward in itself!

✔ **Make note of the objects or events that trigger her fear and aggression — and avoid them!** Events may include your own actions of cornering her, reaching for her, and prodding her into facing something that scares her.

✔ **Remember that the dog has two problems: an inappropriate fear and an inappropriate reaction to that fear.**

  • Treat her fear following my suggestions in the earlier section "Helping a Fearful Dog Be Brave."

  • When you can't avoid a trigger, do what you can to minimize her reaction by having her sit or heel.

Obviously, punishing an already frightened dog doesn't help the situation at all; it just makes the problem worse. But, unfortunately, letting him have his way just rewards his bad behavior, and reassuring or petting him sends the wrong message. People may think they're soothing the savage beast by stroking him gently as he growls and barks, but they're really saying, "Good boy! Get 'em!"

Territorial aggression

Having a pint-sized protector can be nice, but some Poms take their duties a little too seriously. They challenge your guests, your neighbors who are in their own yards, and everyone who walks down the street. They may even extend their territory to their carrying bag, your person, or the car. And this aggression may be directed toward other dogs as well.

Some parts of territorial aggression are learned. For example, if the mail carrier comes in your yard, your dog may spot him and start barking at the intruder. The mail carrier deposits the mail and leaves. But your dog thinks she's scared off the intruder. And so it goes, day after day, until your dog is convinced she's the toughest dog in town.

Normal dogs may bark when a stranger approaches their territory, but they quiet down when the owner tells them to stop. Some dogs, however, cannot be quieted, and some owners are proud that their dog is such a protector. But an indiscriminate protector is a nuisance and a danger, even if she is little. Her barking is irritating, and she can nip and trip people with her aggressive behavior. Stop her in her tracks by doing the following:

✔ Eliminate the possibility for her to act in a territorial manner by removing her

- From the fenced yard when passersby are expected

- From the front door area when you expect company

- From view of the mailbox when you expect the mail carrier

✔ Reward her for sitting and staying when strangers arrive

✔ Have visitors bring her treats

Owners often make territorial aggression worse by trying to reassure the dog or by distracting him with a game or treat — in both cases rewarding him for aggressive behavior. Screaming at the dog is just as bad because the dog thinks you're screaming *with* him, not *at* him.

Getting Him to Drop the Begging

Begging is one of the most preventable behavior annoyances you may face with your Pom. True, those pleading eyes are hard to resist — and it's not like you'll starve if he eats some of your food! So feeding your dog from the table is an easy habit to fall into. The problem comes when he gets insistent or when you realize that those hungry, sad eyes are making you feel guilty at every bite you take.

Your dog repeats actions that bring him rewards. If you give him a treat when he barks at you while you eat, he quickly learns to bark or beg at the table. If you decide to stop (I mean *really* stop) giving him food, he learns it does him no good, so he quits.

The problem is that most people don't operate in this all-or-nothing manner. They don't give him food every time, but when they've had enough of his begging and resolve to stop, they still give in occasionally. This inconsistency makes begging resilient.

Think of the problem this way: When you put a coin in a soda machine, you're supposed to get a soda every time. If one day you don't get a soda, you may try again. But if it doesn't work again, you quit very quickly and deduce the machine is broken. That's an all-or-nothing situation.

Now consider a slot machine. You put your coin in, and you know that you may or may not get a reward. So you put in another coin. And another. You keep hoping that the next time is the jackpot.

When you give in and reward your dogs occasionally for begging, you turn yourself into a human slot machine — and your dog into a gambling addict. When dealing with begging, be the soda machine: all or nothing at all!

Minimizing a Dog's Food-Guarding Response

Dog owners get some funny ideas. One that's sadder than it is funny, though, is training a dog to allow her food to be taken away . . . by repeatedly taking her food away.

The poor dog, trying to eat her meal in peace, keeps having some jerk snatch her food away. She finally growls to let her owner know she doesn't like that move. The owner says, "Aha! I knew it!" and punishes the dog. The dog, already irritated, may take the next step and bite. So the owner decides the dog can't be trusted and punishes her more until the dog finally is subdued.

Although she allows the owner to continue the irritating test, one day a visiting child reaches innocently for her bowl. The dog lashes out at this new food-stealer; she's labeled as vicious and taken to the pound.

Nobody wants a food-guarding dog, but owners who repeatedly test their dogs are essentially teasing them *and* creating the problem. In direct contrast, you want to convince your dog that hands bring food to her bowl; they don't take her bowl away. You do this by one of several methods:

- ✔ Drop special treats into her bowl while she's eating.
- ✔ Give her small portions, wait until the bowl is empty, and then immediately fill it with better treats.
- ✔ Feed her meals one kibble at a time, dropping each into her bowl as she finishes the one before.
- ✔ Never take away any food unless you replace it with something better.

Soon she'll be begging you to come near her food bowl.

If you have more than one dog, they may guard their food and treats from each other. In this case, simply feed them separately; only give them chewies or treats in a private room or in their crates. Dropping a treat between them can start a fight or cause one dog to gulp it down so fast he chokes. Never allow a treat to be abandoned in the house somewhere. It may cause a later dispute, perhaps when you are gone.

Discouraging Disgusting Eating Habits

Your dog hops in your lap and kisses your face all over. Yuck! Why does his breath smell like doo-doo? And what's that brown gunk between his teeth? You look closer. It really is doo-doo! After you run to the bathroom and sterilize your face, take a calming breath before labeling your Pom a sicko. Eating feces is not uncommon for dogs, although it's far more commonplace for cats and horses.

 This menu choice is so common that it has an official name: *coprophagia.* Nobody knows why dogs eat feces, but it doesn't seem to be because of a nutritional deficiency or digestive disorder. Eating feces may be a natural behavior for dogs, perhaps left over from their days as village waste scavengers. Why some dogs do it and others don't is a mystery. Stopping it is a challenge.

The best cure and prevention is diligent feces removal. Here are a few other suggestions:

- ✔ Add hot sauce to the feces (although she may just gobble it down and run for the water bowl!).

- ✔ Use commercially available food additives, usually containing monosodium glutamate, to make the feces taste bad — or at least taste worse.

- ✔ Put a muzzle on her, which stops the eating but not the *trying;* this tactic can lead to messy results.

- ✔ Ask your veterinarian whether the drugs that treat obsessive compulsive behavior may help. Some dogs appear to exhibit a compulsion to eat feces.

 Dogs eat other nonfood objects such as fabrics and rocks. Many of their choices can cause obstructions in the throat or digestive system, though, and require surgical removal to save the dog's life. Prevention is through diligent removal of objects from the dog's reach, possibly supplemented by drug therapy for obsessive compulsive behavior.

Lots of dogs like to eat dirt, which makes you wonder whether the dog is sick or has a nutritional deficiency. But nobody has figured out what they could be deficient in — unless it's dirt!

Putting a Stop to Mounting Embarrassment

Your guest has arrived. Your Pom enters the room, and you can't wait to see the impression he'll make on your company. But when he walks up to her, he starts humping her leg — not exactly what you had in mind!

Mounting is a natural play behavior for dogs — male or female, neutered or intact. They mount each other from any direction, sometimes as a declaration of being top dog. Some dogs become overly enthusiastic and both mount and masturbate at every opportunity. They may use your leg, a pillow, a stuffed animal, or other pets.

Remove the object of his affection immediately and get him to do a more acceptable trick in exchange for a more acceptable reward.

Saying "No" to bad ways of saying "No!"

Unfortunately, many dog trainers still believe in the *dominance* theory, a method of training popular in the '80s and '90s that models wolf-pack behavior. The basis of this method, however, was a study that wasn't representative of normal wolf-pack behavior much less domestic dog behavior.

Nevertheless, trainers still talk about the method and how to be *alpha* (boss) with your dog. For example, they advocate shaking a dog by the scruff of his neck as a way of telling him "No." In reality, wolves don't do anything like that, and the act can permanently injure a small dog.

In order to show him who's boss, advocates also throw a dog to the ground and roll him on his back until he stops struggling. But again, wolves don't do that. This particular act is responsible for many, many dog bites. If somebody suggests these methods to you, please just say "No!"

Part V
The Part of Tens

The 5th Wave   By Rich Tennant

"The breeder said we should just let the puppy keep it until she feels secure in the home."

In this part . . .

Looking for more to do with your Pom? Or just looking for more about Poms? In this part I explain ten fun activities for you and your Pom to share. He may earn some ribbons and titles, but best of all, you may have a new hobby that includes meeting people with similar interests! This part also has a list of little-known Pom facts so you can astound your friends the next time they're trapped on a long car trip with you.

Chapter 16

Ten Cool Activities to Do with Your Pom

*T*he best times with your dog are probably when you share a quiet moment snuggling in front of the television or make a fool of yourself as you play a private game at home. But taking your Pom out for other people to admire is always fun. Fortunately, you have lots of ways to do this.

A Day at the Bark Park

Dog parks let your dog run around with other dogs, and they're a hit in large cities these days. Some parks are public, some are for members only, some you pay for by the visit, some have play equipment, and some have separate areas for big and little dogs.

Avoid parks where your dog would mingle with strange, large dogs or run with lots of out-of-control dogs. Of course, make sure your dog is up on his vaccinations first. Then let the games begin!

Play Fetch

Like most dogs, your Pom probably has fun playing fetch. You need a Pom-sized ball, one small enough for her to easily hold yet large enough that she can't swallow or inhale it. (Err on the side of too large.) You can also use a stuffed toy or a cat toy made from fur or feathers.

Poms aren't natural retrievers because retrieving had little to do with their ancestors' original purpose. As a result, your dog has a better chance of enjoying the game if you teach her early. Follow these steps to quickly train your world-champion retrieving Pomeranian:

1. **Take your dog and two of her favorite toys or balls to the middle of a hallway.**

2. **Throw one toy to one end, encouraging your Pom to get it. When she does, call her back.**

3. **Throw the other toy down the hall in the other direction as soon as she gets back to you.**

4. **Keep this up for a few throws, but quit while she still wants more.**

Another way to teach her to retrieve is to clicker-train her. (Check out Chapter 14 for details on this method.)

1. **Throw a ball. When she takes a step toward it, click and reward her.**

2. **Gradually only click and reward for getting progressively closer to the ball, then touching the ball, then picking it up, and finally bringing it to you.**

This sounds harder to accomplish than it actually is!

Follow Your Nose!

Pomeranians may not be famous as search-and-rescue dogs, but they have an incredible sense of smell and are perfectly capable of sniffing out criminals, wild animals, buried people, and hidden treats. (I suggest you limit your practice, though, to those hidden treats!)

1. **Let your Pom see you hide a treat in an easy place (like under a chair).**

2. **Take him out of sight for ten seconds or so before letting him back in the area. Encourage him to find it, and let him eat it when he does.**

3. **Hide the treat in a less obvious place, still letting him watch you place it. Then repeat Step 2.**

4. **Hide the treat without letting him watch so he has to use his nose to sniff it out. Then repeat Step 2.**

5. **Keep hiding the treasures better and better, and challenge him to find them.**

Most Poms love this game. In fact, it's a good way to make your Pom work for his dinner just like his wild ancestors did. If your dog is overweight, hide his dinner kibble by kibble, helping him burn calories as he eats!

Venture into the Great Outdoors

If you purchased a Pom thinking she was going to be the ideal companion for a trip along the Appalachian Trail, plan on carrying her a good part of the way. But if you're up for shorter hikes, your Pom may be, too. As a matter of fact, Poms can enjoy the thrill of a hike just by walking in a park or even around the block.

Whether you're walking or camping, keep her on an extendable leash and in a harness. And if you camp in a campground, bring an exercise pen to keep her both safe and confined.

While you're at it, enjoy another activity in the wild — boating. The Pomeranian's small size makes her an ideal sailor, but make sure she wears a doggy life vest and knows how to swim. A sturdy fishing net can grab her if she falls out, but she should still know to swim to the boat.

Become a Canine Good Citizen

Your dog, of course, is a good public citizen and a credit to dogdom. If that's really the case, she can earn a Canine Good Citizenship (CGC) certificate from the American Kennel Club (AKC) through a series of simple tests attesting to her civic responsibility.

Basically, she needs to behave around strangers (even when they touch her) without jumping all over them or acting resentful. She also needs to walk on a leash without jerking and freaking out, even when people, dogs, and other distractions go by. For another part of the test, she needs to sit and lie down as well as stay and then come to you when she's on a 20-foot line. Finally, she has to let a stranger hold her leash for three minutes while you're out of sight — without going crazy! You can find complete details, test dates, and test sites at www.akc.org.

You can talk to your dog throughout the test, but you can't use food, treats, or toys during the testing. You also can't force your dog into position, although you can gently guide her.

If your dog potties during the test, it's an automatic failure, so be sure she's empty! If she growls, snaps, bites, or tries to attack another person or dog, she will be dismissed from the test.

In some states the CGC title is helpful in renting apartments or even in getting homeowner's insurance.

Meet and Greet

If your Pom likes to make new friends, take him to a *Meet and Greet,* an organized event where dogs of one or several breeds meet the public. Such events are especially popular for rescue dogs, letting the public see just how wonderful these dogs are. Be sure your dog is freshly bathed and on his best behavior. Then all he has to do is be a petting magnet and an ambassador for the breed!

Because everybody wants to pet a Pom, you need to maintain control over the situation. Keep these tips in mind:

- ✔ Have a table available to set your dog on so that he isn't on the ground in a sea of human feet.
- ✔ Limit the number of people petting him at one time; too many hands can be overwhelming even for a brave dog.
- ✔ Don't allow strangers to hold him; a person may get startled and let go of him.
- ✔ Bring lots of tiny treats for people to give him rather than letting them feed him anything of their own.
- ✔ Take advantage of this great opportunity for him to show off a few tricks!

Contact your local Pomeranian rescue group or club, or a local kennel club, obedience club, or shelter organization, and ask whether they've planned this kind of an event. If they haven't, ask them to consider hosting one. Of course, if it's your idea, you can expect to help out!

Get Some Class!

You may be a firm believer in home schooling, but going to school with other dogs offers your dog advantages he can't get at home.

- ✔ **He gets the important opportunity to socialize with other dogs.** This is especially vital if he's still a puppy. If yours is an only dog, he needs a chance to mingle with members of his own species once in a while. Classes let him do this in a structured environment where no dog is allowed to get out of control.

✔ **He gets to practice his good behavior around distractions.**
Even sitting in a room full of other dogs is challenging compared to sitting in the quiet of his own home. Obedience is
most useful in public.

✔ **You get the chance to work under the eye of experienced
trainers who can suggest better ways to work with your dog.**

✔ **You meet people who also love being with their dogs.**

Classes are available for puppy kindergarten as well as all different
levels of obedience, home behavior, agility, therapy work, canine
good citizen, rally, conformation showing, and other, more obscure
activities. Veterinary offices, grooming shops, local shelters, and
kennel clubs can be helpful in locating a class for your Pom.

Ask questions before signing your pup up for classes. Besides cost
and number of lessons, ask about the training techniques. You
want to hear words like *positive reinforcement, reward based,* or
clicker training. Avoid trainers that require your dog to wear a
choke collar or trainers that talk about being *alpha* or *dominant.*
Other questions to ask are

✔ How many dogs are in the class?

✔ Are small dogs segregated from large dogs?

✔ Are dogs under control?

✔ If dogs are let off the leash for some exercises, is the area
indoors or is it securely fenced?

Let Your Pom Be a Furry Therapist

Can you imagine having to give up your pets? Knowing how much
better your dog makes you feel, why not share that love with
people who can no longer have a dog? Many people would relish a
visit from a well-mannered Pomeranian, maybe just to watch his
antics or share a quiet moment. These people may be in a nursing
home, a children's hospital, or even down the street.

Many towns have groups of people who take their dogs for these
therapeutic visits. They can train you and your dog so you're ready
for any situation and even certify you as a team so you can visit
places dogs aren't normally allowed. The first step in certification
is usually to pass the Canine Good Citizen test (see the previous
section). Of all the activities you can do with your dog, therapy
work is by far the most rewarding.

You can find more information on pet therapy at the Web sites of Therapy Dogs International (www.tdi-dog.org) and the Delta Society (www.deltasociety.org).

Pom Be Nimble, Pom Be Quick . . .

Looking for something a little more active? How about developing your Pom's agility through an obstacle course that he runs against the clock? Agility competitions combine jumping, climbing, weaving, running, zipping through tunnels, and loads of fun!

In an agility course, you and your dog race from one obstacle to the next in a prescribed order. The obstacles include various types of jumps and tunnels, a tall ramp to climb over, a raised plank to run across, and a see-saw to maneuver. Several organizations sponsor trials, each with slightly different obstacles and courses. AKC agility is divided into two types of courses: the Standard course, which includes all the obstacle types; and the Jumpers With Weaves course (JWW), which includes only jumps, tunnels, and weaves, usually in a somewhat more intricate course pattern than the standard. So get jumping!

Join a Flyball Team

Flyball is one of the few dog activities that's actually a team sport. It's a relay race where each team member runs and jumps a series of low hurdles, then steps on a platform to release a ball, and then catches the ball and returns so the next dog on the team can start. It's one of dogdom's most frenetic activities. If you thrive on excitement and team play, flyball may be for you.

Before you say your Pom is too little for any team, consider this: The height of the team's shortest dog determines the height of the jumps for the whole team. So each team has one *height dog*, the one that guarantees the jumps are set low! Sounds like a Pom to me! For additional information, go to www.flyballdogs.com.

Chapter 17

Ten Fun Facts about Poms

The next time you're stuck in traffic and stuck for conversation, how about a little Pomeranian trivia? Memorize this chapter and voila! Instant conversation!

Living in the Lap of Luxury: Royal Poms

Pomeranians have been favored by royalty around the world, but nowhere as much as in England. Consider the following members of royalty and their Poms:

- ✔ Pomeranians were the first royal dogs to live with Queen Charlotte in Buckingham Palace in 1761, and Queen Charlotte is credited with introducing Pomeranians to England.

- ✔ Queen Victoria, granddaughter of Charlotte, is credited with popularizing Pomeranians. A great lover of dogs, she raised and showed at least 15 different breeds during her lifetime, focusing on Pomeranians in her later years.

- ✔ Empress Josephine, wife of Napoleon, is said to have owned several Poms.

- ✔ In 1875, while still the Prince of Wales, King Edward took his Pomeranian, Fozzy, to India.

- ✔ In the late 1800s, the Maharajah of Kapurthala kept Pomeranians and Pekingese.

Famous Pomeranian People Back in the Day

Pomeranians weren't just popular among royalty. These beauties have been hobnobbing with beautiful people for centuries.

- Michelangelo owned a Pomeranian that lounged on a silk cushion while his owner painted the Sistine Chapel.
- Mozart owned a female Pom named Pimperl and dedicated one of his works, an aria, to her.
- Chopin didn't have a Pom of his own, but his lady friend's Pomeranian was so amusing that Chopin was inspired to write his *Valse des Petits Chiens* (Waltz of the Little Dog).
- Isaac Newton's favorite companion was a Pomeranian named Diamond.
- Martin Luther (not to be confused with Martin Luther King) often mentioned his Pom, Belferlein, in his writings.

20th-Century Celebrities and Their Poms

Something about Pomeranians seems to make celebrities want to be seen in their presence. Some actors and singers and their Poms are

- Fran Drescher: Chester and Esther
- Hilary Duff: Macy, Bentley, and Griffin
- David Hasselhoff: Jenny and Killer
- Kate Hudson: Clara
- Sharon Osbourne: Minnie
- Nicole Richie: Foxxy Cleopatra
- LeAnn Rimes: Joey and Raven
- Britney Spears: Izzy
- Tammy Wynette: Killer

Poms on the Big Screen

Poms have graced the following movies:

- *To Die For:* A woman loves her dog more than her husband.
- *Harlem Nights:* A Pom is the constant companion of the main character.
- *Cadillac Man:* A Pom named Chester steals the show.

✔ *Enemy of the State:* Will Smith's character has a white Pom.

✔ *Blade: Trinity:* The movie has a vampire-Pom named Pac-Man.

✔ *Superman Returns:* The villainess adopts a Pom.

✔ *Titanic:* The elderly Rose has a Pom.

Poms in Paintings

Many artistic works feature Poms, among them works by Francis Fairman (*Pomeranians,* which shows four black Poms), Maud Earl (*Pomeranians with Apple* and *Pomeranians in a Park*), Wright Parker (*Roy,* which shows a chocolate Pom), and Henry Crowther (*Pomeranian,* which shows a red Pom). Queen Victoria's Pom, Marco, was painted by Reuben Cole in 1890 and by Charles Burton Barger in 1892. Of special note are the Pomeranian portraits by Thomas Gainsborough, which include *Pomeranian Bitch and Puppy* and *Perdita.*

Titanic Survivors

Two Pomeranians survived the sinking of the Titanic. The first escaped in lifeboat number 7 with her single young owner, Margaret Hays. The other was traveling with Elizabeth Barrett Rothschild and her husband, Martin Rothschild, the leather magnate. Martin went down with the ship, but Elizabeth and her Pom escaped.

The Pom in The Pie and the Patty Pan

Beatrix Potter is best known for writing and illustrating the *Peter Rabbit* books, but she also wrote a story about a black Pomeranian named Duchess in *The Pie and The Patty Pan* in the *Beatrix Potter* book series. (By the way, if you ever spot a Beswick figurine of a little black Pom holding flowers, it's modeled after Duchess and is a collector's item!)

DNA Test for Color

You can see what color your Pom is on the outside, but do you know what colors she might produce in a litter? If you knew whether she and her proposed mate carried certain recessive genes, you'd have a good idea of the outcome. A DNA test now can predict nose color as well as some coat colors by determining whether a dog carries BB, Bb, or bb at one color location on the chromosome, and EE, Ee, or ee at another. Consider these possibilities:

✔ BBEE: Black with black nose; no hidden colors

✔ BbEE: Black with black nose; hidden brown

✔ bbEE: Brown with brown nose; no hidden colors

✔ BBEe: Black with black nose; hidden red/cream coat color

Check out www.healthgene.com for more information.

Pomeranian Paparazzi

Many Poms have made a name for themselves not because of who owned them but also because of their own achievements.

✔ Dick: Dick was the first AKC registered Pom, back in 1888.

✔ Ch. Great Elms Prince Charming II: Weighing in at 4½ pounds, Prince won Best in Show at America's most prestigious dog show, Westminster, in 1988.

✔ Teddy Bear: When an intruder broke into the home of this 15-pound Pom's mistress, Teddy Bear clamped onto the bad guy's hand and wouldn't let go, allowing his owner to run for help.

✔ Ch. Pufpride Sweet Dreams: It's every show dog owner's dream to win a Best in Show. This Pom called Parker won an amazing 42 of them — a record for the breed!

A Pom by Any Other Name . . .

In the United States, the American Kennel Club is the major canine organization, but worldwide, the Federation Cynologique Internationale (FCI) rules. The AKC places the Pomeranian in the Toy group, but the FCI places Poms in the Spitz and Primitive Types group.

This group is subdivided into several sections, with the Pomeranian in the European Spitz section. This section includes the Volpino Italiano, Deutscher Spitz (German Spitz), Wolfspitz (Keeshond), Grossspitz (Giant Spitz), Mittelspitz (Medium Spitz), Kleinspitz (Miniature Spitz), and Zwergspitz (Pomeranian). The Pomeranian is still known as the Zwergspitz (dwarf Spitz) in its native Germany.

Index

housetraining, 74, 97, 203–216
hydrocephalus, 182–183
hyperactive dogs, calming, 244–245
hypoglycemia, 12, 89, 116–117

• I •

ID tags, 71, 193
imidacloprid, flea product, 166
immune system deficiency, 162–163
inbreeding, 39
Independence Day, 85–86
indigestion, senior dogs, 162
indoor yards, 208–209
ingredients, food labels, 124–125
intelligence, personality trait, 26
internal parasites, 155–156, 171–173, 214
Internet, breeder resource, 43
intestinal parasites, 155–156,
    171–173, 214
itching, 171

• J •

Jumpers With Weaves (JWW) course,
    agility trials, 260

• K •

kennel cough, 173
kennel runs, boundary setting, 72–73
kennels, 51–53, 60, 197, 199
keratoconjunctivitis sicca (KCS), 176
kibble, 116, 122–123, 125–126
kidney disease accident cause, 214
kitchens, 79–80
knee (stifle), 23, 183–185
knitting/sewing baskets, 80

• L •

labels, foods, 123–126
lap dogs, personality trait, 25
laundry rooms, 81–82
lawns, 84
leashes, 70, 89, 230–232
legs, patellar luxation, 183–185
lifestyles, ownership issues, 11–16
limbs, puppy selection, 58

Limited Registration (AKC), 36, 158
limping, 153, 176
listlessness, 176–177
litter box, 208
litter identifiers, puppy registration, 60
litters, 39, 59–60
lodgings, pet-friendly travel, 196
lost pets, recovery guidelines, 198
lower back (croup), 23
lufenuron, flea product, 167
lye, 82
Lyme disease, tick concern, 168

• M •

macadamia nuts, health risks, 118
magazines (dog-specific), 43
males
    belly bands, 215–216
    marking behavior, 157, 215–216
    mounting behavior, 252
    neutering, 32, 157–158, 215–216
    ownership pros/cons, 32
    testicle drop, 58
Marco (Queen Victoria's dog), breed
    history, 24
marking behavior, 157, 215–216
mat rakes, grooming equipment, 74
mats (tangled hair), removing, 134–135
medications, 178, 214, 241–242
Meet and Greet events, 258
methoprene, flea product, 167
microchips, ID method, 71, 159
minerals, nutrition requirements, 121
mites, 156–157, 168, 169
money, puppy pickup, 89
motels, pet-friendly travel, 195–197
mounting behavior, 252
mouth, home health check, 154

• N •

nail trimmers, techniques, 144–146
nails (household), 82
nasal discharge, senior dogs, 163
neck, breed standard element, 21
neutering, 32, 36, 38, 157–158, 215–216
newspaper ads, 41–42, 51
newspapers issues, 204
nipping behavior, 109–110, 247

tacks, 82
tattoos, ID method, 71
teeth, 57, 142–144, 154, 163
temperament, breed standard
　　element, 22
temperature, 155, 162, 194
territorial aggression, 248–249
Thanksgiving, 85
therapy dogs, 259–260
thirst, senior dogs, 163
ticks, 156–157, 167–168
time requirements, ownership issue, 11
time of day, puppy pickup scheduling, 88
titers, blood testing, 152
titles, pedigree element, 38–39
toenail clippers, grooming, 73–74
toenails, 144–146, 154
toes (feet), 22–23
toiletries, 81
toilets, 81
tools, 82
toothpaste (meat-flavored), 143–144
Top Notch Toys magazine, breeder, 43
Toy group, breeds, 10
Toy Pomeranians, breed history, 24
toys, 75, 81, 89, 108–109
tracheal collapse, 56, 185–186
training. *See also* obedience training
　agility trials, 260
　clicker training, 224–225
　fearfulness behavior, 239–241
　hide-and-seek activity, 256–257
　obedience commands, 225–232
　object retrieval, 255–256
　organized classes, 258–259
　patience requirement, 15
　puppy introduction timelines, 223
　puppy ownership pros/cons, 34–35
　small dog issues/solutions, 232
　treat uses, 222–225
　tricks, 233–234
travel, 15, 87–90, 192–200
treat sticks, leash training uses, 232
treats. *See also* rewards
　bite-sized bits, 116
　hide-and-seek activity, 256–257
　housetraining uses, 211
　overweight dogs, 128
　training uses, 222–225
trees, 84
tricks, training guidelines, 108, 233–234
tug of war, avoiding, 109

• U •

undercoat, brushing techniques, 132–133
United States, breed history, 24
upper arm, 22–23
upper-level windows, 83
urinary tract infections, 178–179, 214
urination, 153, 163, 214–215
Utility Dog (UD), obedience degree, 39

• V •

vaccinations, 150–153
vases, 79
veterinarians, 43, 58, 71, 76, 86,
　　101–103, 144, 149–153, 157–159,
　　161, 180, 187, 242
vision loss, elderly dogs, 160
vitamins, nutrition requirements, 121
vocalizations, 221–222, 234
vocalizations (yours), commands,
　　218–220
vomiting, 179

• W •

walks, heel position training, 230–232
washable pads, 208
waste removal, equipment, 74
watchdogs, personality trait, 26–27
water, 89, 121
water bottles, grooming equipment, 74
water bowls, 69
water on the brain (hydrocephalus),
　　182–183
Web sites
　AKC (American Kennel Club), 43
　AKC Canine Health Foundation, 182
　alopecia X, 181, 182
　alternative veterinary medicine, 180
　American College of Veterinary
　　Behaviorists, 187, 242
　American College of Veterinary
　　Dermatology, 187
　American College of Veterinary
　　Internal Medicine, 187
　American College of Veterinary
　　Ophthalmologists, 187
　American College of Veterinary
　　Surgeons, 187